James Whitcomb Riley
Age twenty-two

THE
James Whitcomb Riley
Cookbook

by
Dorothy June Williams
Curator, Riley Home, Greenfield, IN
and
Diana Williams Hansen
Food Editor and Consultant

THE HOOSIER HEARTHSIDE COOKERY SERIES

Guild Press of Indiana
6000 Sunset Lane
Indianapolis, IN
46208
317-253-0097

First Printing May, 1990

Library of Congress Number 90-080830

Copyright Dorothy June Williams and Diana Williams Hansen

ISBN 1-878208-03-9

Cover from a 1920 *Ladies Home Journal* advertisement, courtesy of
CPC International Inc, makers of MAZOLA Corn Oil.

Dedication
To John Thomas Williams
Our husband and father,
Who patiently tasted all these things through the years
and helped us learn the joys of cooking.

Art Design: Steven D. Armour

VOLUME I (to come)
The Alice of Old Vincennes Cookbook:
French and Southern Indiana Specialties

VOLUME II
The Conner Prairie Cookbook:
The Hoosier Pioneer Tradition

VOLUME III
The James Whitcomb Riley Cookbook:
Turn-of-the-century Village Fare

Welcome to the world of
HOOSIER HEARTHSIDE COOKERY!

Hoosiers have always been a hospitable bunch, even in the days of the flatboat and the Buffalo Trace. Giant copper or iron pots bubbled over crackling fireplace embers to warm many a pioneer's return from a day clearing fields in the period of Indiana's settlement. Visitors were always welcome around the table.

By 1880, when James Whitcomb Riley began to write his wonderful poems, Indiana cooking was a well established gustatory tradition. The sights and smells of Hoosier chicken frying crispy and brown, ham and waffles hot with melted butter and maple syrup, fried biscuits and apple butter, and juice-laden blackberry or rhubarb pie are a part of American eating tradition. No matter how far a Hoosier may roam, he is never far from Indiana cooking, because he takes the recipes and traditions with him!

Riley was a hobby cook himself, taking his turn at the mixing bowl and poking his head in the oven of whatever home he was living in. Some of the recipes in this book are from his own family; many are favorites in his hometown.

This eating cornucopia pours out its treasures: delicious salads, beverages, cakes, pies and meat-treats trail through all the pages of this book. Some are original from Riley's time, 1890-1916, others have their roots in Hoosier tradition and are updated, even for microwaves, so you may enjoy them in today's busy world.

And . . . may you enjoy the readin' of Riley's poems and the tidbits about life around 1900 in this book, as much as you do the eatin'.

Nancy M. Baxter

Nancy Niblack Baxter,
Editor

Table of Contents

HOME COOKIN' AND JAMES WHITCOMB RILEY

James Whitcomb Riley was born in 1849 in Greenfield, Indiana, and died in Indianapolis in 1916. It was an age of innocence and optimism in America, before the Great Wars, Depression, environmental and "world economy" problems. One of the great pleasures in life was eating, and ladies of the house valued their cooking skills. They vied with one another for the appellation of "Good cook." At box suppers and picnics, a lady was triumphant if her food was the favorite.

Riley's heritage was in Nature, and good-tasting foods were an important part of the life he wrote about. References to foods are sprinkled throughout his entire body of poetry—apples are mentioned in no less than forty of his works. Indiana's unmatched corn is given over to twenty-seven different poems and grapes to twenty-one. Many of Riley's best known works are based on remembrances of favorite foods. Remember the apple so lovingly given to "An Old Sweetheart of Mine," pumpkins in "When the Frost is On The Punkin" and the wonderful cake and pies in "Out to Old Aunt Mary's"?

In his youth, James Whitcomb Riley must have enjoyed a bountiful table. His mother, Elizabeth—to whom he formed a legendary attachment—was an excellent cook; and his father, Reuben, had enough business as a lawyer to provide the victuals. When James Whitcomb Riley was just a baby, his father's brother, Martin Riley, came to stay with his family—Martin had run away from his Indianapolis home. Although Reuben Riley was stern with his younger brother, kindly Elizabeth took "Uncle Mart" under her wing. Whether the following is a typical meal at Elizabeth's table—or just that she felt Martin needed fattening up, here is Martin's description of the dinner served in the Riley home the first night of his visit:

Then came supper—such a supper the prodigal son never feasted upon. Everything—pie, cake, preserves, milk and bread as white as snow—and all the time the mother standing behind my chair, filling my plate as often as I could clear it. (From Marcus Dickey's book, *The Youth of James Whitcomb Riley.*)

Riley's "Uncle Mart" stayed several years in the Riley household. Evidently, he became an accomplished baker, taking over in the kitchen for Elizabeth or "the hired girl" on baking day, when they were too busy with other chores or activities. He even inspired "Bud," as James Whitcomb Riley was nicknamed, to bake, too.

"Bud" spent much of his time in the kitchen rolling dough and making pies, which at first were little more than fragments. After a while he improved so that he "could build pies of legitimate size." "My joy was complete," he remembered later, "when I could fashion a custard pie—and then came the feat worthy of a slight-of-hand performer, of getting it into the oven without spilling." In his poem, "An Impetuous Resolve," Riley declares:

> *When little Dickie Swope's a man,*
>   *He's go' to be a sailor.*
> *An little Hamey Tincher, he's*
>   *A go' to be a tailor;*
> *Bud Mitchell, he's a go' to be*
>   *A stylish carriage maker.*
> *An' when I grow a grea' big man*
>   *I'm go' to be a baker!*

> *An we'll drive off togever*
> *Aslingin' pie crust long the road*
> *Forever and forever!*

Although this poem reflects Riley's early aspirations to the baking trade, that he chose another line of work, poetry, is to our great literary enrichment and entertainment. But his knowledge and love of good food is clearly reflected in his poetry. His descriptions of many familiar dishes adds to the colorful native character of his works, and even gives us a historical picture of the food of Indiana in his time.

In his early twenties, Riley left home to live a vagabond life. He struggled to gain recognition as a poet, supporting himself by various temporary means. He sold Bibles, joined a medicine show, and wrote for newspapers, finally attaining success as a poet-columnist for the *Indianapolis Journal* under the *nom de plume* of "Benjamin Johnson of Boone." The column presented its author as an old farmer. *The Old Swimmin' Hole and 'Leven More Poems* brought him the instant success he had so long craved when it was published by his friend George Hitt of Indianapolis, at Hitt's own expense.

As Riley became more successful, his lifestyle became more dignified, and he spent the last years of his life on Lockerbie Street in Indianapolis. He took the Lockerbie Street address in 1893, and lived there for the last twenty-three years of his life.

George Lockerbie, a Scotsman, had cleared a little farm at the edge of the forest around Indianapolis many years before; his name was later given to a new street by his property. The Nickums, a prosperous German family of grocers, had built a fine brick house on the Lockerbie Street location, and by the time Riley became one of its inhabitants, it was furnished as a Victorian mansion. The home was owned by Major and Mrs. Charles Holstein; Holstein was Attorney General of Indiana, and Mrs. Holstein, a boon companion of Riley's later years, was the Nickums' daughter.

Before he resided at the Lockerbie Street location, Riley had lived in the Dennison House, Indianapolis. During these years, Riley's once-regular routine of three wholesome meals a day became as erratic as his schedule. He always took his meals wherever he might be when he was hungry. After all, he usually ate in restaurants, and he could almost always find some eatery open when he needed food. His poetry, so reflective of

HOME COOKIN' AND JAMES WHITCOMB RILEY

happy earlier years, still contained contented ideas associated with food. But as his eating schedule changed, Riley began to entertain some of his own original views of the best human diet. These unique ideas did not escape the notice of his colleagues at the *Indianapolis Journal.*

"Bread," said one of his later associates, "he considered an invention of the devil, and would have none of it, crackers being a substitute. While business men had lunch, the poet had his breakfast. He was long on oyster stews, and cheese, and mince pie."

Eating habits may have changed since Riley's time, but not the emphasis on the quality and flavor of good food. Here, among historic vignettes of food and home life in Riley's day are updated recipes for foods he might have enjoyed. Most are scratch recipes with easy cooking methods. A goodly proportion use a cooking appliance which Riley would have marveled at—the microwave oven. So, then, on to some good, up-to-date Hoosier home cookin'!

"OUT TO OLD AUNT MARY'S"

W ASN'T it pleasant, O brother mine,
 In those old days of the lost sunshine
Of youth—when the Saturday's chores were
  through,
And the "Sunday's wood" in the kitchen,
  too,
And we went visiting, "me and you,"
           Out to Old Aunt Mary's?—

"Me and you"—And the morning fair,
With the dewdrops twinkling everywhere;
The scent of the cherry-blossoms blown
After us, in the roadway lone,
Our capering shadows onward thrown—
           Out to Old Aunt Mary's!

It all comes back so clear to-day!
Though I am as bald as you are gray,—
Out by the barn-lot and down the lane
We patter along in the dust again,
As light as the tips of the drops of the rain,
           Out to Old Aunt Mary's.

The few last houses of the town;
Then on, up the high creek-bluffs and
  down;
Past the squat toll-gate, with its well-sweep
  pole,
The bridge, and "the old 'babtizin'-hole,'"
Loitering, awed, o'er pool and shoal,
           Out to Old Aunt Mary's.

We cross the pasture, and through the
  wood,
Where the old gray snag of the poplar
  stood,
Where the mammering "red-heads" hopped
  awry,
And the buzzard "raised" in the "clearing"-
  sky
And lolled and circled, as we went by
           Out to Old Aunt Mary's.

Or, stayed by the glint of the redbird's
  wings,
Or the glitter of song that the bluebird
  sings,
All hushed we feign to strike strange trails,
As the "big braves" do in the Indian tales,
Till again our real quest lags and fails—
           Out to Old Aunt Mary's.—

And the woodland echoes with yells of
  mirth
That make old war-whoops of minor worth!
 . . .
Where such heroes of war as we?—
With bows and arrows of fantasy,
Chasing each other from tree to tree
           Out to Old Aunt Mary's!

And then in the dust of the road again;
And the teams we met, and the
  countrymen;
And the long highway, with sunshine
  spread
As thick as butter on country bread,
Our cares behind, and our hearts ahead
           Out to Old Autn Mary's.—

For only, now, at the road's next bend
To the right we could make out the gable-
  end
Of the fine old Houston homestead—not
Half a mile from the sacred spot
Where dwelt our Saint in her simple cot—
           Out to Old Aunt Mary's.

Why, I see her now in the open door
Where the little gourds grew up the sides
  and o'er
The clapboard roof!—And her face—ah,
  me!
Wasn't it good for a boy to see—
And wasn't it good for a boy to be
           Out to Old Aunt Mary's?—

The jelly—the jam and the marmalade,
And the cherry and quince "preserves" she
  made!
And the sweet-sour pickles of peach and
  pear,
With cinnamon in 'em, and all things
  rare!—
And the more we ate was the more to
  spare,
           Out to Old Aunt Mary's!

Ah! was there, ever, so kind a face
And gentle as hers, or such a grace
Of welcoming, as she cut the cake
Or the juicy pies that she joyed to make
Just for the visiting children's sake—
           Out to Old Aunt Mary's!

"OUT TO OLD AUNT MARY'S"

The honey, too, in its amber comb
One only finds in an old farm-home;
And the coffee, fragrant and sweet, and ho!
So hot that we gloried to drink it so,
With spangles of tears in our eyes, you
     know—
          Out to Old Aunt Mary's.

And the romps we took, in our glad
     unrest!—
Was it the lawn that we loved the best,
With its swooping swing in the locust trees,
Or was it the grove, with its leafy breeze,
Or the dim haymow, with its fragrancies—
          Out to Old Aunt Mary's.

Far fields, bottom-lands, creek-banks—all,
We ranged at will.—Where the waterfall
Laughed all day as it slowly poured
Over the dam by the old mill-ford,
While the tail-race writhed, and the mill-
     wheel roared—
          Out to Old Aunt Mary's.

But home, with Aunty in nearer call,
That was the best place, after all!—
The talks on the back porch, in the low
Slanting Sun and the evening glow,
With the voice of counsel that touched us
     so,
          Out to Old Aunt Mary's.

And then, in the garden—near the side
Where the beehives were and the path was
     wide,—
The apple-house—like a fairy cell—
With the little square door we knew so
     well,
And the wealth inside but our tongues
     could tell—
          Out to Old Aunt Mary's.

And the old spring-house, in the cool green
     gloom
Of the willow trees,—and the cooler room
Where the swinging shelves and the crocks
     were kept,
Where the cream in a golden languor slept,
While the waters gurgled and laughed and
     wept—
          Out to Old Aunt Mary's.

And as many a time have you and I—
Barefoot boys in the days gone by—
Knelt, and in tremulous ecstasies
Diped our lips into sweets like these,—
Memory now is on her knees
          Out to Old Aunt Mary's.—

For, O my brother so far away,
This is to tell you—she waits *to-day*
To welcome us:—Aunt Mary fell
Asleep this morning, whispering, "Tell
The boys to come." . . . And all is well
          Out to Old Aunt Mary's.

in Riley's own hand . . .

OLD AUNT MARY'S

WASN'T it pleasant, O brother mine,
In those old days of the lost sunshine
Of youth—when the Saturday's chores were through
And the "Sunday's wood" in the kitchen, too,
And we went visiting, "me and you,"
Out to old Aunt Mary's?—

Relishes and Preserves

SMALL SWEET PICKLES

"Very choice" says this old fashioned recipe, which was stuck into a 1914 cookbook from the ladies of the Bradley Methodist Episcopal Church.

Select cucumbers—do not wash. This is important. Put cucumbers in brine (2 cups salt, 1 gallon water) for 12 days. Froth and scum indicate wholesome working. These put in cold water 24 hours. Put in kettle; cover with equal parts water and vinegar and rounding tablespoon of alum to each gallon of pickles. Let come to a boil. Drain and put in a crock.

1 quart sugar, 1 pint vinegar, 1 stick cinnamon. Boil and pour over pickles. Keep out enough syrup so you can add some every morning. Each morning drain syrup from pickles and heat. Add some of leftover syrup. Do this for nine days then put in jars and cover with hot syrup and seal.

The peculiar taste of sorghum, obtained from cane, was relished by the pioneers who used the thick, golden-brown syrup for sweetening many culinary delights. In the poem, "A Liz Town Humorist," the poet avows, "I chawed on, And Wess says—'Well, You jes' fetch that wife of mine All yer wortermillon—rine (rind),—And she'll bile (boil) it down a spell—In with sorghum, I suppose, and what else, Lord only knows!—But I'm here to tell all hands Them p'serves meets my demands."

COOKING TIPS FOR CHUTNEYS

Some of the relish recipes here are microwaved, some cooked on the stovetop. Both methods can work for all recipes, but you must be sure to use proper techniques for either way. On the stovetop, use a very heavy saucepan to help control the sticking that is likely to occur on the bottom as the mixture thickens. Also turn down the heat after boiling, to prevent uncontrollable burning. In the microwave, you must use appropriate glass bowls or casseroles and be very careful in handling these in and out of the oven. But sticking doesn't occur on the bottom because the heat is divided around the bowl, rather than just on the bottom.

Chutneys add a pleasant zing to plain meals. Like any fruit or vegetable mixture, they should be stored in the refrigerator. Alternately, you can pack them in canning jars to keep on the shelf or give as gifts.

To preserve chutney in canning jars you must first be sure that both the jars and lids are freshly washed and hot (you don't need to scald them) and you must use new seals (the

*I*n a small pioneer home, the dining room might contain a rather small central table which would not hold all the foods prepared for special "company" meals. Therefore, the room was provided with a long rectangular table placed flat to the wall opposite the central table known as "the groaning board." On this table were placed the pickles and relishes, jelly and "red eggs" (hard boiled eggs in beet juice), cake and pie, "float" (floating island, a custard dessert), candy, or whatever else wouldn't fit the center table.

top part of the two-piece lid). Fill the jars to about ½ inch from the top with the boiling hot mixture and adjust the two-piece lid firmly. Carefully lower jars into a large pot of boiling water (there should be enough water to cover 2 inches above the tops of the jars). Cover and return to a boil, then start timing for 10 minutes. After removing from the water, let the jars stand undisturbed for 10 to 12 hours.

Can you sterilize canning jars in the microwave? No, you can't. You must surround each jar with boiling hot water to be sure the heat has evenly penetrated each jar equally.

TOMATO CUMIN CHUTNEY

Spoon some of this on top a block of softened cream cheese for a quick hors d'oeuvre.

- 1 large thick-skinned unpeeled lemon, seeded, quartered and thinly sliced (1 cup prepared)
- 2 pounds fresh firm unpeeled tomatoes, cored, quartered and sliced crosswise into small pieces (5½ cups prepared)
- 1 cup finely chopped fresh onion (1 large)
- 1 cup thin slices celery (3 outside stalks)
- 1 cup dark seedless raisins
- 1 cup sugar
- 1 teaspoon cumin seeds
- ½ teaspoon nutmeg
- ½ teaspoon mustard seeds
- ¼ teaspoon crumbled crushed dried red chili peppers
- 1 tablespoon cornstarch
- 1 tablespoon cold water

In 3-quart microwave casserole, place lemon pieces. Microwave at high (100 percent power) for 3 to 4 minutes, until skin is tender when pierced with a fork. Add tomato, onion, celery, raisins, sugar, cumin seeds, nutmeg, mustard seeds and chili peppers. Microwave at high for 14 to 17 minutes, stirring every 4 minutes, until fruit and vegetable ingredients have softened and blended together (if pierced with fork, celery may still have a slightly firm texture). In small cup or bowl, dissolve the cornstarch in the cold water; stir into chutney until mixture begins to thicken and become clear. Microwave for 2 to 4 more minutes, until chutney is thickened and clear, and no starchy taste remains. Ladle into clean hot half-pint jars, leaving about ½ inch headspace. Wipe jar rims; adjust clean two-piece lids firmly. Process in boiling water bath for 10 minutes (start timing after water has come to a boil). Makes about 6 half-pint jars.

PINEAPPLE PICCALILLI CHUTNEY

If you have your pineapples mechanically peeled and cored at the supermarket, you will need to buy two in order to have enough fruit for this tangy chutney.

- 4 cups fresh pineapple, cut into small dice (about 2 medium)
- 2½ cups sugar
- 1½ cups white vinegar
- 1 cup dark seedless raisins
- 1 cup thinly sliced onion (1 medium)
- 1 cup coarsely chopped green pepper (1 medium)
- ½ cup (4 ounces) chopped pimento
- 1½ teaspoons salt
- 1 teaspoon curry powder
- ⅛ teaspoon cayenne pepper
- 1 teaspoon finely minced garlic (2 large cloves)
- 3 tablespoons cornstarch
- 3 tablespoons cold water

In 3-quart microwave casserole, place pineapple, sugar, vinegar, raisins, onion, green pepper, pimento, salt, curry powder, cayenne, and garlic. Stir to blend thoroughly. Microwave at high (100 percent power) for 20 to 24 minutes, stirring every 8 minutes, until all ingredients have boiled, softened and blended together well. In small cup or bowl, dissolve the cornstarch in the cold water; stir into chutney until mixture begins to thicken and become clear. Microwave for 4 to 6 more minutes, until chutney is thickened and clear, and no starchy taste remains. Ladle into clean hot half-pint jars, leaving about ½ inch headspace. Wipe rims; adjust clean two-piece lids firmly. Process in boiling

*I*n the days after the Civil War, people changed their politics frequently. Reuben Riley had been a Democrat, then he became a member of the new Republican party. Someone saw Jim one day and asked, "Is your father a Democrat or Republican?" "I don't know," was Jim's answer. "I haven't seen him since breakfast."

Riley's first poem was inspired by his love for his mother. He made her a Valentine, and inscribed it with an original verse.

water bath for 10 minutes (start timing after water comes to a boil). Makes about 7 half-pint jars.

oor Reuben Riley suffered a lot with his second son. Riley followed the older boys to the Old Swimmin' Hole, but his father knew that he could not swim. He rushed to the Creek where Jim was apparently at ease on top of the deep water. The worried father found that Riley was holding on to a big root that extended out from a mammoth tree.

PLUM GOOD CONSERVE

With a name as corny as the fields around Indiana.

> 3 pounds blue plums (Italian), seeded and chopped
> 1 cup raisins
> 3 cups sugar
> 1 large or 2 small oranges, chopped, peel and all (Remove seeds)
> 3/4 cup English walnuts
>   Pinch of salt
> 1/4 teaspoon curry powder

In large saucepan or Dutch oven (4 or 5 quart size), stir plums, raisins, sugar and oranges. On high heat, bring to a boil, stirring, and boil hard for about 15 minutes, or until thick. Stir often to keep bottom from sticking. Add the walnuts, salt and curry powder and continue cooking about 5 more minutes, stirring until very thick. Ladle into 6 to 8 (1/2 pint) jars and process as above. Or, store in refrigerator without processing. Makes 6 to 8 cups.

HOLIDAY WATERMELON PICKLES

Cherries give this more color than usual. Very nice accompaniment to beef dishes.

> Rind from large watermelon
> Hot water
> 2 tablespoons salt
> Syrup:
> 3 1/2 pounds sugar
> 1 pint (2 cups) strong vinegar
> 1 teaspoon whole cloves
> 1 tablespoon whole allspice
> Maraschino cherries

Prepare Rind: Cut off the green outer skin, and also remove any pink parts of inner watermelon meat. Cut the remaining (white) part of the watermelon into bite size cubes. For this recipe you need 7 pounds of cubes. In large kettle, cover the watermelon with hot water, add the salt and bring to boil. Boil until melon can be just barely pierced with a fork (not too soft!). Drain thoroughly and put in a large crockery or glassware mixing bowl. Make syrup: in saucepan, stir together the sugar, vinegar and spices. Pour syrup over the watermelon and and let stand overnight at room temperature. The next two mornings, drain off the syrup, reheat it to boiling and pour it back over the watermelon. On the third morning, add a bottle of maraschino cherries (any size, stemmed or not as you wish). Seal melon as given above for chutney and store. Pickle also keeps indefinitely in the refrigerator. Makes about 6 to 8 pints of red and green pickle.

PRESERVING BY PICKLING

Through the years, we have come to think of "pickles" as pickled cucumbers, but in years gone by, especially before freezers, many foods were preserved in brine and syrup. It wasn't easy, as these recipes attest.

PICKLED WALNUTS OR BUTTERNUTS

From 1831. Gather about 100 walnuts or butternuts when soft enough (July). Prick each with large needle, holding nuts with cloth to keep from staining hands. Soak in brine made of 1½ pints salt and a gallon water for 2 to 3 days. Change brine every day. Let stand for 3 days, drain and cover with new brine again. After 3 more days, drain and expose to the sun for 3 days. Put in jars. Cover with syrup made by boiling 1 gallon vinegar, 1 cup sugar, 36 cloves, 18 peppercorns and 12 blades of mace. Pour over nuts while boiling hot. In 3 days, drain off syrup, boil and pour over nuts. Repeat. In a month they will be ready to eat, and will keep for a year. (From *Old Timey Recipes*, 1974)

Be our fortunes as they may,
Touched with loss or sorrow,
Saddest eyes that weep to-day
May be glad tomorrow.
—James Whitcomb Riley

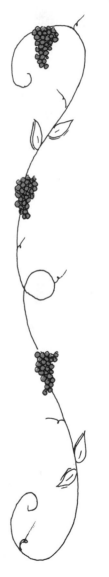

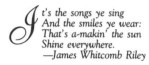

*It's the songs ye sing
And the smiles ye wear:
That's a-makin' the sun
Shine everywhere.*
—James Whitcomb Riley

PICKLED OYSTERS

1 gallon large oysters, freshly opened
  Salt
1 pod red pepper
  Oyster liquor
  Cider vinegar
1 tablespoon whole allspice
2 tablespoons blades of mace
1 lemon, thinly sliced

Put oysters on the stove in their own liquor with salt and red pepper. Let them cook until oysters begin to curl and are just firm. Ladle oysters out of the liquor and plunge them into a bowl of cold water. Repeat once more. Drain oysters and lay out separately on a cloth. Strain the oyster liquor and let it get very cold. To 2 cups oyster liquor add 1 cup cider vinegar. Put in a stone jar and add the whole allspice, whole mace and some thin slices of lemon. Add oysters. There should be enough oyster liquor and vinegar to cover them well. Put in a cool place. Make the day before they are to be eaten. Any oysters that are not eaten may be kept three days. (From *The Williamsburg Cookbook, 1971*)

FRESH RELISHES

Remembering the "relish tray" of crisp vegetables at dinners and restaurants reminds us that relishes are not always cooked to death and stored forever. Many relishes can be made fresh and served immediately. They add appealing texture and color, without a lot of work.

CABBAGE RELISH FOR HAM AND SMOKED SAUSAGES

This is zesty and crunchy.

4 tablespoons (½ stick) butter
4 cups shredded cabbage (about 1 pound)
½ cup chopped onion (1 medium)
3 cups chopped firm tomatoes (2 large)

¼ cup cider vinegar
1 tablespoon prepared yellow mustard
1 tablespoon Worcestershire sauce
1 teaspoon salt
½ teaspoon liquid red pepper sauce
¼ teaspoon ground black pepper
2½ cups chopped green pepper (2 medium)

In 3-quart microwave casserole, place butter. Microwave at high (100 percent power) for ½ minute (30 seconds) to 1 minute, until melted. Add cabbage, onion, tomatoes, vinegar, mustard, Worcestershire sauce, salt, tabasco and pepper. With 2 forks or salad tongs, carefully toss to mix (dish will be full.) Cover and microwave at high for 7 to 10 minutes, stirring after 4 minutes, until cabbage is softened but still slightly crunchy, and volume reduced by about ⅓. Toss in green pepper and serve hot. Makes about 4 to 6 servings.

CLEAR CRANBERRY JELLY

Necessary for Thanksgiving feasting. The natural pectin in the cranberries causes jelling.

24 ounces (two 12-ounce pkg.) fresh cranberries
2 cups water
2 cups sugar

Place cranberries in colander and wash well. In large pan (3 to 4 quart size), pour water and bring to boil on high heat of stovetop. Add cranberries and return to the boil; boil 20 minutes, until cranberries are very tender. Rub berries through a fine sieve to remove skins. Return juice to pan and bring to a boil. Boil 3 minutes, then add the sugar. While stirring, bring to boil again, and boil for 2 minutes. Remove from heat and pour into about 4-cup decorative mold. Cool and chill until set. Unmold to serve. (Note: An interesting and delicious garnish is to surround the unmolded jelly with cream cheese balls which have been rolled in chopped pecans, along with parsley or curly lettuce sprigs.)

Say good-bye er howdy-Do-
What's the odds betwixt
The two?
Comin' - goin' - every
Day -
Best friends first to
Go away!
—James Whitcomb Riley

HERBED ORANGES AND APPLES

A warm relish. If fruit does do not seem very sweet, add another tablespoon of brown sugar.

- 2 tablespoons butter
- 3 tablespoons finely chopped onion
- 2 small apples, unpeeled, seeded and quartered
- 1 large naval orange, peeled, seeded and cut into bite-size chunks
- ¼ cup chopped walnuts
- 2 tablespoons firmly packed brown sugar
- 2 tablespoons raisins
- ¼ teaspoon dried leaf thyme
- 2 tablespoons water

In 2-cup microwave casserole or bowl, place butter and onion. Microwave at high (100 percent power) for 2 to 3 minutes, until onion is softened. Meanwhile, prepare apples and orange. In 1 ½-qt. microwave casserole, arrange apples skin-side-down and orange pieces. To onions, add walnuts, sugar, raisins and thyme; mix well and sprinkle evenly over fruit. Sprinkle with water. Cover and microwave at high for 3 to 5½ minutes, until all parts of apple are tender when pierced with fork, and orange pieces are hot. Spoon sauce over fruit, and serve. (Can also serve cold.) Makes about 4 to 5 servings.

GARDEN FRESH TOMATO RELISH

Good with fresh cooked vegetables like zucchini, corn and eggplant; great on hamburgers and other beef dishes.

- 1 tablespoon prepared mustard
- 1 tablespoon packed brown sugar
- 2 teaspoons white vinegar
- ½ teaspoon seasoned salt
- 2 cups finely chopped tomato
- ½ cup finely chopped celery
- ½ cup finely chopped green pepper
- ¼ cup finely chopped green onion

In 1½-quart microwave casserole, stir together mustard, brown sugar, vinegar and seasoned salt. Microwave at high

(100 percent power) just to warm and blend together. Add tomatoes, celery, pepper and onion. Microwave at high for about 2 more minutes, just to release the juice from vegetables. Stir very well. Refrigerate several hours. Makes about 3 cups.

BEVERAGES

One of the most interesting beverages of James Whitcomb Riley's time was tea. It was stupendous in variety. Riley himself referred to seven kinds of available tea—green, black, Moyune, Formosa, Congou, Amboy and Pingsuey—in his poem "A Cup of Tea," and makes the point that tea is "the safest tipple of them all." "My tea in steam shall twine a fragrant laurel round its rim," Riley writes. But that was just the beginning.

Drinks flavored with herbs or spices, and other foods, were also called tea. Ginger and sage tea were among popular herb teas made at the time. Clover tea was made from clover flowers gathered in the summer, dried and crumbled. It was, quite naturally, sweetened with honey.

There was "light bread tea," made by soaking white bread in milk, then pressing the bread with a spoon before draining off the milk to serve an invalid. (Not to waste anything, the remaining bread was sprinkled with sugar and served as milk toast.)

There was "beef tea," made of beef and water sealed in a jar suspended in water and boiled for 2 hours. It was made for the sick, as was "mush tea," made by adding cooked cornmeal to hot milk, and "whey tea," drained from clabbered milk.

"Rose Hip Tea" made from the seedpods of roses, was known by early settlers as nourishing and acceptably good tasting. Later, during the World Wars, this tea was discovered to be an excellent source of vitamin C.

"Beer" was another drink which could mean several beverages. Unlike tea, beer was carbonated but not always alcoholic. Root beer and ginger beer (ginger ale) were two which weren't. Buttermilk, a distinct beverage all its own, was also popular for its tangy flavor and keeping qualities without refrigeration.

A pitcher of lemonade was the height of desire on a hot summer afternoon. In the new heavy oak iceboxes there were two compartments—at the top was a zinc-lined hold for the big crystal chunks of ice brought by the iceman, and below that was the food compartment. In her kitchen window (or any window visible from the street) the housewife would place a big card with the large numbers on it: 25, 50, 75, 100. The top number indicated how many pounds of ice were needed in the household on ice delivery day. (Occasionally the lady got the number wrong, or the card fell down, or some such—oh my!) As the ice melted, it drained into a floor pan.

17

SWITCHEL

This was also called "haying water," presumably because it was an energy-giving drink for field work. It was cooled in the springhouse on hot work days and, later, could be heated for meals or refreshment.

1   cup pure apple cider
½ cup molasses
1   quart cold water
1   tablespoon ground ginger

Mix vinegar and molasses and add to cold water. Add ginger and mix.

MICROWAVE SPICY TEA PUNCH

To double (10 servings) or triple (15) the recipe, just increase the tea and the sugar. The spices and fruits will flavor the increased amount of punch while it stands before being reheated.

5   cups water, divided
5   tea bags
½ cup packed dark brown sugar
6   whole cloves
2   whole allspice
2   cinnamon sticks
1   thinly sliced large orange
1   thinly sliced small lemon

Into 1½-quart microwave casserole or bowl, place 2 cups of the water, the tea bags (tags over the side of the casserole), sugar and spices. Microwave at high (100 percent power) for 3 to 6 minutes, until piping hot but not boiling, and sugar is dissolved. Remove and let stand for at least 5 minutes to steep. Remove tea bags and pour tea into 2-quart refrigerator beverage container or pitcher. Add remaining 3 cups water and fruits. (Note: Or, if you aren't sure whether the pitcher is heatproof, stir the remaining cold water into the hot steeped mixture before pouring into the pitcher.) Cover and refrigerate several hours or overnight. To serve, strain punch into individual microwave cups or mugs and reheat just until hot and steaming, not boiling. Makes about 5 (8-ounce) cups.

ith an ice pick, the happy housewife would chip off chunks or slivers of ice to add to the lemon juice she had squeezed into a big pitcher and stirred in heaping spoonfuls of sugar. Water was added (not too much—no weak lemonade wanted! Yum! Yum! We may have to sleep on a mattress on the floor in the coolest part of the house tonight, but let's enjoy the frosty lemonade NOW!)

GENUINE HOT COCOA

Boiling the cocoa into a sweet syrup mellows its flavor so it doesn't taste "starchy."

Syrup:
- 1¼ cup cocoa
- 1¼ cup sugar
- ½ cup honey
- ½ teaspoon salt
- ½ teaspoon ground cinnamon
- 1½ cups water
- 1 tablespoon vanilla

In 2-quart microwave casserole or bowl, whisk together cocoa, sugar, honey, salt, cinnamon and water until almost smooth (a few small lumps of cocoa will smooth out as the syrup is heated.) Microwave at high (100 percent power) for 5 to 8 minutes, whisking every 2 minutes, just until syrup begins to boil and ingredients are completely dissolved and smooth. Cool slightly, then stir in vanilla. Pour cooled syrup into a refrigerator storage jar or container (about 1 quart size), cover and refrigerate. Makes about 2¾ cups syrup, enough for approximately 20 cups of cocoa.

TO MAKE EACH CUP OF GENUINE HOT COCOA: In microwave cup or mug, stir sirup and milk, allowing 2 tablespoons sirup for each 8-ounces milk. Microwave at medium high (70 percent power) for about 1 to 1¼ minute, or until just steaming, not boiling. Watch to prevent boilovers.

HOT BUTTERED RUM OR HOT BUTTERED CIDER

The frozen buttery fondant melts and flavors the cider as it's heating. You stir in the rum (or omit rum and make Hot Buttered Cider) just before serving.

Butter Fondant:
- 1 pound confectioners sugar
- ½ cup butter (1 stick)
- ½ teaspoon ground nutmeg
- ¼ cup apple cider or water
- 1 teaspoon vanilla

Ice was delivered in a wagon, the selling of ice being a business. An "Ice and Fuel Company" was in every town selling ice in the summer, and coal (anthracite from Pennsylvania being the most expensive, bituminous or "soft" coal from Pennsylvania or West Virginia being cheaper). Coal was brought in on trains, and the poor folks walked the tracks to see if any had spilled from the coal cars. The ice on the ice wagon was heavily covered with sawdust and heavy burlap.

With the aid of a giant ice pick, the ice men became expert in estimating just how big a chunk would equal the number of pounds ordered. Of course, the weight of the ice was double checked on the ice wagon's scale. With large tongs, the ice man carried the chunk into the kitchen, grunting over the heavier amounts. Delighted children watched for the ice man, and with shouts of joy, pilfered small bits as the ice man chipped away. Ice meant lemonade, or that ice cream could be made in the hand freezer. Refrigeration of course, lessened digestive troubles in a miraculous way.

In 1½-quart microwave casserole or bowl, place sugar, butter and nutmeg. Microwave at high (100 percent power) for 1½ to 2½ minutes, just until butter is soft enough to beat. With mixer at high speed, beat sugar-butter mixture, adding cider gradually as needed to form mixture which is stiff enough to mound from a spoon. Beat in vanilla. On waxed paper-lined cooky sheet, spoon butter fondant in heaping tablespoons. Freeze until very hard, then peel fondant pieces from wax paper and place into rigid freezer container, cover and freeze until needed. Makes about 22 butter fondants.

TO MAKE EACH CUP OF HOT BUTTERED RUM OR HOT BUTTERED CIDER: Place a frozen butter fondant into 8 to 10-ounce microwave cup or mug. Fill mug to about ⅔ full with apple cider. Microwave at high (100 percent power) for about 1¼ to 2 minutes, stirring after half of time, until mixture is steaming hot, not boiling. Remove from oven and serve plain, or to make Hot Buttered Rum, stir in 1 jigger (2 tablespoons) dark rum. (Note, after trying this you may want to make the fondants larger or smaller, depending on flavor desired.)

WASSAIL FROM THE LARGE COFFEE URN

Riley mentions the Wassail Bowl in several of his poems, one entitled, "For This Christmas." Probably a whiskey punch, it was shared with one's friends, served hot, as Riley says, "At tavern-tap and wassail bout, and in ye banquet hall." He proposes for a toast: "God bless you, merry gentlemen—and gentlewomen, too!"

- 1 gallon apple cider
  2-liter bottle ginger ale
- ½ cup tiny round cinnamon red hots
- 1 large whole cinnamon stick, broken
- ¼ cup whole cloves

Into 25 or 30-cup electric percolator, pour twice as much cider as ginger ale to the "fill" line (you might have a little of each left, which can be added after the first few cups are drained off). In the basket place the cinnamon red hots, cinnamon stick and cloves. Allow to perk through a cycle and serve. Makes about 6 quarts wassail.

OLD FASHIONED RECIPE FOR GRAPE WINE

20 pounds grapes
6 quarts boiling water
10 pounds sugar

Stem the grapes. Crush them slightly in a stone jar. Add the boiling water. Let stand 24 hours. Strain and add the sugar. Tie a cloth over the jar; let stand 7 weeks to ferment. Skim carefully once a week for 4 weeks, then let stand for 6 weeks. Bottle tightly and keep in a cool place.

GOOSEBERRY WINE

Wild berries, fruits and even weeds like dandelions were converted into wine. These instructions were handwritten in 1895.

Pick and bruise the gooseberries and to every pound, put a quart of cold spring water, and let it stand three days, stirring it twice or thrice a day. Add to every gallon of juice three pounds of loaf sugar; fill the barrel and when it is done working, add to every twenty quarts of liquor, one quart of brandy and a little isinglass. The gooseberries must be picked when they are just changing color. The liquor ought to stand in the barrel six months. Taste it occasionally and bottle when the sweetness has gone off. (Isinglass is a forerunner of gelatin.)

COUNTRY SYLLABUB from *Miss Leslie's Complete Cookery*, 1863.

Mix half a pound of white sugar with a pint of sweet white wine; and grate in nutmeg. Prepare them in a large bowl, just before milking time. Then let it be taken to the cow, and have about 3 pints milked into it; stirring occasionally with a spoon. Let it be eaten before the froth subsides.

randywine Creek was made famous by Riley's poem, "The Old Swimmin' Hole." This creek had a wide deep spot which provided the best hot weather recreation known to boys in Riley's day. No one really knows how the creek got its name, but a legend survives which attributes its naming to three old soldiers. The time was immediately after the Revolutionary War, and these three survivors were returning home. As they approached the nearest home, they sat together on the grassy banks of a creek to split their last bottle. In a toast, it is said that they dubbed the creek "Brandywine" perhaps from memories of the War, perhaps the liquor—perhaps both!

HORS D'OEUVRES
AND PATÉS

HORS D'OEUVRES AND PATÉS

It is likely, even probable, that James Whitcomb Riley never attended a function known as a "cocktail party." These events began in people's homes when the prohibition of liquor closed the bars. Gradually, hors d'oeuvres began to be served in order to limit or absorb the cocktails.

Today's appetizer table is really a small banquet. There are tiny portions of just about everything you eat as a meal. The meat recipes below can be served as entrees in larger portions. Chunks of chicken, meatballs and small pork riblets are delicious appetizers. You can make these either in the conventional oven, or, because they are small and naturally tender, in the microwave.

MICROWAVED SHRIMP IN THE SHELL

The recipe below starts with this method of cooking the shrimp before their special finishing steps. Bay leaf, garlic and cider vinegar flavor the shrimp and produce a nice aroma.

- 2 pounds raw shrimp in the shell
- 2½ cups water
- 1 large bay leaf
- 1 clove garlic, lightly crushed
- 2 tablespoons cider vinegar

In 2-quart microwave casserole, place shrimp, water, bay leaf, garlic and vinegar. Cover and microwave at high (100 percent power) for 8 to 11 minutes, stirring every 4 minutes, until ends of shrimp look opaque and are tender. Allow shrimp to cool in liquid. Remove shells and sand veins from shrimp, and rinse to clean. You should have about 2 cups cleaned shrimp. Use in recipe below, or serve with one of the following dips:

CATSUP BUTTER: In 1-quart casserole mix 1 cup catsup, ½ teaspoon dry mustard, 1 tablespoon brown sugar, 2 tablespoons vinegar and ⅓ cup butter. Microwave at high about 5 minutes, until hot and well blended.

PINEAPPLE HORSERADISH DUNK: In 1-quart casserole mix 1 jar (12 ounces) pineapple preserves, ¼ cup prepared mustard and ¼ cup prepared horseradish. Microwave

at high for 1 to 2½ minutes, until preserves melt. Stir well to blend.

CHUTNEY DIP: In small bowl stir ½ cup sour cream with ½ cup mayonnaise, 1 teaspoon dill weed and 2 to 4 tablespoons finely chopped chutney or sweet pickle.

SHRIMP IN MUSTARD REMOULADE

This makes a nice self-serve offering when the shrimp are mounded in the center of a large lettuce-lined platter and surrounded with marinated cooked green beans, tomato wedges and a mixture of cauliflower and broccoli florets.

   2 pounds microwaved shrimp in the shell (above)
Marinade:
  ½ teaspoon minced garlic (1 clove)
  ½ cup finely chopped celery (small stalk)
  1 tablespoon chopped chives
  ⅓ cup olive oil
  3 tablespoons lemon juice
  ¼ teaspoon liquid pepper seasoning
  ⅓ cup prepared horseradish
  3 tablespoons yellow prepared mustard
  ¼ teaspoon paprika
  ¾ teaspoon salt
  ½ teaspoon ground white pepper

Prepare shrimp, cool and clean as in recipe above. Leave shrimp whole. In large refrigerator bowl, blend together all marinade ingredients. Add the shrimp and stir to mix well. Chill several hours or overnight. Makes 4 to 6 servings.

DELUXE SHRIMP PLATE

Shrimp Remoulade (above) shares the plate with artichoke and tomatoes, and mushrooms in creamy herb dressing, garnished with crisp bright pea pods.

   Shrimp Remoulade (above)
  ½ pound fresh pea pods, cleaned, ends and strings removed

1 jar marinated artichoke hearts
½ pint cherry tomatoes, halved
1 pound fresh mushrooms, cleaned and sliced
4 to 6 green onions (1 bunch), cleaned and sliced (including some green)
½ cup French dressing
½ cup real mayonnaise
 Dash thyme
 Dash ground black pepper

In 2-quart microwave casserole, place the pea pods and 2 tablespoons water. Cover tightly with plastic wrap. Microwave at high (100 percent power) for 2 to 4 minutes, just until pods have turned bright green. Chill. Make artichoke mixture: In small bowl, toss together the artichoke hearts (include marinade in jar) and cherry tomatoes. Chill. Make mushroom mixture: In medium bowl, place mushrooms, green onions, French dressing, mayonnaise, thyme and pepper. Chill. Assemble plate: Arrange shrimp, artichoke-tomato mixture and mushrooms in three separate mounds on serving plate (or place about ¼ of each mixture on each of 4 individual plates). Between mounds, place the pea pods for decoration. Makes about 4 servings.

ventually it became obvious Riley had a drinking problem, in a day when alcoholism treatment was unknown. One time when Riley was trying to break himself of his drinking habit, he had himself locked in his hotel room to keep from going to the bar. But, as he got thirsty, Riley thought of a way out of his self-imposed prohibition. He persuaded a bellboy to bring a bottle of bourbon and a straw to the door of his room. Once there, it was a simple matter to have the man insert one end of the straw into the open bourbon bottle and the other end through the keyhole, to wet Riley's whistle!

BAKED CHICKEN CHUNKS PARMESAN

4 boned and skinned chicken breast halves (about 2 pounds)
½ cup (1 stick) butter
Crumb mixture:
2 cups bread crumbs
¾ cup Parmesan cheese
2 tablespoons chopped parley
2 teaspoons salt
⅛ teaspoon ground black pepper
 Dash garlic powder

Prepare chicken by cutting each piece into small chunks. In microwave-safe wide shallow bowl, place butter. Microwave at high (100 percent power) for 1 to 2 minutes, or until melted. In large mixing bowl, blend together crumbs, Parmesan, parsley, salt, pepper and garlic. Coat chicken pieces by first dipping in the butter, then in the crumbs.

Space in an open shallow roasting pan, at least 13x9x2-inch in size. Bake at 350 degrees for 40 to 50 minutes, or until tender. Serve with toothpicks.

CHICKEN CHUNKS WITH SHERRY SAUCE

Microwaved chunks of soft-rich chicken with an interesting brown sauce.

- 2 whole boneless skinless chicken breasts, (1¼ to 1½ pounds)
- ½ cup (1 stick) butter or margarine, melted
- 3 eggs
- ½ pound (8-ounces) salted round buttery crackers, finely crushed (about 2½ cups)

Sauce:

- 3 cups chicken broth
- ¼ cup thinly sliced green onion (2 to 4 onions)
- ¼ cup soy sauce
- ¼ cup sherry
- 1 tablespoon sugar
- ⅓ cup cornstarch
- ¼ cup sliced almonds

Prepare chicken by trimming all fat and connective tissue, and cutting into chunks. Each of the meaty half-breast pieces should yield about 6 or 7 chunks. In small bowl, stir together the butter and eggs. Coat chicken chunks with butter-egg mixture, then roll in cracker crumbs until all chunks are coated. Arrange coated chunks in 12x8x2-inch microwave dish (dish will be crowded but coating prevents pieces from sticking together). If desired, drizzle any left-over butter-egg mixture and sprinkle leftover crumbs over chicken. Cover dish with wax paper and microwave at high (100 percent power) for 7 to 10 minutes, until thickest pieces show no pink when cut through. Keep chicken pieces covered while making sauce: In 1½ to 2-quart microwave measuring bowl or casserole, whisk together the chicken broth, green onion, soy sauce, sherry, sugar and cornstarch. Microwave at high for 9 to 12 minutes, whisking every 2 minutes, until mixture is thickened and clear. Stir in sliced almonds. To serve, remove chicken pieces to

A mong the tales told about Riley's alcoholic debauchery in youth is the following: One dark night as Riley and a friend were stumbling across the court house yard, having just successfully navigated their way towards the town pump, they were hailed by a friend. "I'd like you to meet Durbin Davis," said the friend. "Durbin's one of the local musicians in town," he explained. James Whitcomb Riley, unable to properly evaluate his surroundings, grasped the handle of the pump and shook it vigorously. "Glad to meet you, Durbin," he said.

plate or bowl and drizzle with sauce. (Or, if desired, offer the sauce as a dip for the hot chicken pieces.) Serve with toothpicks or small forks. Makes about 24 to 28 chunks.

BABY RIBLETS WITH PICKLE BARBECUE SAUCE

In early American kitchens, pickles provided the "sweet" in sweet and sour sauces for meat.

- 1½ lb. pork loin baby back ribs
- 1 can (8 oz.) tomato sauce (1 cup)
- 3 tablespoons vinegar
- 3 tablespoons sugar
- ¼ teaspoon tabasco sauce
- 1 tablespoon Worcestershire sauce
- ½ cup chopped mixed sweet pickles
- 1 tablespoon juice from sweet pickles
- 1 tablespoon cornstarch

With sharp knife, cut between each rib so that each rib is an individual piece. You should have about 12 pieces. In 12x8x2-inch dish, place riblets. Cover with wax paper. Microwave at high (100 percent power) for 12 to 15 minutes, turning over and rearranging after 6 minutes. Meanwhile, in small bowl combine the tomato sauce, vinegar, sugar, tabasco sauce, Worcestershire sauce, pickles and juice and cornstarch; stir well. After ribs have partially cooked, drain fat from dish, turn ribs over and rearrange, then distribute sauce over top. Microwave at high for 12 to 15 more minutes, turning and rearranging as before after 6 minutes. Ribs are done when no pink remains in meat. Makes 5 to 6 hors d'oeuvre servings.

BOURBON GLAZED HAM BALLS

- 1 lb. ground cooked ham
- ½ lb. ground fresh pork
- 3 slices soft bread, cubed
- 2 tablespoons bourbon, divided
- ½ cup water
- 1 egg

In "What Chris'mas Fetched the Wigginses," Riley states the eating philosophy of the day, defined as "hospitality." "Hospitality" meant a person "Got to eat whatever's set; got to drink whatever's wet."

Guile was used in the old days to get "licker" Riley tells us. "I've went more (miles) so's to come back By old Guthrie's still-house, where MINORS has got licker there—That's pervidin' we could show 'em Old folks sent fer it from home."

benezer Hiram Stedman, a Kentucky papermaker, had this to say about bourbon back in 1878: "Them days the Bank officers and welthy men woold Come down and Fish, up the Creek a week at a time. They Came prepaired to Enjoy the Sport. They Brot the Best provisions and alwais the Best of old Burbon not to drink to Excess, But to Make one Feel Renewed after the toils of Fishing. The president of the Bank, alwais Kept his Black Bottle in the Spring and the Mint grew Rank and Compleatly Hid the Bottle. I never saw one of them in the least affected by using What is now Called poison and the Reason was it was pure Whiskey. Then the effects produced in drinking the pure Whiskey! In the Early days of Kentucky one Small drink woold Stimulate the Whole Sistom. One Could feel it in their feets, hands, and in Evry part. There was a warm Glow of Feeling, a Stimulus of Strength, of Beaurency (bouoyancy) of feeling, a Something of Reaction of Joy in place of Sorrow. It Brot out Kind feelings of the Heart, Made men sociable. And in them days Evry Boddy invited Evry Boddy That came to their house to partake of this hoesome Beverage." Kentucky Hospitality, Federation of Women's Clubs, 1976

¼ cup minced green pepper
¼ cup minced fresh onion
1 teaspoon dry mustard
¼ teaspoon pepper
⅛ teaspoon ground cloves
⅓ cup (packed) brown sugar
1 tablespoon catsup
½ tablespoon white vinegar

In large mixing bowl mix together ham, pork, bread, 1 tablespoon of the bourbon, water, egg, green pepper, onion, dry mustard, pepper and cloves. Shape mixture into about 24 meatballs, using a heaping tablespoon meat mixture for each. Arrange meatballs in 12x8x2-inch microwave oblong dish. Cover with wax paper. Microwave at high (100 percent power) for 9 to 11 minutes, gently rearranging ham balls to redistribute less cooked pieces towards the outside of the dish after about 5 minutes. Be sure all meaty areas are fully cooked (no pink interior). In small bowl, stir together remaining 1 tablespoon bourbon with brown sugar, catsup and vinegar. Drizzle over ham balls and return to microwave for about 2 to 4 more minutes, gently stirring after 2 minutes, until lightly glazed. To serve, transfer finished ham balls to serving platter and serve with toothpicks. Makes 24.

MARINATED VEGETABLES

These tangy savories offer a nice "bite" to complement rich meat tidbits, and the more bland cheese offerings. And they have the advantage of being made ahead and refrigerated until serving. They're colorful, too.

Remember that the natural acid in vinegar or lemon juice, while adding a pleasing "nip" to antipasto mixtures, also affects the color of green vegetables, turning them olive color over time. While the flavor of antipasto vegetables is deep and zesty, their colors will have mellowed somewhat, due to the marinade.

Also see Salads for other marinated vegetable ideas.

BRUSSELS SPROUTS WITH CHILIES

- 1 pound fresh small cleaned and trimmed Brussels
  sprouts
- ¼ cup water

Marinade:

- ½ cup tarragon vinegar
- ½ cup olive oil
- ½ teaspoon minced fresh garlic (1 clove)
- 1 tablespoon sugar
- 1 teaspoon salt

  Dash of hot pepper sauce
- 3 medium green onions, including part of green top,
  thinly sliced crosswise

  4-ounce jar sliced pimentos

  4-ounce can chopped mild green chilies

In 1½-quart microwave casserole, place Brussels sprouts
and water. Cover. Microwave at high (100 percent power)
for 6 to 9 minutes, stirring every 4 minutes, until largest
sprouts are barely tender when pierced with a fork. Meanwhile, make marinade: in medium size bowl or 1-pint measuring cup, stir together the vinegar, oil, garlic, sugar, salt,
hot pepper sauce and green onions. When Brussels sprouts
are fork tender, drain them well, then return to the casserole. Toss with the prepared marinade. Cover and chill
several hours or overnight, stirring frequently. Just before
serving, drain sprouts. Toss with drained pimento strips
and chilies. Makes 8 or more appetizer servings. Note: One
10-ounce package frozen Brussels sprouts may be substituted for fresh. Place in 1-quart microwave casserole with 2
tablespoons water and microwave at high (100 percent
power) for about 8 to 10 minutes. Stir after about 4 minutes.

VEGETABLES ANTIPASTO

- ⅓ cup olive oil
- ¼ cup water
- ⅓ cup lemon juice
- ½ teaspoon dry mustard
- 6 peppercorns
- ½ teaspoon dried thyme

*According to Marcus Dickey, Riley's official bi-
ographer, the poet never wrote a line of his beautiful poetry under the influence of liquor. The Dickey biographies
are unbelievably detailed and complete. Other books about
Riley were written by Minnie Belle Mitchell, Richard
Crowder and Jeanette Nolan, among others.*

*When James Whitcomb Riley was asked for a good recipe for
cider, he replied, "Be sure to use the right proportion of
wormy apples!"*

½ pound fresh asparagus, (small bunch) tough ends removed, cut into 1 or 2-inch pieces

¼ small cauliflower (¼ pound), cut into small florets

1 medium carrot, scraped and sliced thin

½ small red pepper, seeded and thin-sliced lengthwise

½ cup halved pitted medium ripe olives (about 1½ ounces)

Make marinade: In a 1½-quart microwave casserole, stir together the olive oil, water, lemon juice, mustard, peppercorns and thyme. To marinade add asparagus, cauliflower and carrot. Cover casserole and microwave at high (100 percent power) for 3 to 5 minutes, just until slightly softened. Add red pepper slices and olives; toss to mix. Recover and refrigerate 1 to 2 hours, stirring occasionally. Makes about 3 cups. (Note: you can substitute broccoli for the asparagus (you'll need about ½ bunch) if you wish.

HERBED CHERRY TOMATOES

⅔ cup oil

¼ cup tarragon vinegar

¼ cup chopped fresh parsley

½ cup sliced green onions (include some green part)

¼ teaspoon dried marjoram
    dash curry powder

1 teaspoon salt

¼ teaspoon ground black pepper
    1 to 2 pints small cherry tomatoes, washed, stems removed

½ cup halved stuffed green olives, drained

In large non-metal bowl or casserole, stir well oil, vinegar, parsley, onions, marjoram, curry, salt and pepper. Add tomatoes and olives, mixing well to blend. Marinate in refrigerator for at least 4 hours, or for 2 to 3 days before serving. Drain before serving. Makes about 2 to 4 cups.

A lthough not considered as unhealthful as they frequently are today, cigarettes ware still frowned upon by some folks in Riley's time, as we learn from the poem, "While Cigarettes to Ashes Turn." The parents of a young girl do not approve of the man who is courting their daughter. "He smokes—and that's enough," says Ma; "And cigarettes at that!" says Pa.

PATÉS—THE ORIGINAL COUNTRY CROCK

A good old fashioned cheese crock is a treasure at busy times like the holidays. So is a delicious rich chicken liver paté. These can be made at leisure when no one's around. The cooking's between you and the food, and there are no guests to want your attention. Best of all, they require absolutely no last minute work, just the gathering of a few crackers or melba toast as accompaniments.

You can use your microwave to good advantage in the preparation of these make-ahead foods. Some of these hors d'oeuvres start with raw scratch foods, and almost all of them require softened or melted butter or cheese.

Here are favorite renditions of these old reliables. If you have time to prepare extras, they make wonderful home-made gifts.

BRANDIED CHEESE CROCK

This improves with age, so make it a week or two ahead of time. Taste the mixture before you pack it into the crock or bowl. Add a personal touch of flavor—a dash of hot pepper sauce, a pinch of curry powder, a bit more garlic, or some chopped pecans.

- 1 pound sharp cheddar cheese, shredded (4 cups)
- 1 package (3-oz.) cream cheese
- 3 tablespoons brandy
- 2 tablespoons olive oil
- 1 teaspoon dry mustard
- 1/2 teaspoon finely minced garlic (2 cloves)
- 1/2 teaspoon salt

In 2-quart microwave bowl or casserole place cheeses. Microwave at medium (50 percent power) for 2 to 5 minutes, stirring every 2 minutes, until softened. Stir in brandy, oil, mustard, garlic and salt. With electric mixer, beat well until thoroughly blended. Mixture will be soft and creamy. Pack into a 3 to 4 cup crock or bowl which has a tight

*E*ven those in high places loved a "chaw" of tobacco in Riley's time. In the poem, "Down to the Capital" an old one-legged veteran of the Civil War goes to Washington, D.C. to visit his Representative, Old Flukens. Both men had been Forty Niners, and had panned for gold together. Rep. Flukens stuck it out, and hit it rich. The old man is dazzled by the company his old friend now keeps. "They's people there from all the world—Jes' ever' kind 'at lives, Injuns and all! and Senators and Ripresentatives. . ." The old man and his flossy friend spend the night talking over old times. To the old man's surprise, his friend says: "My God," says he—Fluke says to me, "I'm tirder'n you; Don't putt up yer tobacker tel you give a man a chew. Set back a lettle furder in the shadder—that'll do; I'm tirder'n you, old man, I'm tirder'n you."

fitting lid, or cover with plastic wrap. Keep refrigerated. Serve with crackers or cocktail rye rounds. Makes about 3 cups.

PATÉ OF CHICKEN LIVERS

For best flavor, take this from the refrigerator about 30 minutes before serving. It is a dense, meaty paté—best on buttered crackers or bread. The bits of raw onion lend a nice texture.

- 1 pound chicken livers
- 1 cup water
- 4 peppercorns
- 6 tablespoons (¾ stick) butter, softened
- 1 tablespoon finely chopped onion
- 1 tablesoon lemon juice
- 1 tablespoon bourbon
- ½ teaspoon salt
- ½ teaspoon dried thyme
- ¼ teaspoon ground nutmeg

In 2-quart microwave casserole, place livers. With tines of fork, prick each liver to release steam as livers microwave. Add water and peppercorns. Cover casserole and microwave at medium (50 percent power) for 16 to 20 minutes, stirring after 8 minutes, until tender. Insides of livers may be just slightly pink. Drain livers, discarding peppercorns. Puree livers in food processor fitted with steel knife. In small mixing bowl, beat butter, onion, lemon juice, bourbon, salt, thyme and nutmeg until blended. Stir in the pureed liver. Pack mixture into well greased 1½ to 2-cup mold. Cover and chill thoroughly, then turn out onto serving plate. (Or, if desired, pack mixture into attractive serving crock or bowl and chill, covered, until serving.) Garnish with ripe olives and chopped hard cooked egg. Makes about 1½ cups.

CORAL SHRIMP BUTTER PATÉ

Offer melba toasts or firm unseasoned crackers. Make up to 5 days ahead. Take from refrigerator about an hour before

serving to become spreadable. You can buy broken shrimp
for this.

- 2 pounds cooked cleaned shrimp
- ½ pound soft butter (2 sticks)
- 1 teaspoon very finely minced or scraped onion
- ½ teaspoon ground mace
- ¼ teaspoon salt
  Food color

Chop shrimp medium fine. In medium mixing bowl, beat
butter with onion, mace and salt until light and fluffy. Mix
in the chopped shrimp. (Check color, and add few drops
red and yellow food color to tint pale coral if desired.)
Spoon mixture into 3 to 4 cup bowl and cover tightly with
plastic wrap. Refrigerate until serving. Garnish top with
chopped parsley. Makes about 3 cups.

MILADY'S GAZETTE: HOUSEKEEPING
IN RILEY'S DAY

GAZETTE: HOUSEKEEPING IN RILEY'S DAY

In James Whitcomb Riley's day, housewives followed a regular routine. Monday was wash day, and on that day, dinner consisted of bean soup. To make bean soup, the housewife bought dried beans (navy beans, Northern beans or limas) from the grocery, picked out the bad ones (sometimes even small pebbles, too) and put them to soak in a large pot of water overnight on Sunday night. Rising early on Monday morning, she put them in a large kettle with lots of water, a large peeled onion, and a big chunk of bacon or ham. Her only anxiety was that they should boil dry, and she would look at them occasionally and give them a stir. That evening, exhausted from doing the family washing, all she had to do was make a batch of cornbread to go with the beans. The family knew there was no use in complaining, for Mother was too tired to think of anything else. Next Monday would be the same.

Tuesday and Wednesday were given over to ironing. The clothes had been hung out to dry on a clothesline of rope or wire, and various manipulations were necessary, especially if there had been rain showers. It was a trick to take down some of the clothes when just damp enough to iron; if they got too dry they had to be dampened. Every housewife watched the clotheslines of her neighbors to see if the clothes had the proper whiteness, and were hung properly. Heavy garments might take a long time to dry, and badly needed clothing, such as underwear, might need to be taken inside and hung in front of the stove to speed up the drying process.

White things were "blued" to make them whiter. Blueing (nowdays it's called whitening agent and is incorporated into modern deterents) came in little hardened powdery balls of bright blue. Starch came in big lumps which were crushed, then boiled with water to the desired thickness. For heavy starch, such as for dress shirts, a lot of starch was used; a lighter mixture sufficed for handkerchiefs (this was before Kleenex, remember!), thin collars, aprons, curtains and other household articles.

Ironing was a chore because the heavy irons had to be heated on the stove, and seemed always to be too hot or too cold. At first these pointed oval tools had wooden handles which were detachable, but later on the handle was designed as part of the iron. The attached handle made later electric irons a vast improvement. The more flounces and ruffles a dress had the more it was admired, so many hours were spent at the ironing board, using the tip of the heavy iron to get the fullest effect of the ruffles. There was quite a sense of achievement, of course, when a beautiful, full skirted dress was finally "turned out." Some of these skirts were several yards around.

Besides ironing clothes, sewing and mending them was another chore for the Tuesday or Wednesday schedule. Socks were darned on an egg-shaped darner of wood which fitted well into the heel. Maybe an older person, a grandmother or great aunt who was an excellent darner would be pressed into service. New clothing, too, had to be hand made. Precious dress patterns were passed around, and the cutting and fitting of clothes was also squeezed into the weekly schedule. Maybe even late at night, a dressmaker would be found in the home making something for a very special occasion. [continued p. 40]

"Lorain" cooks a whole meal to perfection while you are miles away

It cooks her Sunday dinner

while she attends church

"Before I discovered the 'Lorain' Oven Heat Regulator we had to take our Sunday dinners out. Now I put the whole dinner in the oven at 9 a. m., set the regulator for four-hour cooking, and go to church. When I return at 1 p. m. a steaming-hot dinner is ready, cooked to perfection."

The Franklin Churn.

This is a wonderful invention, and churns butter in from one to five minutes from sweet or sour cream or sweet milk.

It is one of the best inventions ever offered to the public, and should be seen and tested to be fully appreciated.

No butter maker can afford to be without this churn.

The prices are in reach of every one. Prices $5, $6 and $8.

You can secure the churn at J. V. COTTEY'S Grocery Store, Greenfield, Ind.

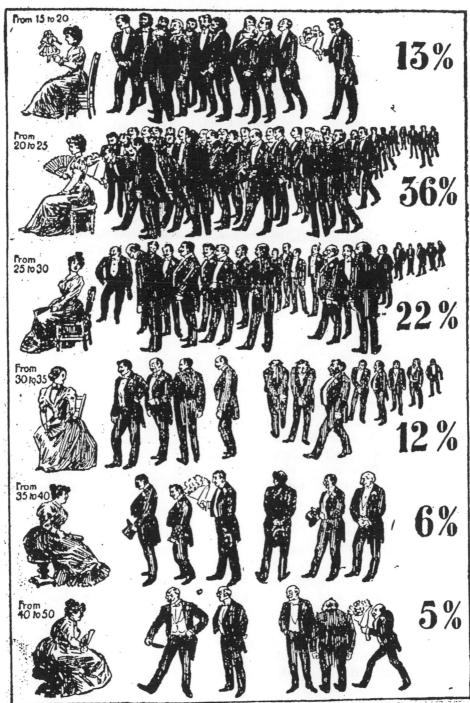

From 15 to 20 — 13%

From 20 to 25 — 36%

From 25 to 30 — 22%

From 30 to 35 — 12%

From 35 to 40 — 6%

From 40 to 50 — 5%

WOMAN'S CHANCES OF MARRYING AT VARIOUS AGES.

GAZETTE: HOUSEKEEPING IN RILEY'S DAY

[continued from p. 35]

By Thursday some marketing was necessary, and the housewife would take her basket on her arm and sally forth downtown. Even a small village had more than one grocery store. The freshest vegetables and small size staple items were put into the housewife's basket for her own personal delivery home. Heavy items like a 25 pound sack of flour or big bag of salt were delivered later, by the grocer's wagon. Flour and salt both came in cloth sacks which were saved and used to strain the fruit from the colander into the saucepan when making jelly.

The housewife had to go to the meat market, also. Only the wealthy could afford steak, although twenty-five cents' worth would feed a family of three. The poorer ladies would get a nickel's worth of liver, and ask for a soup bone which the butcher would throw in for free, usually with meat clinging to it. A big dog might accompany the shopper, too, giving the butcher the chance to treat him to a bone to be carried proudly in his mouth along the street. If a soup bone was ordered over the phone, there was "no charge." Incidentally, phone calls were made by lifting the receiver and telling the local operator the name of the person whom you wished to call. Later, simple numbers were given to phones. (Until the middle 1950's, your cookbook authors had a phone which could be called by instructing the Greenfield operator to ring 49.)

Friday was cleaning day. A mop was covered with cloth and waved overhead, taking care of the week's cobwebs. Beds were changed, floors mopped, windows and mirrors washed and everything "slicked up" for the weekend. To the housewife, spring house-cleaning was a headache of enormous dimensions. She dreaded it all year. Every closet was emptied, every drawer turned upside down and all the carpets were taken up. As perhaps an early version of today's wall-to-wall carpeting, individual carpets were tacked down over a floor from one wall to the other. At spring housecleaning time all the tacks were removed and the strips of carpet were hung over an outside clothesline. Here a carpet beater—a large wire fan-like device—was applied for several hours while the year's dust flew in clouds. At least a week was given over to spring housecleaning, and more by the fastidious.

Saturday was baking day. In very strict households, where religious beliefs allowed no work at all to be done on Sundays, the cooking for the entire weekend had to be done. This included meats, vegetables, enough bread, always several pies and at least one large cake. It must be said that pie was the favorite dessert of the home-cooking period. An experienced housewife probably had pie dough on hand, thus the filling was no more trouble than stirring up a cake which, after all, had to be iced.

By this time, Sunday had arrived. Sunday was the day when man, like God, rested. No work was to be done and the family went to church. Often people entertained each other after church. After dinner, the ladies did the dishes in a dishpan and hand dried them with towels, while the men nodded in their chairs. In later years, the men might go hunting on Sunday afternoon—hunting had become a sport rather than a necessity.

Then the company finally got in their buggy and departed and the housewife waved thankfully, for it was understood that leftovers were the fare for Sunday evening, and Mother could nurse her headache wherever she chose. But don't forget to put the beans to soak for Monday; the next week would come round soon enough.

1¾ Pounds of Dirt
from a 9 x 12 rug

JAMES WHITCOMB RILEY'S POEMS IN WHICH APPLES ARE MENTIONED

The Child World
The Way The Baby Came
Old Indianny
August
Told By The Noted Traveler
Philiper Flash
The Mad Lover
Pomona
Bewildering Emotions
An Old Sweetheart of Mine
Unknown Friends
'Mongst The Hills O' Somerset
Song For November
The Old Days
The Child's Home Long Ago
A Cup of Tea
A New Year's Time At The Willard's
A Fruit·Piece
The Hoosier in Exile
When The Frost is On The Punkin'
When June Is Here
Orchard Lands Of Long Ago
Them Old Cheery Words
The Days Gone By
Out To Old Aunt Mary's
Rubiayat of Doc Seifers
The Bear Story
George A. Carr
The Robins' Other Name
Autumn
The Raggedy Man
Albumania
Knee Deep in June
A Homemade Fairy Tale
Billy Goodin'
A Masque of the Season
A Song of Long Ago
Old Man's Nursery Rhyme
The Little Old Apple Tree
Moonshiner's Serenade

THE NUMBER OF TIMES POPULAR FOODS ARE MENTIONED IN RILEY'S POEMS

Apples	40		Milk	15
Bread	12		Mush	3
Biscuits	4		Peaches	12
Butter	4		Preserves	2
Corn	27		Pie	18
Candy	7		Pears	13
Coffee	7		Pumpkins	8
Cake	8		Potatoes	4
Chicken	9		Strawberries	4
Fish	15		Turkey	5
Grapes	21		Tea	6
Gingerbread	2		Wine	24
Honey	35		Watermelon	8

"Here is the ticket, it's clear
Which stands for a league of good cheer
For this candidate
I candidly state
I'll vote every day in the year"

EVERYBODY
FOR IT

Many authentic banquet or "special meal" menus of the late 19th century list a first course of soup. Most of these were light soups, but sometimes a creamed variety appeared. For everyday meals, however, soup was likely to be the main dish—it was too much trouble to serve both soup plus another main dish.

Today, soups may not be made in the gargantuan amounts of yore, and many of these adapt in small amounts to the microwave. Creamed soups work well because they don't stick to the dish even after boiling. This is because microwave energy enters the food around all the edges; it's not just concentrated at the bottom.

After cooking, most soup mellows in flavor and tastes delicious after a day or two of refrigeration. Try to use it up within about two days, however, or freeze it.

CREAMY WHITEFISH CHOWDER

You can use 1 to 2 pounds of fresh cleaned fish fillets in this soup. With the 2 pounds, it will be very thick, and you will need to add up to a cup more milk to thin it to a thick stew consistency.

- 2 pounds fresh whitefish fillets
- 1/4 cup butter (1/2 stick)
- 1 teaspoon salt
- 1/2 teaspoon coarsely ground black pepper
- 2 medium white potatoes (1 pound), peeled and cubed (3 cups)
- 3 large carrots, scraped and diced (2 1/2 cups)
- 1 large onion, peeled and cut in large dice (1 1/2 cups)
- 2 medium stalks celery, sliced (1/2 cup)
- 2 cups cut corn (3 ears fresh, or 10 ounces frozen)
- 1/4 cup flour
- 2 cups milk (plus additional milk as necessary to thin soup)

In 8-inch square microwave dish, place fish, butter, salt and pepper. Cover dish with plastic wrap and microwave at high (100 percent power) for 5 to 8 minutes, breaking

rom The Century Cook Book (1894): GOLDEN RULES FOR THE KITCHEN Without cleanliness and punctuality good Cooking is impossible. Leave nothing dirty; clean and clear as you go. A time for everything, and everything in time. A good Cook wastes nothing. An hour lost in the morning has to be run after all day. Haste without hurry saves worry, fuss and flurry. Stew boiled is Stew spoiled. Strong fire for Roasting; clear fire for Broiling. Wash Vegetables in three waters. Boil fish quickly and meat slowly.

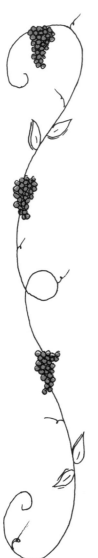

up fish and rearranging underdone pieces towards outside edges of dish every 3 minutes. Fish is done when all pieces are opaque and will flake easily. Set aside. In 3-quart microwave casserole, place potatoes, carrots, onions, celery and corn. Microwave at high for 15 to 18 minutes, until vegetable chunks are tender but firm. To the chunks, add the flour and toss until flour is evenly distributed. Add the milk and microwave at high for 5 to 8 minutes, stirring every 3 minutes, until mixture has boiled and is smooth. Add the flakes of fish and all of the juices and seasonings in the cooking dish. Add additional milk (up to 1 cup) as necessary to thin the chowder to desired consistency. Stir and reheat for 2 to 3 minutes, until hot. Makes about 12 to 15 appetizer servings, about 8 entree servings.

PUREE OF BROCCOLI SOUP

Don't throw out your broccoli stalks—make this soup! A puree is a soup thickened by vegetables instead of starchy thickener. The food processor helps puree this mixture easily. Stop when some small chunks of crisp-tender broccoli remain; they give nice texture.

- ½ cup chopped onion (1 small)
- ½ cup chopped celery (1 large stalk)
- 1 cup chopped peeled potato (2 medium)
- 2 cups chopped stalks and leaves of broccoli
- ¼ cup chopped fresh or dried parsley
- 4 cups beef bouillon
- 1 teaspoon salt
- ¼ teaspoon ground black pepper
- ⅛ teaspoon ground nutmeg
- 3 drops liquid hot pepper seasoning
- ¼ cup butter
- 1 cup cream

In 3-quart microwave casserole, place onion, celery, potato, broccoli, parsley, bouillon, salt, pepper, nutmeg, hot pepper seasoning and butter. Cover and microwave at high (100 percent power) for 20 to 24 minutes, stirring after 10 minutes, until soup is simmering well and chopped pieces of broccoli are slightly softened. Blend in food processor or blender until only small particles of broccoli remain. Or, for softer pieces, let hot soup stand, covered, for about 20 minutes, before pureeing. Stir in cream. Makes about 6 to 8 servings.

EMERALD VICHYSSOISE

A cold soup to make ahead of time. Serve with hot bacon or herb-cheese muffins.

- 3 tablespoons chopped green onion, including some of green tops (2 medium)
- ½ cup chopped onion (1 small)
- 2 tablespoons butter
- 3 cups peeled and diced potatoes (3 medium)
- ½ cup sliced celery
- ½ cup (packed) chopped parsley
- 3 cups chicken broth
- ½ teaspoon dried thyme or 1½ teaspoons fresh
- 2 cups peeled and chunked cucumber (1 medium)
- 1 pint (16 ounces) sour cream
- 1 teaspoon salt

In 3-quart microwave casserole place green onion, onion and butter. Microwave at high (100 percent power) for 2 to 3 minutes, stirring every minute, until onions are wilted. Add potatoes, celery, parsley, chicken broth and thyme. Cover and microwave at high for 14 to 17 minutes, stirring after 7 minutes, until potatoes are just tender. With slotted spoon, remove cooked vegetables to blender or food processor (leave reserved liquid in the 3-qt. casserole). Add cucumber to cooked vegetables; puree until smooth, adding a little vegetable liquid if necessary. Add sour cream and salt; blend smooth. Gradually pour blended mixture into the reserved vegetable liquid in 3-quart casserole. Stir to blend well. Cover and chill at least 3 hours. Serve in chilled bowls, decorated with thin slices of unpared cucumber. Makes 6 to 8 servings.

RUBY PLUM SOUP

A sweet cold soup garnished attractively with a swirl of sour cream. This may seem very strong when tasted hot, but chilling it tames its flavor. A good use for old or imperfect plums.

4 cups diced peeled and seeded ripe plums (2 pounds, about 8 medium)

2 cups red port wine

1 stick (3 inch) cinnamon

¼ cup sugar

½ teaspoon vanilla

⅛ teaspoon ground allspice

Small pinch salt

Topping:

½ cup sour cream

additional 2½ tablespoons sugar

In 3-quart microwave casserole, place plums, wine and cinnamon stick. Cover and microwave at high (100 percent power) for 10 minutes, until steaming hot. Stir well, then microwave at medium high (70 percent power) for 10 to 12 more minutes, until plums have softened. Remove cinnamon stick. In food processor, whir mixture, half at a time, until well blended (mixture will not be completely smooth). Stir in sugar, vanilla, allspice and salt. Cover and chill. Just before serving, make Topping: Stir together sour cream and sugar until sour cream thins. Divide soup into 7 or 8 (about ½ cup) servings, and spoon sour cream over each serving. With knife, spiral the sour cream attractively through each serving. Serve immediately. Garnish each bowl with fresh mint sprig, if desired. Makes 7 to 8 servings.

CHICKEN VELVET SOUP

This recipe is a standard at the famous Tea Room of L.S. Ayres' Department Store in Indianapolis. Ayres' opened for business in 1907, and Riley probably shopped there. In the store's early years, it was thought that food was served from informal food stands before the Tea Room opened in 1929.

6 tablespoons butter or margarine

6 tablespoons flour

½ cup milk

½ cup light cream

3 cups chicken broth

1 cup finely chopped cooked chicken

Dash pepper

EARLY RECIPE FOR SHAMPOO—"An excellent shampoo is made of salts of tartar, white castile soap, bay rum and lukewarm water. The salts will remove all dandruff; the soap will soften the hair and clean it thoroughly, and the bay rum will prevent taking cold." (from The Century Cookbook, 1894)

Riley's own taste in reading was varied. His favorite book was "Arabian Nights" from which he got the format for his own long poem "A Child World." He also liked Longfellow's Poems; "Tales Of The Ocean," and McGuffey's Fifth reader. These books developed Riley's imagination.

In saucepan, melt butter or margarine. Blend in flour, then stir in milk, light cream and chicken broth. Cook over medium heat, stirring constantly, till mixture thickens and comes to a boil. Reduce heat. Stir in finely chopped cooked chicken and dash pepper. Return soup to boiling and serve immediately. Makes about 5 cups soup.

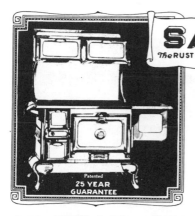

"Hired Girls" were an integral part of life in Riley's day. There were few commercial jobs open to young girls except perhaps school teaching. So those of an adventurous nature jumped at the chance to come to town to serve as hired girl to some tired mother of a large family. Big families were greatly desired in those days—"Lots of boys for the fields, lots of girls for the kitchen." Room and board was often the only pay a hired girl received; a sum such as $3.00 per week was accepted with delight. The Rileys had several hired girls, including Mary Alice Smith (later immortalized as "Little Orphant Annie"). Floretty and 'Lizabuth Ann are mentioned in the poems. "Our hired girl, she's Lizabuth Ann; an' she can cook best things to eat." Lizabuth Ann also flirted with the Raggedy Man, we learn in the poem, and she made parched corn for him while he played his "maccordeun (accordion)."

"THE RAGGEDY MAN"

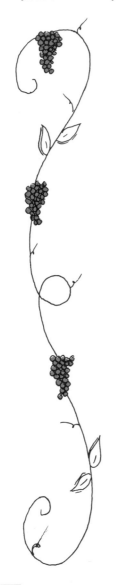

*If you want somepin',
And jes dead-set
A-pleadin' fer it
With both eyes wet,
And teary won't
Bring it,
W'y you try sweat.*
—James Whitcomb Riley

O THE Raggedy Man! He works fer Pa;
  An' he's the goodest man ever you
    saw!
He comes to our house every day,
An' waters the horses, an' feeds 'em hay;
An' he opens the shed—an' we all ist laugh
When he drives out our little old wobble-ly
    calf;
An' nen—ef our hired girl says he can—
He milks the cow for 'Lizabuth Ann.—
    Ain't he a' awful good Raggedy Man?
      Raggedy! Raggedy! Raggedy Man!

W'y, The Raggedy Man—he's ist so good,
He splits the kindlin' an' chops the wood;
An' nen he spades in our garden, too,
An' does most things 'at *boys* can't do.—
He clumbed clean up in our big tree
An' shooked a' apple down fer me—
An' 'nother 'n', too, fer 'Lizabuth Ann—
An' 'nother 'n', too, fer The Raggedy
    Man.—
    Ain't he a' awful kind Raggedy Man?
      Raggedy! Raggedy! Raggedy Man!

An' The Raggedy Man one time say he
Pick' roast' rambos from a' orchurd-tree,
An' et 'em—all ist roast' an' hot!—
An' it's so, too!—'cause a corn-crib got
Afire one time an' all burn' down
On "The Smoot Farm," 'bout four mile
    from town—
On "The Smoot Farm"! Yes—an' the hired
    han'
'At worked there nen 'uz The Raggedy
    Man!—
    Ain't he the beatin'est Raggedy Man?
      Raggedy! Raggedy! Raggedy Man!

The Raggedy Man's so good an' kind
He'll be our "horsey," and "haw" an' mind
Ever'thing 'at you make him do—
An' won't run off—'less you want him to!
I drived him wunst way down our lane
An' he got skeered, when it 'menced to
    rain,
An' ist rared up an' squealed and run
Purt' nigh away!—an' it's all in fun!
Nen he skeered *ag'in* at a' old tin can . . .
    Whoa! y' old runaway Raggedy Man!
      Raggedy! Raggedy! Raggedy Man!

"THE RAGGEDY MAN"

An' The Raggedy Man, he knows most
    rhymes,
An' tells 'em, ef I be good, sometimes:
Knows 'bout Giunts, an' Griffuns, an' Elves,
An' the Squidgicum-Squees 'at swallers
    the'rselves:
An', wite by the pump in our pasturelog,
He showed me the hole 'at the Wunks is
    got,
'At lives 'way deep in the ground, an' can
Turn into me, er 'Lizabuth Ann!
Er Ma, er Pa, er The Raggedy Man!
    Ain't he a funny old Raggedy Man?
    Raggedy! Raggedy! Raggedy Man!

An' wunst, when the Raggedy Man come
    late,
An' pigs ist root' thue the garden-gate,
He 'tend like the pigs 'uz *bears* an' said,
"Old Bear-shooter'll shoot 'em dead!"
An' race' an' chase' 'em, an' they'd ist run
When he pint his hoe at 'em like it's a gun
An' go "Bang!—Bang!" nen 'tend he stan'
An' load up his gun ag'in! Raggedy Man!
    He's an old Bear-Shooter Raggedy Man!
    Raggedy! Raggedy! Raggedy Man!

An' sometimes The Raggedy Man lets on
We're little *prince*-children, an' old King's
    gone
To git more money, an' lef' us there—
And *Robbers* is ist thick ever'where;
An' nen—ef we all won't cry, fer *shore*—
The Raggedy Man he'll come and "splore
The Castul-Halls," an' steal the "gold"—
An' steal *us*, too, an' grab an' hold
An' pack us off to his old "Cave"!—An'
    Haymow's the "cave" o' The Raggedy
    Man!—
    Raggedy! Raggedy! Raggedy Man!

The Raggedy Man—one time, when he
Wuz makin' a little bow-'n'-orry fer me,
Says "When you're big like your Pa is,
Air *you* go' to keep a fine store like his—
An' be a rich merchunt—an' wear fine
    clothes?—
Er what *air* you go' to be, goodness knows?"
An' nen he laughed at 'Lizabuth Ann,
An' I says "'M go' to be a Raggedy Man!—
    I'm ist go' to be a nice Raggedy Man!"
    Raggedy! Raggedy! Raggedy Man!

*We say, and we say and
    we say,
We promise, engage and
    declare,
Till a year from tomorrow is
Yesterday,
And yesterday is — Where?*
    —James Whitcomb Riley

Salads

SALADS

LEAFY GREEN SALADS

Salads based on leafy greens like lettuce were not common in Riley's time. Rather, there were plates of sliced cucumbers or onions, dressed with salt, pepper and vinegar, or pickled vegetables, like beets. Also, leftover vegetables might be served cold with oil and vinegar so they wouldn't go to waste. In the spring, there were fresh greens to wilt in the frying pan along with cider vinegar, sugar, butter and seasonings. Spring greens were thought to have healthful properties and people ate them to get over whatever ailed them in the winter. People also knew that when the greens came up, the time was right to dose your family with sulphur and molasses.

Sometime after about 1915, leafy greens began to be used for salads, and in 1918 an interesting recipe called French Salad, presumably served on lettuce, was printed. It called for ten cents worth of ham and ten cents worth of cream cheese to be put through a grinder with ten cents worth of sweet pickles. This mixture was seasoned with salt, sugar and pepper and topped with mayonnaise. With about thirty cents of ingredients, it would serve about 6 people.

LETTUCE SLICES WITH COTTAGE CHEESE DRESSING

After removing the core and coarse outside leaves of lettuce, cut the head into ½ inch slices. These slices are attractive and easier to prepare than tossed salad.

- 1 pound (16 ounces) small curd creamed cottage cheese
- 1 cup mayonnaise
- ½ teaspoon ground black pepper
- 1½ teaspoons finely minced onion
- ½ teaspoon salt
- 1 large head lettuce
  Paprika

Make dressing: Stir together cottage cheese, mayonnaise, pepper, onion and salt. Refrigerate until serving. To serve salad: Place ½-inch slices of lettuce on individual salad

Riley's poems mention "salad" only once, and that is in a later poem. Head lettuce was not grown in early gardens; the common variety was leaf lettuce. This grew in great abundance, and along with radishes and onions, was very welcome in the spring. Lettuce could not be cooked, so the housewife prepared "Wilted Lettuce." A slice of ham was fried in grease, the ham removed, then a cupful of sugar and a cupful of vinegar were added in the skillet. Into the hot grease went as much carefully cleaned leaf lettuce as the housewife could heap in. The lid was popped onto the skillet, the lettuce turned and tossed a few times, then the gas turned off while the lettuce "wilted." Very tasty.

A pioneer fruit salad or dessert was called "Ambrosia." Oranges were peeled into segments and a layer put in a pretty dish. Over this went a layer of fresh coconut, next some marshmallows or a layer of powdered sugar. Repeat until the dish was filled to the top. Ambrosia was a Greek term; "Food for the Gods."

plates. Just before serving, cover each with about ⅓ cup dressing. Garnish with paprika. Makes about 6 to 8 salads.

GREENS AND WALNUT SALAD

Microwave warm salads in an attractive microwave table ready dish. Greens reduce in volume as they wilt, so it's OK to start with a very full dish.

- 8 strips bacon
- 1 pound fresh spinach, trimmed and washed
- ½ cup thick sour cream
- 1 tablespoon mild distilled white vinegar
- 1 teaspoon sugar
- ¼ teaspoon salt
- ⅛ teaspoon ground white pepper
- ⅓ cup coarsely chopped walnuts

On microwave bacon rack or paper towel-lined glass dish, arrange bacon in a single layer. Microwave at high (100 percent power) for 6 to 8 minutes, until very crisp, rotating dish if necessary. Save 1 tablespoon bacon fat. Remove bacon to paper towels to cool. Place damp spinach in 3-quart microwave casserole (if spinach is completely dry, sprinkle with 2 tablespoons water.) Cover. Microwave at high for 3½ to 5½ minutes, stirring every 2 minutes, just until spinach is wilted and slightly cooked. Meanwhile, in small (2-cup) bowl, stir together 1 tablespoon of the reserved bacon fat, sour cream, vinegar, sugar, salt, and pepper. Drain spinach very well, lightly pressing to drain excess moisture. If desired, remove spinach to salad bowl or individual plates, top with walnuts, then sour cream dressing. Crumble bacon over all. Makes about 4 servings.

GREENS AND RED CABBAGE SALAD

This was served at the Williams' family reunion celebrating Tom and June Williams's Fiftieth Wedding Anniversary.

- 2 pounds spinach, trimmed and washed
- ½ small head red cabbage, finely shredded (3 cups)
- 1 large white onion, cut into rings

*O*ne Sunday as Riley happened to be present at the Methodist Sunday School when no one was there to take the minutes, Riley was asked to take the absent secretary's place and record the minutes. The result was so flowery with such items as "Mrs. Pinkney wore a large pink feather-trimmed hat" that he was never again asked for his assistance.

A great treat early in the spring was dandelion greens. Taking a big dishpan, the bonneted housewife would march out to dig the young dandelion plants. Carefully cleaned and cooked with a hunk of bacon, they were tasty indeed after a long vegetable-scarce winter. Not all the plants were eaten, however. Perhaps more of them were drunk, for dandelion wine was a coveted specialty.

½ pound small yellow squash, cut ¼-inch thick
1 bottle (16 ounces) creamy garlic and herb salad dressing

Tear spinach coarsely into large pieces. Line salad bowl with spinach. Arrange red cabbage, onion and yellow squash in center. Cover and refrigerate. At serving time, pour dressing over vegetables and toss to mix well. Makes about 12 servings.

CABBAGE CUTTERS

Cabbage salads, especially cole slaw, are possibly the oldest salads in America. There are many interesting old cabbage cutters on farms around early America. Some of them used a hand pumping device to raise and lower a blade to chop the cabbage. Others (like our food processors) used a hand crank which caused circular blades to whir against the cabbage in a barrel. For sauerkraut, people used a large metal board with a blade set in the center, on the order of the hand vegetable shredders of today.

REAL COLE SLAW WITH OLD FASHIONED BOILED DRESSING

3 cups finely shredded cabbage
1 egg
¼ cup vinegar
1 tablespoon sugar
1 teaspoon salt
¼ teaspoon pepper
½ teaspoon dry mustard
1 tablespoon butter
2 tablespoons light or heavy cream

Shred cabbage into salad bowl and set aside. In small cup or bowl, beat the egg with a fork and set aside. In small saucepan, place vinegar, sugar, salt, pepper, mustard and butter. Bring to boil over high heat, stirring constantly. Pour a little of the hot mixture into the egg, mix well and stir this back into remaining mixture in saucepan. Cook, stirring constantly over medium heat, until mixture boils

Cottage cheese was a food made by housewives in early days. Families with German heritage called it "schmeirkase" and made it frequently. Sour milk was heated to a certain degree, then the colorless liquid called whey was poured off, and the curds were worked up with cream into cottage cheese. Riley spells it in the phonetic way "smearcase" in the poem "Name Us No Names No More" which describes the joyous feelings of children who consider everything funny. Incidentally, for those interested in genealogy, Riley gives the name of several early families of his day that the children considered "funny." "Bowersox" was one.

and thickens. Remove from heat and immediately pour over cabbage. Chill and serve cold. Makes about 6 servings.

COLORFUL CABBAGE SALAD

2 cups finely shredded cabbage
½ cup sliced small onions
1 cup fresh or canned pineapple chunks
4 ounces chopped pimento
½ cup sliced stuffed olives
1 cup shredded mild cheddar cheese
1 cup mayonnaise
2 tablespoons lemon juice
Salt and pepper

In large salad bowl, toss to combine cabbage, onions, pineapple, pimento, olives, cheese, mayonnaise and lemon juice. Add salt and pepper (especially pepper) to taste. Refrigerate for at least 2 hours before serving. Makes about 6 servings.

COLD VEGETABLE SALADS

Cold vegetables dressed with vinegar and oil were considered a creative way to use up leftover food. Today, these would be called salads. If the dish needed sweetening, sugar or sweet French dressing could be used. Also see other cold vegetable mixtures in appetizer chapter.

GREEN BEANS AND EGG SALAD

Egg Salad:
4 hard cooked eggs, shelled and chopped
3 tablespoons mayonnaise
2 tablespoons sweet pickle relish
1 teaspoon prepared mustard
2 teaspoons vinegar
¼ teaspoon salt
Bean Salad:
3 cups cooked fresh green beans

The word salad originally came from "sal" meaning salt. Greens were the food which you sprinkled with salt before you ate them. In Riley's day salt was precious. It was used in preserving many foods, like ham and bacon as well as put in foods for the table. Salt was bought in small cloth sacks, and if any were spilled, it was thought to be bad luck. This had to be warded off by throwing a pinch of salt over the right shoulder, in keeping with age-old superstitions.

½ cup olive oil
¼ cup tarragon or other white herb vinegar
    Salt and pepper
½ cup minced onion
4 slices crumbled crisp bacon

Make egg salad: In medium bowl, stir together all ingredients. Chill. Make bean salad: Ahead of time, cook beans to crisp-tender stage and chill. In small jar or bowl, shake or stir oil, vinegar, salt and pepper and onion; chill. Just before serving, mix oil mixture with the beans and toss with the crisp bacon. To serve, in lettuce lined 1-quart serving bowl, heap the beans. Garnish with a wreath of egg salad spooned on top of beans. Makes about 4 to 6 servings. (Note: beans stay brightest green if refrigerated alone. The acid in the dressing causes beans to turn olive color.)

CAULIFLOWER ORANGE SALAD

2 cups raw cauliflorets
2 cups orange wedges, cut into bite-size pieces
¼ cup finely chopped green pepper
1 tablespoon onion juice
Dressing:
½ cup lemon juice
¾ cup olive oil
1 teaspoon salt
1 teaspoon paprika

In salad bowl, toss cauliflorets, orange wedges, green pepper and onion juice. Make dressing: In small jar, shake together the lemon juice, olive oil, salt and paprika. Toss the cauliflower mixture with dressing. Chill. Makes about 6 to 8 servings.

GOURMET POTATO SALAD

2 hard cooked eggs
3 cups cubed boiled potatoes
2 tablespoons finely chopped onion
½ teaspoon salt
    Dash black pepper

⅔ cup sour cream
2 tablespoons cider vinegar
1 tablespoon dijon mustard
½ teaspoon celery seed
2 tablespoons mayonnaise
⅓ cup sweet pickle relish
¼ cup finely chopped fresh parsley

Prepare eggs by separating hard cooked whites and yolks. Dice the whites into mixing bowl. Add cubed potatoes, onion, salt and pepper. Toss to mix. In small bowl, mash the yolks and stir in the sour cream, vinegar, mustard, celery seed, mayonnaise and pickle relish. Lightly toss the sour cream mixture with potato mixture. Chill. Garnish with chopped parsley over the top. Makes 4 to 6 servings.

*"*urds and Whey" was an early form of cheese (cottage cheese). As far as "store cheese" was concerned, it was considered quite a delicacy, and not in common use at all. Big whorls of cheese came from Pennsylvania, to be cut up by the grocer and sold by the pound. The grocer had scales with a balance on one side and weights on the other. When the desired amount of cheese was put on the balance side, the scale balanced with the weights. In Riley's day, chafing dishes were the rage, and "Welsh Rarebit" was the height of culinary achievement. This was a cheese sauce with mustard and other spicy accents. It was served over toast.*

TOSSED ZUCCHINI SALAD

1 pound zucchini
2 cups water
½ teaspoon salt
1 clove garlic, minced
½ cup chopped onion
½ cup chopped green pepper
½ cup sliced celery
Red French dressing

On cutting board, quarter the zucchini lengthwise, and cut crosswise into bite-size pieces. In saucepan, put water and salt; bring to boil and drop in zucchini. Cook for just 3 minutes, until bright green. Remove pan from heat and let stand about 2 minutes more, until crisp tender. Drain zucchini and, in salad bowl, toss with the minced garlic, onion, pepper and celery. Chill. When ready to serve, toss vegetables again with French dressing. Makes about 6 servings.

MARINATED MIXED VEGETABLES

So popular for more than 30 years. Keep in your refrigerator to serve anytime.

- 2 pounds fresh green beans or 2 (10-oz.) pkg. frozen
- 2 cups cooked fresh corn or 1 (10-oz.) pkg. frozen
  - 10-ounce package frozen peas
- 1 cup sliced celery (2 large stalks)
- 1 medium onion, chopped
- 1 green pepper, diced
  - 4-ounce jar sliced pimento

Dressing:
- ¾ cup distilled white vinegar
- ¾ cup salad oil
- 2 tablespoons water
- 1 teaspoon salt
- ½ teaspoon pepper
- ½ teaspoon paprika

In large saucepan, cook beans in boiling salted water about 7 minutes. Drain and cut in 2-inch lengths. For all frozen vegetables used, thaw before making salad. In large shallow glass baking dish (flat dish gives vegetables more even contact with marinade), mix the beans, corn, peas, celery, onion, pepper and pimento. In screw-top glass jar, place dressing ingredients. Close jar and shake to mix well. Mix well with vegetables. Cover dish with plastic wrap and refrigerate several hours or overnight. (Note: For brightest colors of vegetables, serve within a day.) Makes about 10 servings.

FRUIT SALADS

In 1905 a housewife won a national recipe contest with a jellied salad, and "congealed" salads became popular after that time. As reliable electric refrigerators came into the household, gelatin salads were very frequently made because they were attractive and could be made as much as three days ahead of serving. After about 1920, fancy "composed" salads were popular, and salads which looked like butterflies, candles and holiday shapes (even Santa Claus) were served.

Circa 1896, Fanny Farmer of the Boston Cooking School predicted in her cookbook that in the near future an important part of the educational process would deal with learning about the human diet. "Then," Ms. Farmer wrote, "mankind will eat to live, will be able to do better mental and physical work, and disease will be less frequent."

CRUNCHY PINEAPPLE CRANBERRY MOLD

To unmold easily, dip in hot water about 15 seconds, then invert over serving plate.

> 1-pound 4-ounce (20 ounces) can crushed pineapple
> 6-ounce package lemon flavored gelatin
> ½ cup lemon juice
> 3 tablespoons grated orange peel
> 2 cans (1 pound each) whole cranberry sauce
> ½ cup chopped walnuts

Drain pineapple and add enough water to syrup to make 1½ cups liquid. Heat liquid to boiling and pour over gelatin, stirring well to dissolve. Stir in pineapple and remaining ingredients; turn into 7-cup ring mold. Chill until firm. Unmold and serve, if desired, with dressing made by stirring together ½ cup each mayonnaise and sour cream. Makes 8 to 10 servings.

OVERNIGHT FRUIT SALAD

On special occasions, spoon this into a raspberry ring (recipe below.)

Dressing:
> 1-pound 4-ounce (20 ounces) pineapple chunks in syrup
> 3 egg yolks, beaten
> 2 tablespoons sugar
> ⅛ teaspoon salt
> 1 teaspoon cornstarch
> 2 tablespoons lemon juice
> ¼ teaspoon grated lemon peel
> ½ cup sour cream
> ⅛ teaspoon almond extract
> 1 teaspoon vanilla

Salad:
> 11-ounce can mandarin oranges
> ½ cup sliced fresh dates
> ½ cup halved maraschino cherries
> 2 cups miniature marshmallows
> ½ cup whipping cream

he idea of vitamins in food was fairly new at the time, and they were called "accessory food factors" in the proper diet. Ms. Farmer wrote: "By observation and experiment it has been determined that certain foods possess health-giving factors, although other foods of nearly identical chemical composition do not possess them. These factors are called 'vitamins' and at least eight, with different functions in promoting growth and health, have been recognized. They are present in foodstuffs in such small quantities that they have not yet been isolated or measured. One theory is that they are a form of energy and therefore cannot be isolated or measured as if they were part of the physical composition of food. Whatever their nature, their importance is believed to be very great, since serious disorders result when foodstuffs containing them are omitted from the diet."

The Boston Cooking School Cookbook

Make dressing: Drain pineapple, saving at least ¼ cup syrup. In top of double boiler, beat together egg yolks, sugar, salt, cornstarch, lemon juice and lemon peel. Cook over hot water, stirring, until mixture is thick. (You can improvise with two saucepans, to suspend the mixture over hot water.) Cool. Blend in the sour cream and flavorings. Make salad: In large mixing bowl, blend the drained pineapple, oranges, dates, cherries and marshmallows. Mix with dressing, cover and chill overnight. When ready to serve, whip cream in chilled bowl with chilled beaters. Fold cream into salad. If desired, serve in Raspberry Sherbet Ring, below. Makes 6 to 8 servings.

RASPBERRY SHERBET RING:

6-ounce package raspberry flavored gelatin
2   cups boiling water
1   pint (2 cups) raspberry sherbet

Dissolve raspberry gelatin in the boiling water. Immediately add the raspberry sherbet, stirring until sherbet melts. Turn into 5-cup ring mold. Chill until firm.

APRICOT PECAN SALAD

8-ounce can crushed pineapple
3-ounce package apricot gelatin
18-ounce package cream cheese, cut into large chunks
4-ounce jar baby food apricots
½   cup chopped pecans, divided
1½ cups frozen whipped topping, thawed

Place undrained pineapple in 1-quart measure. Microwave at high (100 percent power) for 2 to 3 minutes, until hot. Stir in dry gelatin until dissolved. Add cut-up cream cheese and stir in along with pureed apricots. Cool to room temperature. Fold in ¼ cup nuts and the topping. Pour into an 8-inch square dish and distribute remaining nuts over top. Refrigerate until set. Makes about 9 servings.

SUGARLESS FRUIT GELATIN

    10-ounce package unsweetened frozen strawberries
 4 bananas
16 ounce can crushed pineapple undrained
    6-ounce package unsweetened strawberry gelatin
 1 cup boiling water

Into blender or food processor (with steel blade) place strawberries, bananas and pineapple. In measuring cup or bowl stir together gelatin and boiling water; add to blender or food processor and mix until smooth. Pour into 13x9x2-inch pan and refrigerate. Variation: If desired, place half of salad in pan, cover with dollops of sour cream and spread; cover with rest of salad, more sour cream (use up to a pint of sour cream). Or, spread top (or part of top) with a layer of frozen whipped topping, thawed. Makes 12 to 15 servings.

GRAPE-PEAR SALAD

    3-ounce package lemon gelatin
 2 cups purple grape juice
 6 pear halves
½ cup drained cottage cheese
¼ cup chopped pecans

In small saucepan, stir together lemon gelatin and grape juice. Heat until dissolved, then chill until thickened. When chilled, arrange pear halves hollow side up in 8-inch round glass dish. Distribute cottage cheese among cavities and sprinkle tops with pecans. Carefully spoon chilled gelatin over pears. Chill until set. Makes about 6 servings.

SPICED PEACH SALAD

 3 (16-ounce) cans sliced peaches in syrup
 1 cup distilled white vinegar
 2 cups sugar
 6 whole cinnamon sticks
 2 teaspoons whole cloves
 2 (6-ounce) packages orange gelatin
    Water
⅔ cup dark seedless raisins

Drain peaches, saving syrup in medium saucepan. To saucepan, add vinegar, sugar, cinnamon and cloves. Bring to boil and simmer 8 to 10 minutes to dissolve sugar and release spices. Strain syrup into 1-quart measure and add water, if necessary to make 1 quart. Very carefully pour hot mixture back into pan and stir in gelatin to completely dissolve (Note: if mixture has cooled, heat briefly to help dissolve.) When dissolved, add 3 cups cold water, the drained peach slices and raisins. Stir well and pour into 13x9x2-inch pan to chill until set. Makes 12 to 15 servings. (Note: if a thinner salad is desired for more servings, divide most of mixture in 13x9x2-inch pan, and rest into 9-inch square pan.)

In 1865 Riley played the snare drums in a military band in Greenfield. A wagon like this proudly drew the band in the parade. This picture is 1925 Riley Day.

Vegetables

DRIED VEGETABLES FROM THE INDIANS AND PIONEERS

Drying foods was the earliest method of preserving them. Canning, pickling and preserving are much newer methods. Drying required no special equipment or recipes, so it was easier and cheaper than other methods. Many people dried vegetables for the winter even after newer processes were invented. Dried beans, for example, were strung on thread like a necklace and hung from the rafters of a well ventilated barn or other place to shrivel and turn greenish-grey. They were cooked much like we cook dried navy beans today, by soaking, parboiling and long simmering with smoked meat. The beans were supposed to be strung in the center about ¼ inch apart from each other so they could dry evenly. Sometimes when they were skewed just right on their string, they looked like mens' pants on a clothesline, thus the oldtime name, "Leatherbritches Beans."

MICROWAVING VEGETABLES

The recipes below are from "The Microwave Way" cooking column by Diana Williams Hansen. University studies on vegetables have shown that using less water and shorter cooking times in a microwave preserves vitamin C over conventional cooking methods using more water and time. However, you can cook most of these vegetables on the stovetop, watching and stirring, if you wish. Don't overcook!

Microwaving techniques vary with the vegetable. Onions are usually precooked to soften so their flavor can mellow the overall dish. Carrots, on the other hand, are frequently precooked just because they're hard and crisp and take longer to soften than other vegetables. Tomatoes and zucchini, which are "watery" vegetables, cook quickly because microwave energy is attracted to the water in foods. But sometimes with tomatoes, you cook them longer just so they'll wilt and become saucy.

Roastin' Ears—Called "corn on the cob" by some; to Hoosiers the term is always "roastin' ears." Writes Riley in "The Boy Lives on Our Farm," "Sometimes he drives TWO horses, when He comes to Town and brings A wagonful o' 'taters (potatoes) nen, An' roastin' ears an' things."

Some of the most interesting vegetable recipes are made up of more than one vegetable for appearance, flavor and texture contrast. However, mixtures using several vegetables necessarily make large amounts. If you don't need as much at one sitting, remember that microwave-reheated vegetables are almost as good as the first time around. Some vegetable combinations make good omelet fillings or vegetarian entrees covered, perhaps, with cheese.

GREEN BEANS WITH WALNUT SAUCE

   1 pound fresh green beans, strings removed and cut in 1-inch pieces, or two packages (10 ounces each) frozen
      Water
  ½ cup chicken broth
  3 tablespoons minced green onions (2)
  ½ teaspoon minced peeled garlic (1 small clove)
  1 tablespoon catsup
  1 teaspoon salt
  2 tablespoons tarragon vinegar
  ½ cup finely chopped walnuts

In 1½-quart microwave casserole, place beans. For fresh beans, add ½ cup water, cover and microwave at high (100 percent power) for 9 to 13 minutes, stirring every 4 minutes, until beans lose their raw taste. For frozen beans, add 2 tablespoons water and microwave at high for 6 to 10 minutes, breaking up after 2 minutes, until tender and bright green. Let stand while combining sauce. In 2 to 4-cup microwave casserole or bowl, place chicken broth, onion, garlic, catsup, salt and vinegar. Microwave at high for 1 to 3 minutes, just until steaming hot. Stir in walnuts. Toss sauce with freshly cooked beans. Makes about 4 servings.

BROCCOLI AND RUTABAGA STICKS

When preparing broccoli, using the florets is the easy part. You can eat them raw with a creamy dip, marinate them (see Appetizers) or toss them in salad. Too often the stalks wither in the refrigerator before being thrown away. One

rom Indiana's The Court House Cookbook, Volume 1, comes this very old recipe for Baked Bean Rarebit, which uses up that last cupful of baked beans. "Press ½ pint cold baked beans through a sieve and mix with ½ teaspoon salt and ¼ teaspoon paprika. Melt 2 tablespoons butter in a saucepan, add beans and when hot stir in ½ cup milk gradually. When smooth add 3 heaping tablespoons soft cheese, chopped fine, and 1 teaspoon Worcestershire sauce. Stir until cheese is melted, then pour over very thin toasted slices of brown bread."

answer is to julienne the stalks for an attractive and easily-microwaved presentation. Peel the stalk first to remove the tough outer layer. Cut it crosswise, then cut each half lengthwise into slim even sticks (like celery sticks.) A bunch of broccoli yields 1 to 1½ cups of julienne strips from the stalks. You can substitute white turnip for all or part of the rutabaga. This microwave time is based on about 3 cups julienne vegetables.

- 1½ cups julienne strips of broccoli stalk
- 1½ julienne strips of rutabaga (1 small, peeled and cut)
- 2 tablespoons water
- ½ teaspoon sugar
- ½ teaspoon salt
- ¼ teaspoon ground white pepper
- 2 tablespoons butter

In 1½ to 2-quart microwave casserole, place broccoli, rutabaga and water. Microwave at high (100 percent power) for 10 to 14 minutes, stirring after 5 minutes, until pieces are barely tender when pierced with a fork. Add sugar, salt, pepper and butter and toss to mix well. Serve hot. Makes about 4 to 6 servings.

CROPS FOR THE ROOT CELLAR

Root crops like beets, carrots, turnips and rutabagas were a blessing to the 1900's housewife because they could stay in the garden to be used up as needed until the frost. They didn't have to be hastily gathered and canned or preserved at a specific time (whether convenient or not!), as did the more delicate above-ground vegetables. And when you did go to preserve them, all you had to do was put them in the cool root cellar.

ZESTY SWEET AND SOUR BEETS

Cook beets whole, with the skin and root end intact and about 2 inches of stem. Otherwise, beets can "bleed" their color into the cooking water. The skin slips off easily after cooking.

1 pound beets (about 5), stems cut to 2 inches and leaves removed

1 cup water

Sauce:

1 tablespoon cornstarch

3 tablespoons sugar

½ teaspoon salt

1½ tablespoons vinegar

3 tablespoons prepared horseradish

2 tablespoons butter

Wash and clean beets, cutting all but 1 to 2-inches of stem, but do not peel. In 1½-qt. casserole, place beets and water. Cover and microwave at high (100 percent power) for 10 to 14 minutes, until tender when pierced with fork. Into separate measuring cup, measure ¾ cup of the beet juice and reserve. Drain away the rest of the juice. Let beets cool until you can easily handle them. When cool, slip off the skins. Into another container, dice the beets into large pieces. Make sauce: In same 1½-qt. microwave casserole, place cornstarch, sugar, salt, reserved beet juice, vinegar, horseradish and butter. Stir very well to blend cornstarch. Microwave at high for 4 to 7 minutes, stirring every 2 minutes, until clear and thickened. Add diced beets and gently blend. Serve warm or cold, garnished with spoonful of sour cream, if desired. Makes 4 to 6 servings.

TANGY HORSERADISH CARROTS

An attractive way to cut carrots is called the "roll cut"— cut a slender, pared carrot crosswise on the diagonal, then roll the carrot ½ turn so the opposite side is up before making the next cut in the opposite diagonal direction. Pieces should be approximately pyramid-shaped. The age and size of the carrot determine the best cooking time; you might have to add time for older carrots.

2 pounds carrots, cleaned and cut into chunks (about 5 cups)

½ cup water

Sauce:

⅓ cup coarsely chopped onion

1 tablespoon butter
½ cup mayonnaise
2 tablespoons prepared horseradish
½ teaspoon salt
¼ teaspoon pepper
½ teaspoon dried dill weed

In 2-qt. microwave casserole or bowl, place carrots and water. Cover with vented plastic wrap. Microwave at high (100 percent power) for 10 to 14 minutes, until crisp-tender when pierced with fork. Drain. Make sauce: In 2-cup (1 pint) measuring cup or bowl, place onions and butter. Microwave at high for 1 to 2 minutes, until onions are almost tender. Stir in mayonnaise, horseradish, salt and pepper, and dill. Pour over carrots and toss to mix well. Makes 6 to 8 servings.

CORN AND COUNTRY TOMATOES

This tastes good just as it comes from the oven. But it you wish, you can add the suggested butter and/or cream which are traditional additions to country-cooked vegetables.

2 cups slices of peeled fresh onion (2 medium)
2½ cups (1 pound) coarsely chopped fresh tomatoes (2 medium large, cored)
3 cups sliced fresh okra (¾ pound)
1 teaspoon salt
1 teaspoon oregano
½ teaspoon cumin seed
⅛ teaspoon cayenne pepper
3 cups fresh cut corn (5 ears, tips cut from kernels, ears scraped with dull side of knife to capture all the corn solids and "milk")
1½ cups large dice green pepper (1 large)
"Enrichers" (optional): 2 tablespoons butter and/or 1 cup light cream

In 3-quart microwave casserole, place onion. Cover and microwave at high (100 percent power) for 2 to 3 minutes, until wilted. Add tomatoes, okra, salt, oregano, cumin and cayenne. Stir well and continue microwaving at high for 4 to 7 more minutes, until tomatoes are soft and saucy and okra is soft and sticky. Stir well, then stir in the corn and

any later poems were nostalgic, thoughtful. In "At Broad Ripple" he writes,
"The river's story flowing by—forever sweet to ear and eye
Forever tenderly begun,
Forever new and never done.
Thus lulled and sheltered in a shade
Where never feverish cares invade
I bait my hook and cast my line
And feel the best of life is mine."

green pepper. Cover and continue microwaving for 8 to 11 minutes, until corn is still crisp but has lost its raw taste. If desired, stir in one or both of the "enrichers" just before serving. Makes about 8 servings.

CAULIFLOWER WITH PIMENTO COTTAGE CHEESE SAUCE

A food that has practically disappeared today was once a "snack" for cold winter afternoons: parched corn. Grains of corn were carefully spread out on a flat pan or cookie sheet, and allowed to dry in a "warm" oven for several hours.

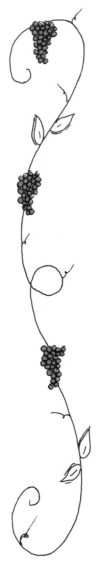

1½ pound whole head fresh cauliflower, green leaves and cone-shaped core removed
¼ cup water
1 tablespoon butter
1 tablespoon flour
½ cup milk
1 cup small curd cottage cheese
½ cup sharp cheddar cheese
2 ounces chopped pimento with juice (small jar)
½ teaspoon dried dill weed
½ teaspoon salt
⅛ teaspoon ground black pepper

In 1½-quart microwave casserole, place cauliflower and water. Cover with plastic wrap and microwave at high (100 percent power) for 7 to 11 minutes, rotating ½ turn after 4 minutes, until cauliflower is tender. Let stand, covered, while making sauce. In 1-quart microwave mixing bowl or casserole, place butter and flour. Microwave at high for about 2 minutes, whisking after 1 minute, until butter and flour mixture is well combined. Add milk and microwave for 2 to 5 more minutes, whisking every minute, until sauce is boiling, thickened and smooth. Stir in cottage cheese, cheddar cheese, pimento, dill weed, salt and pepper. Microwave sauce at high an additional 2 to 4 minutes, just until the cheeses are partially melted and sauce is hot and well combined. Remove cauliflower to a serving plate, and spoon some of the sauce over the top. Cut cauliflower in wedges to serve, and pass additional sauce. Makes about 6 servings.

VEGETABLES

MICROWAVING POTATOES

Potatoes are the most popular fresh food for microwaving. They are very easy to cook in their natural skins, rapidly and with little water, thus preserving vitamins and minerals. You can microwave potatoes as many ways as you cook them conventionally. From the microwave, potatoes will be more moist on the outside and inside and cooked in about a tenth of the conventional baking time.

Round or oval potatoes microwave better than long thin ones (just as with baking) because the ends are less apt to overcook. Always vent the jackets of potatoes by pricking them. Space apart—in a circle if more than two. Allow 3 to 6 minutes at high (100 percent power) for a single potato, and about 3 minutes per potato for additional ones.

BROCCOLI AND CHEESE TOPPING FOR MICROWAVED POTATOES

    1 package (10-oz.) frozen broccoli spears
    3 tablespoons water
Sauce:
    1/4 cup (1/2 stick) butter
    1/4 cup flour
    1/4 cup finely chopped onion
    1 teaspoon salt
    1/2 teaspoon dry mustard
    1/8 teaspoon cayenne pepper
    2 cups milk
    2 cups shredded sharp cheddar cheese (8 ounces)

In 1-quart microwave casserole place unwrapped broccoli and water. Cover and microwave at high (100 percent power) for 7 to 9 minutes, until just tender. Let stand until slightly cooled, then slice spears into large pieces. Set aside until just before serving. Make sauce: In 1-quart microwave measuring cup or bowl, place butter, flour, onion, salt, mustard and cayenne. Microwave at high for 2 to 3 minutes, whisking every minute, until mixture is well blended and slightly dry. Gradually whisk in the milk. Microwave at high for 3 to 6 more minutes, whisking every minute, until mixture boils and thickens smoothly. Whisk

in the cheese until melted. Fold the broccoli into the cheese sauce and serve over potatoes which have been cut open. Makes enough sauce for 4 to 6 potatoes.

GARLIC AND ONION BUTTER FOR NEW POTATOES

Cook small new or red potatoes about 8 to 12 minutes per pound at high (100 percent power), in a single layer in ½ inch of water, and in a covered microwave casserole. Prick each one before cooking, and expect larger ones to take more time per pound than smaller ones.

  ⅓ cup butter
  ¼ cup finely chopped onion (1 small)
  2 medium cloves garlic, minced
  ½ teaspoon leaf thyme
  ¼ teaspoon salt
  ⅛ teaspoon white pepper
  ½ cup chopped parsley (small bunch)

In 1-quart microwave bowl or casserole, place butter, onion, garlic, thyme, salt and pepper. Microwave at high (100 percent power) for 2 to 3½ minutes, stirring every minute, until onion is translucent and cooked. Add this mixture along with chopped parsley to 1 to 1½ pounds of microwave boiled "new" potatoes (about 12 to 16) and toss gently to coat each potato. Makes 3 to 4 servings.

TWICE BAKED SWEET POTATOES WITH PEANUT TOPPING

These taste almost like sweet potato pie, and are very easy to serve. Make them ahead of time and refrigerate until their final heating.

Topping:
  2 thin slices wheat bread, torn into small pieces (1 cup lightly packed)
  ½ cup coarsely chopped salted peanuts
  ⅓ cup butter or margarine
  3 tablespoons (packed) light brown sugar

¼ teaspoon ground nutmeg
Filling:
 4 same-size medium sweet potatoes (about 2 pounds)
 ¼ to ¾ cup milk (depending on moistness of
   potatoes)
 1 tablespoon lemon juice
 ⅛ teaspoon ground black pepper

Make topping: In 8-inch round microwave dish or pie plate, scatter bread pieces. Microwave at high (100 percent power) for 2½ to 3½ minutes, stirring every minute, until very dry and pieces crumble easily. With fingers, crush pieces into fine crumbs. Add the peanuts, butter, brown sugar and nutmeg. Stir well and continue microwaving at high for 2 to 3 more minutes, stirring every minute, until well blended and crumbly. Set aside. Microwave potatoes: Scrub potatoes well and pierce each several times with fork. Arrange in circle on piece of paper towel in microwave oven. Microwave at high for 12 to 15 minutes, until potatoes can be pierced with fork (they will still remain firm). Remove from oven and let stand until cool enough to handle. With sharp knife, cut thin slice lengthwise off top of each potato. With small spoon, scoop flesh from each into medium mixing bowl. To potato flesh, add milk, lemon juice and pepper and whip with electric mixer until very light and fluffy. Pile about half of filling into potato shells, then divide a scant half of the topping over filling. Finish filling shells with rest of whipped potato. With back of spoon, make rather deep indentions in the filled potatoes to hold the remaining topping, then divide topping over potatoes. Place filled potatoes in shallow 8-inch round dish and, when ready to serve, microwave at high for about 2 to 4 minutes, or until hot through. Makes 4 servings.

FRESH TOMATO PUDDING

You can use firm (wintertime) tomatoes in this. Leave the skins on for texture, or peel as desired, and puree with a food processor. This would "plop" and spatter on a range top as it boils, so microwaving it is cleaner and requires less stirring. Increase the sage to ½ teaspoon if you wish.

1½ cups fresh white or rye bread cubes, packed (3 slices)
⅓ cup melted butter
1¼ cups finely pureed fresh tomatoes (2 medium)
2 to 4 tablespoons brown sugar (depending on sweetness of the tomatoes)
¼ teaspoon salt
¼ teaspoon rubbed sage
⅛ teaspoon black pepper

In 1-quart microwave casserole, place bread cubes. Distribute melted butter evenly over cubes. In small bowl, stir together tomato puree, brown sugar, salt, sage and pepper. Pour over bread and stir well. Microwave at medium high (70 percent power) for 9 to 12 minutes, stirring after 4 minutes, until bread has thickened the pudding. Stir and let stand a few minutes before serving in sauce dishes. Makes about 4 to 5 servings.

HERBED ZUCCHINI AND CARROT CASSEROLE

Freshly buttered and herbed croutons thicken this attractive vegetable dish.

Croutons:
3 cups fresh white bread cubes (6 slices)
½ cup butter (1 stick)
½ teaspoon thyme
½ teaspoon basil
½ teaspoon salt
1 teaspoon minced fresh garlic (2 cloves)
Vegetables:
1 cup half-slices of onion (2 small)
1 cup short julienne strips of carrot (2 medium)
3 cups sliced zucchini (2 medium)
2 cups (1 pint) sour cream (16 ounces)

Make croutons: In 12x8x2-inch dish, place the bread cubes. Microwave at high (100 percent power) for 4 to 6 minutes, until dried and almost crisp. Push bread to one side and add the butter to the unoccupied area in the dish. Return to microwave at high for 1 to 2 minutes, until butter has almost completely melted. Stir butter with bread cubes, along with thyme, basil, salt and garlic. Continue microwaving at high for 4 to 7 more minutes, until cubes are very dry (they will continue to crisp after being removed from oven). Microwave vegetables: In 2-quart microwave casserole, place the onion and carrot. Cover and microwave at high (100 percent power) for 3 to 5 minutes, until onions are wilted and carrots are slightly cooked. Add zucchini, cover and continue microwaving for 4 to 7 more minutes, until zucchini is crisp-tender. Stir in the sour cream along with about half the croutons, which have been crumbled slightly. Top with the remaining croutons (also crumbled slightly) and continue microwaving at medium high (70 percent power) for 7 to 10 minutes, until hot throughout. Makes 6 to 8 servings.

GOOD LUCK VEGETABLES

Traditions built around eating certain foods for luck are older than James Whitcomb Riley's time, and they exist to today. Early 1900's references suggested stuffed cabbage as being especially lucky if eaten at New Year's. In the southern part of Indiana and points south, blackeye peas must be eaten for good luck, along with a form of pork such as bacon, which is in this popular recipe.

HOPPING JOHN (Rice and Blackeye Peas)

    6 slices bacon
    2 cups coarsely chopped onion (1 very large or 2
      medium)
    ¾ cup long grain rice
    1 cup dried blackeye peas
    1½ teaspoon salt
    ¼ teaspoon pepper
    6 cups water

With scissors, cut bacon slices into dice into 3-quart microwave casserole. Cover with paper towel. Microwave at high (100 percent power) for 4 to 6 minutes, until very crisp. Without draining bacon fat, add the remaining ingredients to the casserole. Cover with wax paper (casserole

lid might be too tightly fitting, and cause spillover). Microwave at high for 20 minutes, until very hot and boiling, then stir well and continue microwaving at medium (50 percent power) for 17 to 21 minutes, until peas are firm but tender. Mixture will be very moist. Let stand about 15 minutes to dry somewhat and for flavors to blend. Makes about 6 to 8 servings.

Note: You can vary traditional Hopping John by adding celery and/or bay leaf before cooking. Also, add a dash of cayenne pepper, if you wish. Other versions include cut up fresh or canned tomatoes, although the tomato variation is not traditional. (Note: To make this without a microwave, cook in saucepan on stovetop approximately same time. You may have to add more water, so check cooking about every 15 minutes. Alternately, precook rice and peas (or use canned), saute onion in bacon fat on stovetop, combine ingredients excluding the water and bake at 350 degrees for about 30 to 40 minutes.)

MOZIS ADDUMS' "RESIPEE FOR CUKIN CON-FELL (cornfield, or Blackeye) PEES"

From the 1874 cookbook *Housekeeping in Old Virginia*. It is quoted as follows from Marion Flexner's famous cookbook, *Out of Kentucky Kitchens*.

"Gether your peas 'bout sun-down. The folrin day, 'bout 'leven o'clock, gowge out your pees with your them nale, like gowgin' out a man's eyeball at a kote house. Rense your pees, parbile them, then fry 'em with som several slices uv streekt middlin (Bacon), incouragin uv the gravy to seep out and intermarry with your pees. When modritly brownm, but not scorcht, empty into a dish. Mash 'em gently with a spune, mix with raw tomarters sprinkled with a little brown shugar and the immortal dish ar quite ready. Eat a hepe. Eat mo and mo. It is good for you genral helth uv mind and body. It fattens you up, makes you sassy, goes throo and throo your very soul. But why don'y you eat? Eat on. By Jings. Eat. Stop! Never, while thar is a pee in the dish.—Mozis ADdums."

JUNE'S LUCKY STUFFED CABBAGE ROLLS

6 large cabbage leaves, from outer layers of cabbage
   Boiling Water
½ cup chopped onion
5 strips bacon, cooked drained and crumbled
3 cups bite size shredded rice cereal, crushed (1 cup)
1 pound lean ground beef
1 egg
1 teaspoon salt
¼ teaspoon pepper
⅛ teaspoon basil
Topping:
½ cup sour cream
1 tablespoon flour
10-ounce can condensed tomato soup
¾ cup shredded sharp cheddar cheese

Place cabbage leaves in large kettle or heatproof bowl and pour the boiling water over them to cover. Let stand until pliable, about 8 to 10 minutes. Meanwhile, make filling by combining the onion, crumbled bacon, rice cereal, beef, egg, salt, pepper and basil. Divide into 6 equal mounds and shape into logs. Drain cabbage leaf and over the heavy vein, place a log of meat. Fold sides to center and roll up the cabbage roll. Place seam side down in greased 2½ quart casserole. Repeat to make all 6 rolls. Make topping by stirring sour cream, flour and tomato soup. Spread over rolls. Cover and bake at 350 degrees for 30 to 45 minutes, until rolls are tender and no traces of pink appear in meat. Add cheese, and bake until melted. Makes 6 rolls.

Riley's Old Swimmin' Hole. James Whitcomb Riley is in the center in a black hat. Tom Randall and a reporter from *Harper's Magazine* are the other two men.

FISH

FISH AND SEAFOOD

"As a food, fish ranks just below meat on the one hand and above vegetables on the other. It is easier of digestion but less nutritious than meats, if salmon is excepted, which is extremely hearty food, and should be eaten sparingly by children and those whose digestion is not strong. But, though it is not recommended that fish should be the only animal food of which one partakes, its value as a part of the diet is indicated by the larger proportion of phosphorous which it contains, and which renders it especially fitted for the use of those who perform much brain work. There can be no doubt that fish might with advantage enter much more largely into our family diet than it does at present, as it would not only afford a pleasant variety in fare, but would also supply certain elements of blood which are not obtained in sufficient quantity from either meat or vegetables." *The New Buckeye Cook Book (1880)*

Other than tuna, which was available canned, fish was not common to Hoosiers on a daily basis in Riley's time. However in the summertime the lakes and streams in Indiana would sometimes yield fish for baking or frying. It has not been until the last few years, when omega 3 and fatty acids entered the vocabularly, that fish has enjoyed the popularity it now does.

The delicacy and natural tenderness of fish and seafood make it a perfect microwave food. Most gourmets, if they cook no other food in the microwave, do microwave fish because it preserves the moisture and natural texture of this meat.

POACHED FISH WITH VEGETABLES

With microwaving, fish does not need to be completely covered with liquid to keep it moist. The acid in the wine and lemon juice helps reduce the odor of fish which otherwise could easily spread with the steam which forms during poaching.

ags, bones, bottles to-day?" was a cry heard at the turn of the century. The rag-man's cart was well known. Also travelling about were men with fresh fish, the Jewell Tea Company selling its spices and extracts, the "strawberry" man, scissors grinders, occasional gypsies, and patent medicine men on their wagons.

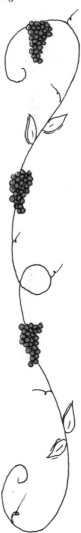

From The Century Cook Book (1894): An Excellent Cough Syrup. Take five cents' worth each of sweet spirits of nitre, paregoric, syrup of squills and sweet oil; put all in a pint of molasses, dose, a teaspoonful several times a day. The book also gives a recipe for Cough Troches (Cough Drops): One ounce of powdered licorice-root, one ounce of powdered gum-arabic, one ounce of powdered cubeds, mix all together with one pound of pulverized sugar, add enough water to make a stiff paste like bread dough; roll out thin and cut in shape with an open top thimble; arrange upon sheets of foolscap, and set away to dry.

- 2/3 cup rose or dry white wine
- 1/3 cup lemon juice
- 1/4 teaspoon salt
- 1/2 teaspoon dried dill weed
- 12 whole peppercorns
- 3 medium carrots, scraped and sliced
- 2 large green celery stalks, sliced
- 1 small onion, sliced
- 1 lb. orange roughy or flounder fillets, fresh or defrosted

In 8-inch square microwave dish, place wine, lemon juice, salt, dill and peppercorns. Stir to dissolve salt. Add vegetables and stir again. Cover with plastic wrap and microwave at high (100 percent power) for 8 to 10 minutes, until carrots are still slightly firm when pierced with a fork. Add fish fillets, thickest areas to edges of dish, and spoon vegetables over top. Recover and microwave at high for 2 minutes. Turn fish over and again spoon vegetables over top. Recover and continue microwaving at high for 1 to 3 minutes, until fish turns opaque and thin areas flake easily. Let stand several minutes, covered, to finish cooking the thick areas and so that fish can absorb flavor from the poaching liquid. Serve fish and vegetables with some of the poaching liquid (discard peppercorns) spooned over the top. Makes about 4 servings.

CRUMB COATED FISH FILLETS

The coating ingredients in this recipe will accommodate a pound of thin flounder fillets from a block-size frozen package. Thicker fillets, whether fresh or frozen, won't have as much surface area per pound, so will need less coating. The outside coating of the fish should be soft and flavorful and have a good brown color after microwaving. These are good as is or in sandwiches.

- 3 eggs
- 1/2 cup butter, melted (1 stick)
- 1 1/2 teaspoons onion salt
- 2 cups cornflake crumbs
- 1 lb. frozen flounder fillets, defrosted

In small wide bowl beat together eggs, butter and onion salt. In small shallow bowl place cornflake crumbs. With fingers, dip each fillet into crumbs, then egg mixture, then crumbs again. Arrange in 12x8x2-in. microwave dish with thin areas overlapping. Microwave at high (100 percent power) for 8 to 10 minutes, rotating dish ½ turn if necessary after half of time. Makes 4 to 6 servings. (Note: If you are microwaving large thick fillet pieces, an 8-in. square dish may be adequate to hold all pieces.)

Riley was often asked why he never married. "When I was young," he replied, "I had plenty of girls but no money. When I was old, I had plenty of money but no girls!"

"Tuna Fish A La Apartment" was a recipe contributed by Marjorie H. Walker of Greenfield to a Tri Kappa Cookbook in 1928. It suggested that you mix 1 can tuna fish with 1 can asparagus, cover with white sauce, season to taste, bake 30 minutes. This recipe serves 4, she said. About 40 years later, Ms. Walker founded The Hancock County Historical Society. She was also on the original committee to furnish the Riley Home when it first became a historic site in 1939.

PLANKED WHITEFISH was a 1928 recipe by Ora H. Thayer. The Thayer Building still stands today on Greenfield, Indiana's Main Street on The National Road, U.S. 40.

Clean and split a 3-pound whitefish. Put skin side down on oak plank 1-inch thick and longer and wider than fish, sprinkle with salt, pepper and brush with melted butter. Bake 25 minutes in hot oven. After taking from oven spread with butter and garnish with parsley and lemon. Serve off of the plank. Serves 8.

MUSHROOM SOLE FILLETS IN WHITE CHEESE SAUCE

Add partially-cooked slivered carrots, for color, to the top of the fish before steaming it, if desired. Get the freshest fish possible. Even frozen fish should be stored no more than 3 months.

- 1 tablespoon butter
- 2 tablespoons thinly sliced greens onions
- 1 pound sole or flounder fillets, defrosted and cut into serving pieces (see note for defrosting)
- 1½ cups (about 6 ounces) sliced fresh mushrooms
- ¾ cup sauterne or chablis wine
- 2 tablespoons flour

*I*t was customary in Riley's day to read poems at funerals. When his dear friend, a daughter of Lee O. Harris, died, Riley sat up all night composing a poem for her services. There was one word he was not satisfied with, but he finally had to turn the poem in to the minister. A little later he thought of the word he wanted but the funeral had begun. He concentrated on the desired word and had it in mind when the minister read his poem. Low and behold the minister did not read the written word, but in its place supplied the one in Riley's mind!

¼ cup (4 tablespoons) whipping cream
1 teaspoon salt
⅛ teaspoon pepper
½ teaspoon lemon juice
1 cup (4 oz.) shredded Swiss cheese
  Chopped parsley

In 12x8x2-inch microwave dish, place butter and green onions. Microwave at high (100 percent power) for about 1 minute, until butter is melted. Distribute butter and onions evenly over dish, then arrange fillets over onions with thickest areas to edges of dish and tails overlapping in center. Add mushrooms over top of fish; pour wine on top. Cover with plastic wrap, turning back one corner to vent. Microwave at high for 7 to 9 minutes, rotating dish ¼ turn every 3 minutes, until fish flakes with a fork. Meanwhile, combine flour, cream, salt and pepper in 1-quart microwave casserole until smooth. When fish is done, carefully drain the poaching liquid into the flour mixture and stir well. Recover fish and keep warm while cooking sauce. Microwave sauce in casserole at high for 2 to 3 minutes, stirring every minute, until thickened. Add lemon juice. Pour sauce over fish, then sprinkle with cheese. Microwave at high for 2 more minutes, until cheese has melted and entree is hot. Sprinkle with chopped fresh parsley. (Note: To defrost 1-lb. paper-wrapped package of frozen fish, microwave it at the defrost setting (about 30 percent power) for about 4 to 8 minutes, turning over and rotating the package after half the time. Time depends on the thickness of the fish and power level used (the higher the power the shorter the time.) After defrosting, fish should be cool and even frosty. If still a little bit too frozen, place the fish under cool running water to separate.

SEAFOOD

OYSTERS

As the national network of railroads became established across the country, ocean foods became popular in middle America. One of the most popular was oysters, which were shipped in barrels to farms and towns very often. Although definitely an "upscale" food, oysters were common enough to be served frequently at parties, and especially during the holidays. When James Whitcomb Riley wrote for *The Indiana Journal*, he treated himself to oysters frequently. In the early 1900's the John and Anna Williams family (their son, Tom Williams was our husband and father) thought it was good luck to eat oyster stew on Christmas eve. We lament with the environmentalists the pollution of our waters which has reduced the availability of oysters today.

ysters, as one of Riley's favorite foods, are mentioned several times in his poems. Oysters were eaten only in months with an R in them. In the poem, "Grendfather Squeers," we read, "His teeth were imperfect—my grandfather owned That he couldn't eat oysters unless they were 'boned'."

CHRISTMAS EVE OYSTER STEW

  1 pint oysters, thawed if frozen
 ¼ cup (½ stick) butter
  1 quart milk
 1½ teaspoons salt
 ⅛ teaspoon pepper
    Paprika

Drain oysters. In medium saucepan, melt butter. Add drained oysters and cook at medium heat just until edges curl, about 3 or 4 minutes. Add milk, salt and pepper and bring almost to the boiling point (bubbles will rise to the surface.) Remove from heat. Shake paprika lightly over each serving and and serve hot with oyster crackers or soda crackers. Makes about 6 servings.

HOLIDAY SCALLOPED OYSTERS

  4 cups (1 quart or about 36 ounces) oysters, thawed
    if frozen
 ¾ cup melted butter
  2 cups fine soda cracker crumbs (about 40 squares)
 ½ cup fine chopped fresh parsley
  1 teaspoon salt
 ⅛ teaspoon pepper
 ⅛ teaspoon nutmeg
 ¼ cup cream or milk

Reserving ¼ cup oyster liquor in measuring cup, drain oysters. In small mixing bowl, mix together butter, crumbs

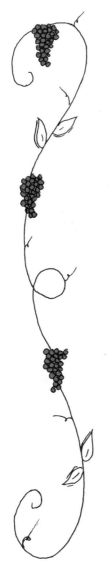

uns were fired off and firecrackers exploded in Hoosier villages on Christmas and New Year's Day until after the turn of the century. Oyster dressing has survived as a favorite to this day for the Christmas turkey.

and parsley. In cup, mix salt, pepper and nutmeg. Assemble oysters: In 10x6x2-inch dish, layer ⅓ of buttered crumbs. Top with half of oysters and half of seasonings. Repeat with ⅓ of crumbs, other half of oysters and seasonings. Put the last ⅓ of crumbs on top and spread evenly. To reserved oyster liquor, mix in cream or milk; pour over the assembled casserole and with knife, poke holes through layers to help liquid be absorbed. Microwave at high for 13 to 15 minutes, rotating dish if necessary after 7 minutes, until oysters are firm when pierced with fork. Makes about 6 servings. (Note: This can be baked in a conventional oven at 350 degrees for about 30 to 40 minutes, until oysters are firm.)

SHRIMP

"Shrimps are caught in immense quantities along the seashore from early spring til late autumn, but are chiefly used for bait and for lunches for the parties of children who have unlimited time to pick them from their paper-like shells. If one can take the trouble to pick them out, they are really more delicate in fibre and finer flavored than their larger cousins from the Gulf. Tinned shrimps should always be rinsed in lightly salted water and well drained and aired before they are used."...1904 *Gold Medal Cook Book.*

CHIVE BUTTERED SHRIMP

- 1 pound raw shelled deveined shrimp
- ½ cup (1 stick) butter, melted
- 2 tablespoons white wine
- 1 tablespoon chopped chives
- ¼ teaspoon minced garlic (1 clove)
- 2 drops tabasco

In 2-quart microwave casserole, place shrimp (Note: If shrimp have been frozen and defrosted, drain very well on paper towels so water doesn't dilute butter sauce.) Add butter, wine, chives, garlic and tabasco and stir well. Cover casserole and microwave at high (100 percent power) for 5 to 7 minutes, stirring every 2 minutes, until shrimp are evenly pink and firm but tender. Serve as appetizer with cocktail picks or on bed of rice or pasta. Makes 3 to 4 entree servings.

PINEAPPLE SWEET AND SOUR SHRIMP

This is one of the few recipes in this book which might not have been served in Riley's time in Indiana. Canned pineapple was beginning to be popular at that time; however, fresh pineapples were generally unavailable. Pineapple was thought to be mostly for salads or for pineapple upside down cake, or to glaze a ham. This recipe uses a whole small to medium fresh pineapple which has been peeled and cored at the supermarket, part chopped for the sauce and the rest chunked to add texture to the finished dish. Fresh pineapples vary in sweetness. Taste the pineapple you use in this dish and be prepared to add a little more sugar if the fruit is not very sweet.

- 1 medium pineapple peeled and cored (about 1¾ pounds after peeling)
- ¼ cup chopped onion (1 small)
- ¼ cup sugar
- 2 tablespoons cornstarch
- ¼ cup cold water
- ½ cup mild white vinegar
- 1 pound cooked peeled and deveined medium to large shrimp, defrosted and drained if necessary (about 2 pounds raw unpeeled)
- ½ cup (4 ounces) chopped pimento, undrained
- 1 teaspoon minced fresh garlic (2 cloves)
- 2 tablespoons soy sauce
- 10 drops liquid pepper seasoning
- 1 cup large dice green pepper (1 medium)
- 3 strips bacon, microwaved crisp and crumbled
- 3 or 4 green onions, sliced

Prepare pineapple: Cut peeled pineapple in half and remove core. In food processor, chop half of the pineapple medium fine (you should have about 1 cup). On cutting board with sharp knife, cut the other half into bite-size chunks (you should have about 1½ cups). Make sauce: In

1½-quart microwave casserole, place the onion. Microwave at high (100 percent power) for 1 to 1½ minutes, just until hot. Add sugar, cornstarch, cold water and vinegar. Microwave at high for 2½ to 4 minutes, until mixture is smooth, clear and very thick. Add shrimp and stir well to distribute, and to warm the shrimp. Add chopped pineapple, pimento, garlic, soy sauce and liquid pepper seasoning. Microwave at high for 5 to 7 minutes, stirring every 2 minutes, until all ingredients are hot. Stir in the green pepper and pineapple chunks well and let mixture stand for 5 to 10 minutes before serving. Garnish with bacon crumbles and green onion slices. Serve over hot cooked rice, with chopsticks, if desired. Makes 4 to 6 servings.

Note: If you wish, you can substitute canned pineapple for fresh. Use an 8-ounce can of crushed pineapple for the sauce, and an 8-ounce can (or part of a 20-ounce can) pineapple chunks or tidbits, drained, to stir in after cooking. You will probably want to increase the sugar; try ⅓ cup and add more only if necessary.

MEATS
(Beef and Pork)

MEATS (BEEF AND PORK)

BEEF

In James Whitcomb Riley's Indiana, meat usually meant beef.

In 1888, *The New Buckeye Cookbook* published the latest word on meat cookery. "Broiling steak," it advised, "is the very last thing to be done in getting breakfast or dinner; every other dish should be ready for table, so that this may have the cook's undivided attention. Never take lid from broiler without first removing it from fire, as the smoke and flames rush out past the meat and smoke it."

"Roasting," the book laments, "is almost unknown in these days of stoves and ranges—baking, a much inferior process, having taken its place." Original roasting, the book continues, is actually rotissing on a spit, the meat being basted periodically with drippings and salt water. For oven roasting, a bright and hot fire is recommended. If you don't have a trivet, support the roast on three clean bits of hard wood or bones "laid crosswise of the roast," and always keep the thickest part of the meat in the hottest part of the oven.

On doneness of meat, the book has this to say: "Take care that every part of the roast, including the fat of the tenderloin, is cooked so that the texture is changed. Most persons like roast beef and mutton underdone, and less time is required to cook them than for pork and veal or lamb which must be very well done. Underdone meat is cooked throughout so that the bright red juices follow the knife of the carver; if it is a livid purple it is raw, and unfit for food."

BEEF TENDERLOIN MADIERA

1 whole tenderloin, about 3 to 5 pounds
  Cooking oil, paprika, cracked black pepper
Sauce:
  1 quart beef broth (two 16-ounce cans)
  1 bay leaf
  ½ teaspoon chopped garlic
  1½ teaspoons sugar

* like the other foods of early settler's times, meat had to be procured, processed, and canned. They did not seem to grind up much beef, but a grinder was always used when making pork sausage. When the hog was butchered, the scraps, and less desirable cuts (not those loins and rib parts) went into the sausage grinder. Preserved by salt and sage, the top of the crock protected with a "lid" of lard, sausage could be eaten for some time after the fresh cuts of meat were gone. There remained the hams to hang up in the smokehouse over a well-laid fire of hickory smoke. Hams were wrapped heavily in cloth, then hung down from the rafters of the back porch for many months.*

 ⅓ cup cornstarch
   Water
 2 tablespoons madiera wine

oasted cheese or Scotch Rare-bit was another dish which was often served in Greenfield during the late 1800's. Besides Scotch Rare-bit, old cookbooks gave recipes for Welsh Rare-bit.

Prepare beef: trim any silvery membrane. Rub all outside surfaces with oil, then with paprika and pepper. Place in roasting pan and fold the thin ends underneath to protect them from overcooking. Let stand until about one hour before serving. Make sauce: In saucepan, stir broth, bay leaf, garlic and sugar. Over high heat, bring to boil, reduce heat and simmer 5 minutes. In small bowl or cup, stir cornstarch with enough water to thin. Pour into broth mixture and allow to boil for about 1 minute only. Remove from heat and stir in wine; keep warm. Time roast beef to cook about 35 minutes for medium-rare doneness, then let stand about 10 minutes before carving. To roast: Preheat oven to 450 degrees (this takes 10 to 15 minutes). Add roast and bake for 10 minutes. Reduce the heat to 350 degrees and bake for another 25 minutes. Internal temperature should be about 125 degrees, and will rise to about 135 degrees upon standing. (You can test doneness by making a small cut into center, which would be concealed by slicing anyway.) Any pan drippings can be strained into the sauce. Makes about 10 to 12 servings.

GARLICKY RIB EYE BEEF

 5 pound eye of rib beef roast
 ¼ cup milk
 3 pieces toasted white bread without crust
 4 cloves garlic, minced
 3 egg yolks
 ¼ cup olive oil
 1 teaspoon lemon juice
 ½ teaspoon water

With sharp knife, cut roast vertically into serving-size slices, stopping about an inch from the bottom of the roast (10 or more slices.) Make garlic paste: In small bowl soak milk and bread until crumbly; wring any excess milk and place bread in small bowl. Add garlic and egg yolks and mix thoroughly. Gradually add olive oil, stirring smooth. Stir in lemon juice and, water to make spreadable. Spread paste between slices of roast. With heavy butcher's string, tie roast several times to reform roast securely. Roast at 325 degrees for about 2½ hours, until medium done. Makes 10 or more servings.

SLOW COOKED SMOKY BEEF BRISKET

Taste the sauce as you mix it and correct seasoning to your own liking. Be sure it's tangy enough, and smoky enough.

  1 beef brisket, about 4 pounds
Sauce:
1½ cups catsup (about 12 ounces)
1½ tablespoons brown sugar
1½ tablespoons Worcestershire sauce
2½ tablespoons liquid smoke (Wright's)
1½ tablespoons cooking oil
1½ teaspoons salt
  ½ teaspoon pepper
  ¼ to½ cup water

For this recipe, you will be using the broiler pan of your electric range. Place the bottom part of the pan on a shelf in the middle of your oven (not preheated), and pour in water to reach about halfway up sides. Place top insert (the slotted tray) on kitchen counter, and on it, place large wide strip of heavy duty aluminum foil (big enough to wrap the brisket). With sharp knife, trim brisket of all fat. Place meat in center of foil. Make sauce: In small bowl, stir together all ingredients, adding only enough water to thin to spreading consistency. Spread over meat and loosely wrap, sealing edges very firmly. Place slotted tray over bottom portion of broiler pan. (Separating the pan makes carrying the package of meat and sauce easier.) Bake at 225 degrees for 14 hours, checking doneness after about 8 to 10 hours and replenishing water at that time. When done and very tender, remove meat to cutting board and slice diagonally. Makes about 10 to 12 servings. Serve with sauce which forms in packet. Makes about 10 servings. (Note: You could also cook this recipe in a crock pot. Also, for best slices which hold together for sandwiches, make this ahead of time and refrigerate at least a day. Slice across the grain.)

Pot pies were often served as a way to use leftover meat or fowl. They were good because they contained a lot of meat, not just a few bites. They might have chunks of potato, carrot, onion, turnip or whatever vegetable the housewife happened to have. Several Riley poems mention pot-pies; for instance the Widder Gray, and her girl Han' (Hannah) "Well jest a glance O' the widder's smilin' countenance, A-cuttin' up chicken and big pot-pies, Would make a man hungry in Paradise!" (Needless to say, this artful cook did not remain a "widder" long.)

HORSERADISH POT ROAST

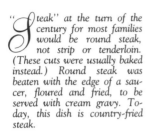

"Steak" at the turn of the century for most families would be round steak, not strip or tenderloin. (These cuts were usually baked instead.) Round steak was beaten with the edge of a saucer, floured and fried, to be served with cream gravy. Today, this dish is country-fried steak.

3 to 4 pound beef chuck roast
Shortening
⅓ cup prepared horseradish
Salt and pepper
Water
6 to 8 small onions
6 to 8 medium carrots
6 to 8 lengths of celery
3 medium potatoes, halved

In heavy Dutch oven brown roast in shortening over medium heat. Spread horseradish over top surface and sprinkle with salt and pepper. Add about ½ inch of water to pan, cover and cook over low heat for 2 to 2½ hours, adding more water if necessary. When meat is almost tender, add vegetables and continue cooking for additional hour. (Note: or, if desired, brown meat in skillet, transfer to oblong baking pan to season. Add vegetables and cover tightly with foil. Bake at 325 degrees for about 3 to 3½ hours.) Makes about 6 servings.

To make kettle gravy: remove meat to serving platter and keep warm. Skim excess fat from juices; pour off broth and measure. For about 6 servings you need about 2 to 3 cups broth, depending on your family's taste. Return broth to kettle and heat. For each cup of broth in kettle, shake together ¼ cup cold water and 2 tablespoons flour in small covered jar. Stir into hot broth, bring to boil and boil 1 minute, stirring constantly. Serve with roast and vegetables.

OLD FASHIONED FRESH HORSERADISH SAUCE FOR BEEF is as good now as it was then. Fresh horseradish is harvested in the fall; look for it in the produce section of the supermarket or roadside stands. Scrape and clean the outside of the root and remove all defects. Grate enough to make ¾ cup. Place in saucepan with 1 cup milk, 1 tablespoon butter, dash of salt, and "the inside of an ordinary slice of bread." (Do not use the crust as it makes the mixture brown.) Slowly bring to a boil, stirring occasionally, and boil for about 10 minutes to thicken. Add more milk if mixture gets too thick. Makes about 1¼ cups.

If you do not use the horseradish immediately, grate it into white wine vinegar or distilled vinegar. Do not use cider vinegar or other colored vinegar, which discolors horseradish. Refrigerate horseradish and horseradish sauce to store it.

DEVILED SWISS STEAK

Electric range companies used recipes like this to promote "Thrift Cookers" (a sunken kettle on the stovetop for slow cooking) during the War years.

- 3 pounds top round steak (1½-inch thick)
- ½ cup flour
- 1 teaspoon dry mustard
- 1 teaspoon salt
- ¼ cup (½ stick) margarine or solid vegetable shortening
- 1 onions, peeled and sliced
- 2 tablespoons Worcestershire sauce
- 1 cup water

Place steak on cutting board. In small bowl or cup, mix the flour, mustard and salt. Sprinkle about half of flour mixture over top surface of steak and, with wooden kitchen mallet, edge of sturdy saucer or edge of foil covered brick, pound the flour into the steak to break the fibers and tenderize the meat. Turn over and repeat flour and pounding on other side of meat. In large skillet with melted margarine, brown both sides of meat on stovetop at medium high heat until rich brown. Place meat in casserole or baking pan to fit. Cover with sliced onions, sprinkle with Worcestershire sauce and pour water around meat. Cover tightly with lid or aluminum foil. Bake at 375 degrees for 1½ to 2 hours, until very tender. Makes 6 to 8 servings.

(NOTE: For an old fashioned "meat and potatoes" meal, scrub well and prick 6 to 8 large potatoes. Place in oven, on shelf, and bake with meat. Large potatoes take about 1¼ hours, so you may wish to let meat bake for about 30 minutes before adding the potatoes. If they're done too early, wrap closely in aluminum foil (or put in covered cas-

Hash inevitably followed a meal of roast meat, preferably beef. This was often a Tuesday meal, as Sunday's roast should not be kept very long in the ice box. Chunks of the roast and slices of potato were simmered in water flavored with any leftover brown gravy. Sometimes bits of carrot and onion were added. Hash was yummy but looked down upon. In one of the jingles in "A Session with Uncle Sidney," Riley writes, "Our dog Dash, Et the Hash."

serole) and keep warm. However, skins are most crisp just as potatoes are removed from oven.

BURGUNDY STEW

  2 pounds stewing beef, cut in 1½-inch chunks
1¼ cups burgundy wine, divided
  2 (10-ounce) cans beef consomme, undiluted
  1 teaspoon salt
  ½ teaspoon garlic salt
  ¼ teaspoon pepper
  1 large onion, sliced
  ½ cup fine dry bread crumbs
  ½ cup all purpose flour

In 3-quart heavy casserole, stir together beef, 1 cup of the wine, consomme, salt, garlic salt, pepper and onion. In small bowl, mix the crumbs and flour. Stir into casserole mixture. Cover tightly and bake at 300 degrees for 3 hours, or until beef is tender. Just before serving stir in the remaining ¼ cup wine for flavor. Makes about 6 servings.

LEFTOVER BEEF PIE

"Leftover meat can be exciting," exclaimed food editorials to the thrifty housewife of the early 1900's. During the first half of this century, through depression and wars, women have had to watch their pennies. Leftover beef is a challenge, also, because in the refrigerator it can become very firm and dry. A good remedy to this is to grind the meat to tenderize it then mix with some seasoned sausage for moisture. Bake between pie crusts for texture contrast.

    Pastry for double 8-inch crust
  1 pound well trimmed leftover beef roast or steak
  1 medium onion, peeled
  ½ pound well seasoned sausage
  1 egg
  ¼ cup water

Preheat oven to 425 degrees. Roll out bottom pastry and fit into 8-inch pie plate. Using grinder or food processor, grind

*C*hildren in the early 1900's were brought up on gravy. Considered healthful, its base was the grease in which meats had been fried or roasted. To this grease about an equal amount of flour was added, a "pinch" of salt, and, stirring constantly, a thick paste was made. Then milk, or water was carefully added, a little at a time. When the desired thinness was achieved, the gravy was allowed to "bubble up" to cook the flour, and that was it, an essential for almost every meal, even breakfast. Riley verified this, in his poem "Rabbit:" "(Rabbits) Skinned and hung fer a night or two On the old back-porch where the pump's done froze—Then fried 'bout right, where your brekfust's at, With hot brown gravy and shortenin' bread— Rabbits like those Ain't so p'ticular (particularly) pore, I guess, Fer EATIN' purposes!"

or chop the leftover beef along with the onion. In large skillet on surface unit at medium high heat, or in large microwave casserole in microwave at high power, cook the sausage until completely browned. Drain sausage well and return to skillet or casserole. Stir in ground cooked beef, onion, egg and water. Roll out and adjust top crust. Bake about 35 to 45 minutes, until well browned. Serve with chili sauce, catsup or Tomato Sauce, below. Makes about 6 servings.

Tomato Sauce: In 2 to 4-cup microwave casserole or bowl, place 2 tablespoons onion. Microwave at high about 1 to 2 minutes, until wilted and started to soften. Add 2 tablespoons chopped green pepper and stir well. Stir in 8-ounce can tomato sauce and heat about 2 to 3 minutes, until hot through.

GROUND BEEF

Ground beef dishes are much more popular today than they were in James Whitcomb Riley's time. Early housewives had much better things to do than to finely chop by hand a haunch of homegrown beef for supper, so roasts and stews were more common. One of the very first published recipes for meat loaf appeared in 1900 and called for "4 pounds of the round" to be very finely chopped and mixed with 1 pint bread crumbs, 2 tablespoons chopped parsley, 1 level teaspoon pepper, 4 eggs, 1 good-size onion and 2 teaspoons salt. The mixture was to be packed into a square bread pan until it took the shape of the pan, then turned out of the pan onto a greased roasting dish for baking in a moderatly quick oven (about 375 degrees) for 2 hours, basting every 15 minutes with a little hot stock. After cooking, the housewife was told, the loaf should be allowed to let it "stand away" until perfectly cold. It was to be served in thin slices with horseradish cream or cold tomato sauce.

MEAT LOAF

Elsie D. Mitchell, daughter-in-law of Minnie Belle Mitchell and author of *Hoosier Boy*, (Riley's childhood) gave this recipe to a Greenfield church cookbook in the early

Fried mush was a frequent accompaniment to meat. Refined white corn meal was used to make the mush found in every household. This meal was carefully stirred into rapidly boiling salted water for soft mush, care being taken to avoid lumps. This was eaten with sugar and cream, maybe for breakfast; or there would be oatmeal made by the same method from prepared oats. For fried mush, a stiffer mixture was prepared (all the corn meal that could be absorbed into the boiling salted water.) This was poured into a greased crock to "set."

1900's. Ms. Mitchell's home, next door to the James Whitcomb Riley birthplace, eventually became the Riley Museum.

or supper, slices were cut out of the mush crock and fried until brown in hot grease. "Meat fryin's" was the term for fat fried out of bacon. Besides bacon fat, there was hog lard to use for frying. "The Happy Little Cripple" says: "At evening when the ironin's done, an Aunty's fixed the fire, An' filled an' lit the lamp, an' trimmed the wick an' turned it higher—she sets the kittle on the coals, an' biles an' makes the tea, An' fries the liver and the mush, an' cooks an egg for me."

1 pound beef and pork ground
1 medium onion chopped
2/3 cup chili sauce
2/3 cup cracker crumbs
2 eggs
1/2 to 1 teaspoon salt
1/8 teaspoon pepper
Milk

Mix meat, crumbs, eggs, chili sauce, onion, salt and pepper. Add enough milk to hold above together. Shape into loaf and cover with crumbs, lumps of butter on top. Lay 1 or 2 bay leaves on top. Put in baking pan, add a little hot water; bake 1 1/2 hours in moderate oven. Serve with hot tomato sauce. Serves 6.

GARDEN MEATLOAF MICROWAVE

This is good hot or cold and makes delicious sandwiches. If you have a large microwaveable mixing bowl, start with sauteeing the onion and celery in it, then add all the remaining ingredients. Otherwise, use directions below and mix the meatloaf in any bowl or pot you have.

1/2 cup chopped onion
1/2 cup chopped celery
1/2 cup chopped green pepper
1 cup chopped fresh tomato
2 tablespoons packed brown sugar
2 tablespoons brown mustard
2 teaspoons tarragon or cider vinegar
1 teaspoon salt
2 pounds extra-lean ground beef
2 cups soft wheat bread crumbs, packed (4 slices)
2 eggs
Glaze: 1 tablespoon packed brown sugar mixed with 1 teaspoon each brown mustard and vinegar

In 2-cup microwave bowl or container, place onion and celery. Microwave at high (100 percent power) for 3 to 5 minutes, until onion is slightly transparent. In large mixing bowl, place green pepper, tomato, brown sugar, mustard, vinegar and salt. Add the precooked onion-celery and stir together well. (This is the garden relish, and is a delicious garnish for roasted and grilled meats and meat sandwiches.) To the relish, add the beef, crumbs and eggs and mix with hands until thoroughly blended. Place in 9-inch microwave ring mold. Or place in 10-inch quiche dish which has high sides and, with fingers, displace about a 2-inch circle in the center of the meat to form a ring shape. Spoon Glaze over top and lightly smooth over surface. Cover loaf with wax paper. Microwave at high for 17 to 21 minutes, rotating ½ turn if necessary after 10 minutes, until meat is thoroughly cooked and juices are clear. Meat thermometer stuck halfway between center and edge of the ring should read 170 degrees. Makes about 8 servings. (Note: You can bake this meatloaf in a conventional oven at 375 degrees for about 1 hour to 1 hour 10 minutes. Use conventional oven-safe cooking container.)

Things got pretty basic at the Fanny Farmer Boston Cooking School in the late 1800's. In her cookbook used at the school, Ms. Farmer defines baking as cooking in an oven. For the most simplified baking, she goes on, the oven should have a heat regulator. In measuring ingredients for baked goods, dry ingredients are "measured level" and a cupful of liquid ingredient is defined as "all the cup will hold." She even defines stirring and beating. Stirring means using a circular motion to mix ingredients in ever-widening circles in the mixing bowl. Beating, on the other hand means "turning the ingredients over and over" from top to bottom. Stirring was horizontal mixing, beating was vertical mixing.

STUFFED GREEN PEPPERS

These were known as "Baked Mangoes" in 1914, when the Cosmos Society of the Bradley Methodist Church ran this recipe for them in a cookbook: "Fill green mangoes with well seasoned hamburg steak. Place in pan with 1 cup boiling water. Serve with cream gravy."

- 4 tablespoons (½ stick) butter
- 2 medium onions, chopped
- 1 pound ground round or ground chuck beef
- 4 large ripe tomatoes, cored and chopped
- 1 teaspoon salt
- ¼ teaspoon ground black pepper
- 2 cups fresh bread crumbs
- 10 medium green peppers, tops cut off and ribs and seeds removed from interiors
- ⅔ cup dry bread crumbs

In large skillet on stovetop, melt butter at medium high heat. Add onions and cook until wilted, then add ground beef and cook until meat is brown through and onions are soft. Add tomatoes, salt and pepper; allow to simmer about

10 minutes. Add the fresh bread crumbs. Meanwhile, par-boil the green peppers in pot of boiling water about 3 minutes each. When cool enough to handle, stuff each pepper with the beef-tomato filling. Space evenly in greased 13x9x2-inch baking dish. Sprinkle tops with the dried bread crumbs. Bake at 350 degrees F. for 40 to 45 minutes, until peppers are tender and hot through. Makes 10 peppers. (Note: to freeze for later, set the stuffed peppers individually in muffin cups and freeze separately overnight. Then, wrap each pepper individually in plastic wrap and put several (as much as you need for a meal) in plastic freezer bags. Before baking frozen peppers, space in greased baking dish and allow to stand at room temperature about 30 minutes before baking.

HAMBURGERS

James Whitcomb Riley might have eaten a hamburger during his travels, especially after they were introduced in the nineteenth century at two world's fairs. By about 1911, hamburgers on buns were considered good for picnics or a snack by the beach. It was not until after 1920 that hamburger stands began to be popular, and the rest is history.

HAMBURG STEAK

From the *Ladies Society Cookbook* of the First M.E. Church, Greenfield, Indiana, 1901.

For this purchase three-quarters of a pound of the round of beef, and have the butcher chop it very fine. Form the meat into a cake three-quarters of an inch thick, lightly flour the upper side, turn that side against the wires of a broiler, lightly flour the other side, and broil slowly. Place the steak when done upon a hot serving dish, and season with butter, salt and pepper. It requires careful handling, but if treated as directed, it will not stick to the broiler.

HAMBURGERS AU VIN

When microwaving hamburgers, it takes a little longer to cook lean meat mixtures than those with greater fat content.

- 1 pound ground beef
- 2 cups sliced fresh mushrooms
- 1/4 cup (1/2 stick) butter
- 1/4 cup sherry or rose wine
- 1/4 cup water
- 1 tablespoon cornstarch
- 1/8 teaspoon salt

Divide ground beef into 4 patties and lightly shape each one 3/4-inch thick. Microwave or grill: To microwave place on plastic meat rack, arranging patties evenly in a circle, and cover with wax paper. Microwave at high for about 5 to 7 minutes, turning patties over, rearranging and recovering after about 3 minutes. Set aside, covered, while making sauce. In 1-quart microwave casserole, place the mushrooms and butter. Cover. Microwave at medium high (70 percent power) for 2 to 3 minutes, until mushrooms are starting to darken and soften. In small cup or bowl, stir together sherry, water, cornstarch and salt; gradually stir this mixture into the hot mushrooms. Continue microwaving for 3 to 5 minutes, stirring every 2 minutes, until sauce is clear and thickened. Arrange hamburger patties on a serving plate and divide the sauce over each. Makes 4 servings.

SNAPPY BURGERS WITH BROWN SAUCE

- 1 cup crushed gingersnap cookies, divided
- 1 1/2 pounds lean ground beef (20% fat or less)
- 2/3 cup soft bread crumbs (1 slice)
- 1/3 cup finely chopped onion
- 1/3 cup lemon juice, divided
- 3 tablespoons water
- 1/2 teaspoon salt
- 1/4 teaspoon pepper
- 1 1/2 cups beef broth
- 1/3 cup packed brown sugar

In large mixing bowl, place ⅓ cup of the gingersnap crumbs, beef, bread crumbs, onion, 3 tablespoons of the lemon juice, water, salt and pepper. With hands, mix to blend well. Shape lightly into 6 patties, ¾ to 1 inch thick. Microwave or grill. To microwave, arrange in 12x8x2-inch microwave oblong dish. Cover with wax paper. Microwave at high (100 percent power) for about 7 to 10 minutes, turning over, rearranging and recovering burgers after about 4 minutes. Let stand, covered, while making sauce: In 1-quart microwave casserole, stir together remaining ⅔ cup gingersnap crumbs, beef broth, brown sugar and remaining lemon juice (2⅓ tablespoons). Microwave at high for 6 to 9 minutes, stirring every 3 minutes, until sauce has thickened. Drain burgers of fat, if necessary, then distribute hot sauce over each. Recover with wax paper and let stand a few minutes before serving for burgers to absorb flavor of sauce. Serve with noodles, if desired. Makes 4 to 6 servings.

BEAR'S PAWS (From *The Practical Cookbook*, 1904)

Bear's paws are by many considered to be a great delicacy, in fact the best part of the bear. Clean the forepaws very nicely, boil in salted water until tender, dip them in melted butter, egg, and then in bread crumbs, broil with frequent basting until lightly brown. Garnish with lemon slices and capers and send to the table with any kind of a spice gravy. Sometimes the paws are pickled in vinegar and savory herbs for a day beforehand; then boil in bouillon and part of the marinade instead of water before broiling them.

FRICASSEED RABBIT (1823)

The best way for cooking rabbit is to fricassee them. Take a couple of fine ones and disjoint them. Put them into a large stewpan, season them with cayenne pepper and salt, some chopped parsley and some powdered mace. Pour in a pint of warm water (or veal broth if you have it) and stew over a slow fire till the rabbits are quite tender, adding some bits of butter, rolled in flour, when the rabbit is about half done. Just before taking from the fire, enrich

etween the ages of 22 and 25, Riley experimented with growing a mustache. He finally achieved a fine droopy one, but it was dark red in color, while his hair was almost colorless, it was so light. "I look like a walrus," he said disgustedly, and shaved it off.

the gravy with a jill or more of thick cream with some nutmeg grated into it. Stir the gravy well, but take care not to let it boil after the cream is in, lest it curdle. Put the pieces of rabbit on a hot platter and pour the gravy over them.

PORK

Besides beef, pork was the mainstay of the family's diet, especialy in wintertime. Finding a use for all the parts of the hog was one of the major creative achievements of the early American farm family. The hooves became pickled pig's feet; the head became souse or scrapple, the entrails were scraped for use as sausage casing, the fat became either lard or an ingredient in soap. The bristles were used in making brushes, or as a strengthener for plaster. Some people made an ointment from the gall bladder to cure frost bite. Then of course there was the delicious meat—pork loin, hams, pork chops, bacon, salt pork and delicious herb-scented sausage.

If you were to purchase pork, says *The Gold Medal Cook Book* (1904), find a dealer "who has all his meat tested by a microscopist." The book then advised buying young meat which might be more lean, and cooking it until thoroughly done—a recommendation which still stands today.

MUSHROOM SAUSAGE PIE

Savory meat pies were common in Riley's day—today we would call this a quiche.

      Pastry for 9-inch single crust
   1 pound hot pork sausage
   ¼ cup (½ stick) butter
   ¾ pound (12 ounces) fresh mushrooms
   Rich custard:
   1 cup whipping cream, not whipped
   2 egg yolks, beaten
   1 tablespoon flour
   1 tablespoon melted butter
   1 tablespoon lemon juice

FHB!" was a familiar signal in the early days. Families were very hospitable, and loved to invite others to a meal. At the same time, some food items were scarce and expensive, no doubt just the thing you wanted to impress the company with. When these items were passed, "FHB" was hissed in the ears of the family. "Family Hold Back!" (Don't take seconds of the roast!)

½ teaspoon salt
½ teaspoon pepper
Garnish: ½ cup freshly grated Parmesan cheese

Preheat oven to 450 degrees. Roll out and fit pastry into 9-inch pie plate. Without pricking, bake the crust about 8 to 10 minutes, until lightly brown. As it bakes, air pockets underneath the pastry can cause it to puff up and crack, so check the pastry every 2 to 3 minutes, and push it down to fit the shape of the pie plate if this happens. Let stand while making filling. In large skillet, fry the pork sausage and drain off fat well. In same skillet, melt the butter and add mushrooms and cook briefly. Spread the sausage and mushrooms evenly in the pastry. Make rich custard; in medium mixing bowl, whisk together thoroughly the heavy cream, egg yolks, flour, melted butter, lemon juice, salt and pepper. Pour this mixture evenly over the pie filling. Bake the pie for 30 to 40 minutes at 375 degrees, until rich brown and set. As you remove from the oven, sprinkle the Parmesan cheese over the top. Serve warm. Makes about 6 to 8 servings.

SAUSAGE RICE CASSEROLE

Serve this with sliced turkey or cheese-topped vegetables for a little more protein. For a main dish casserole, you can double the sausage to serve 8 people.

1½ cups cooked white rice
1½ cups cooked wild rice
1 pound seasoned "hot" sausage
1 large onion, chopped fine
½ pound fresh mushrooms (8 ounces), cleaned and quartered
Sauce:
2 tablespoons flour
¼ cream or milk
½ teaspoon salt
Dash black pepper
1 teaspoon dried oregano
¼ cup dried parsley
1½ cups chicken broth (12 ounces)
Topping: ¾ cup slivered almonds

Pigs' feet were considered a delicacy when the hog was butchered. On a cold winter's day, the meal might be this unusual treat. Pigs' feet had meat on them and a lot of gelatinous substance. They were boiled with greens or soup beans for several hours and served with corn bread.

Using package directions, cook the rice and cool (should have about 6 cups). In large skillet, cook the sausage until completely done. Drain, saving drippings. To 2 tablespoons sausage drippings, add onion and fry until limp, then add mushrooms and cook lightly. In greased 3-quart casserole, layer ⅓ of rice, half of sausage and onion-mushroom mixture, ⅓ of rice, rest of sausage and onion-mushrooms and top with last ⅓ of rice. Preheat oven to 350 degrees. Make sauce: In saucepan off heat, stir together flour, cream or milk, salt, pepper, oregano and parsley until smooth. Gradually stir in chicken broth and bring to boil, stirring, until slightly thick. Pour sauce over casserole. Sprinkle top with nuts. Bake for 25 to 30 minutes, until brown and hot throughout. Makes 8 to 10 servings.

WILLIAMS' EASTER EGG 'N BACON DISH

As long as we can remember our daughter and sister, Rosemary, has made this dish for the family on Easter morning, after the egg hunt. She adjusts this to the number we're serving.

　　10-oz. can cream of mushroom soup
　½　cup real mayonnaise
　½　cup milk
　1　teaspoon chopped chives
　6　hard cooked eggs
　8　slices bacon, fried or microwaved crisp, crumbled

Preheat oven to 350 degrees. In small mixing bowl, blend together soup with mayonnaise, milk and chives. Into greased baking, layer about ⅓ of sauce and slice 3 eggs into sauce. Continue layering ⅓ of sauce, remaining 3 eggs and rest of sauce. Top with the crisp bacon crumbles. Bake for about 20 minutes, until bubbly. Makes about 4 servings.

"Green beanpot" was a standard dish which had a lot of variables, fresh beans, "shellouts," onions, corn—the one essential was smoked pork—ham or saltpork. It cooked half the day so everything blended.

TRI-COLOR PORK CHOPS

eddlers and hucksters came to village and country homes alike. In their wagons were kitchen items, flavorings, needles and pins, darning cloth, toys and scissors. The boys in the family would rush out with chickens to trade for the variety of wares.

4 (1-inch thick) pork chops
4 (1-inch thick) onion slices
4 (1-inch thick) green pepper rings
1 bottle (12 ounces) chili sauce

Score fat on pork chops and arrange in 8 or 9-inch square baking pan. Arrange the onion slices and pepper rings over chops. Distribute chili sauce evenly over top. Cover tightly with aluminum foil or pan lid. Bake at 350 degrees for about 1 hour, or until chops are completely done through (test one by cutting near bone—there should be no pink.) Makes four chops.

FRUIT STUFFED PORK CHOPS

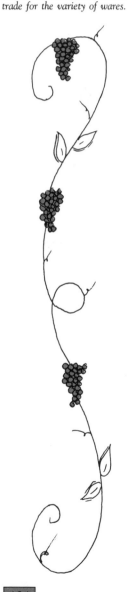

½ cup diced celery
1 cup dried bread cubes
1 cup diced peeled apple
½ cup crunchy peanut butter
¼ cup seedless raisins
½ teaspoon salt
⅛ teaspoon ground black pepper
¼ teaspoon cinnamon
6 (1-inch thick) rib pork chops, with pockets slit for stuffing
½ cup cider or apple juice

Preheat oven to 450 degrees. Stuffing: In 1½-quart microwave casserole, place celery. Microwave at high (100 percent power) for about 1 to 2 minutes, until softened. Add bread cubes, apple, peanut butter, raisins, salt, pepper and cinnamon. Mix well and use to stuff pork chops. Carefully arrange in 13x9x2-inch baking pan or ovenproof dish. Place chops in preheated oven until browned, about 10 to 20 minutes. Pour off pan drippings. Pour the cider evenly over chops, cover pan or dish with aluminum foil or cover and continue baking about 45 minutes, or until tender. Makes 6 chops.

MEATS (BEEF AND PORK)

PORK TENDERLOIN WITH MUSTARD CREAM

12 slices (¾-inch thick) pork tenderloin
  Salt and ground black pepper
  All-purpose flour
⅓ cup butter, divided
⅓ cup mild white vinegar
2 cups whipping cream
½ cup dijon or coarse brown mustard
1 teaspoon dried dill weed

On cutting board, place each tenderloin slice between sheets of wax paper. With wooden kitchen mallet or foil covered brick, pound and flatten pieces until they are about ½ inch thick and 2 to 3-inch in diameter. Sprinkle with salt, pepper and flour. In heavy skillet on stovetop at medium high heat, melt half the butter and cook the tenderloin pieces until completely done through (no pink). Remove to warm platter. To skillet, add the vinegar and bring to a boil to loosen all the browned areas in the skillet. Let boil until only about half of liquid remains, then add cream, mustard, dill weed, and other half of butter. Stir until well blended. Taste for salt and pepper, then pour over pork. Makes 4 to 6 servings.

FANCY MOLDED MUSTARD—Delectable with ham, turkey and other meats.

1 package unflavored gelatin
1 tablespoon water
4 eggs
¾ cup sugar
2 tablespoons dry mustard
¾ cup cider vinegar
¼ cup water
2 tablespoons grated horseradish
1 pint whipping cream

In small cup or bowl, stir gelatin and 1 tablespoon water. Let stand few minutes to soak. Meanwhile, in top of double boiler, beat the eggs well. To eggs, add sugar, mustard,

ide meat was the term for unsmoked bacon. "Fresh side" was sliced, sometimes dipped in batter and fried. In Riley's poem "Coon Dog Wess," we read: "Wife come traipsin' (a lagging walk) at the rag-tag-and bobtail of the crowd, Dogs and childern, with a bag, cornmeal and some side-meat, Proud and as independent—My! Yit a mild look in her eye."

ame meant rabbits, squirrels or birds. They were fixed a variety of ways; one of the easiest was fried like chicken.

vinegar, water and horseradish. Stir in soaked gelatin. Fill the bottom of the double boiler with hot water and cook and stir the mixture until it thickens enough to coat a silver spoon. Remove from heat and cool mixture to room temperature. Then, whip the cream until stiff and fold it in. Pile the mixtue into a 1-quart fancy gelatin mold and refrigerate until set. Makes about 3 cups. (Note: If you don't have a double boiler, substitute 2 saucepans, one which fits inside the other, with water in the larger bottom pan.)

CARAMEL HAM AND WALNUTS

2 ham slices (2 pounds total)
1 tablespoon vinegar
3 tablespoons dark brown sugar
2 tablespoons cooking oil
½ cup chopped walnuts
2 cups boiling water
½ cup sherry

On tray or large piece of aluminum foil, rub ham slices with vinegar, then sugar, coating all surfaces well. Let stand up to 2 hours before cooking. In large heavy saucepan, place oil. Over high heat, quickly brown the ham slices. Brown sugar will caramelize, which adds to flavor and color of the meat. When both sides have caramelized, add the walnuts, water and sherry. Cook slowly, uncovered, until liquid has evaporated and ham is tender. Pile nuts over ham to serve. Makes about 6 servings.

RED EYE GRAVY When ham slices are fried plain, removed from the frying pan and a little water added to the pan to loosen the flavorful drippings, the result is the old time Red Eye Gravy. This pinkish-brown liquid is usually not thickened, but rather poured over the hot ham as a way to return the moisture and flavor which might have been lost otherwise.

MEATS (BEEF AND PORK)

HOG JOWLS AND TURNIP GREENS

Mustard, kale and turnip greens are cooked same as spinach. Smoked hog jowl is cooked with greens. Season well with red pepper and salt. Cook until tender, drain and serve on platter with meat in center and poached eggs. Always serve with cornbread.

—Reprinted from *Old Timey Recipes* (1974)

HAM BROCCOLI STRATA

Named for its layers of ingredients, this is an attractive main dish idea to serve many people for lunch. Refrigerate overnight and served freshly baked.

- 16 slices white sandwich bread
- 1 to 1½ pounds thin sliced cooked ham
- 2 (10 ounces each) packages frozen chopped broccoli
- 2 to 3 cups (8 to 10 ounces) grated sharp cheddar cheese

Custard:
- 6 eggs
- 2 cups milk
- ½ cup (1 stick) butter or margarine, melted
- 2 tablespoons mild yellow mustard
- 2 tablespoons grated onion

Make this the night before you intend to serve it to allow all ingredients to blend before baking. Remove bread crusts. In greased 13x9x3-inch pan, layer half the bread, half the ham, half the broccoli (one package), half the cheese. Repeat layers. Make custard: In medium mixing bowl, whisk thoroughly to blend the eggs, milk, melted butter, mustard and onion. Pour mixture evenly over top of strata. Cover with plastic wrap and refrigerate overnight. About 1½ hours before serving, bake strata at 350 degrees for about 1 hour. Makes 8 to 10 servings.

Venison was very rare in Indiana in 1900; almost all of the early deer had retreated by 1830. There are more deer today in Indiana than in pioneer times.

HOW TO CURE A HAM (From *The Blue Grass Cook Book*, 1875)

Kill your hogs when the wind is from the northwest. The night before you salt the meat, take a string of red pepper and make a strong tea. (Let it remain on the stove over-night.) Put in the tea 2 heaping tablespoons of saltpetre to every two gallons. Take this strong tea and pour on the salt. Salt the meat lightly for the first time to run off the blood. Let the meat lie packed 3 days--longer, if the weather is very cold. Then overhaul the meat and put 1 teaspoon of pulverized saltpetre on the flesh side of each ham and rub in well. Then rub with molasses mixed with salt. Pack close for 10 days. After this overhaul again, rubbing each piece, and pack close again. Hang the meat in 3 weeks from the time the hogs were killed. Before hanging, wash each piece in warm water, and while wet roll in hickory ashes. Then smoke with green hickory wood, and tie up in cotton bags in February.

FAVORITE BOURBON SAUCE FOR HAM

10-ounce jar red currant jelly
1/4 cup butter
1/2 teaspoon dry mustard
2 teaspoons dijon or brown mustard
1/4 cup bourbon

In 1-quart microwave casserole, place jelly. Microwave at high (100 percent power) for 4 to 5 minutes, stirring every 2 minutes, until melted. Stir in remaining ingredients and let stand to blend. Serve with ham. Makes about 1 1/2 cups.

Poultry

BIRDS OF THE BARNYARD

"Poultry is not as nutritious as beef and mutton," read the 1904 *Gold Medal Cookbook*, "but its tenderness and flavor renders it most agreeable as a change in the usual bill of fare; neither has it as much fat, except in the case of geese or ducks, but but this can be supplied in the way of butter or cream. Game with dark meat should be cooked rare, as venison, canvas-back duck and almost all birds, while the white-fleshed animals, turkeys, chicken, etc., should be well done."

Gourmet chefs nowadays try to buy "free ranging" chickens because they are more flavorful than chicken grown under standardized conditions. But back in Riley's day all chickens were free ranging. You had to catch one from the chicken yard before you could cook it. Chickens were so commonly home grown that butchers frequently assumed that you had your own, and carried little poultry in their shops. Or, you had a source of chickens, sweet milk and fresh eggs each week from a farm nearby. Because of the effort it took to dress chickens, they were often served just on weekends, with beef over the week.

Low calorie, low fat chicken has mushroomed in popularity since cholesterol—something James Whitcomb Riley never heard of—was discovered.

CHICKEN SMOTHERED WITH SWEET ONIONS

Keep the chicken and onions separate until just before serving, for best appearance. While the chicken is baking, slowly simmer the onions until very tender and light brown.

- ¼ cup slivered almonds
- 3 pound frying chicken, cut up
  Salt, pepper, paprika
- ¼ cup (½ stick) butter
- 5 large onions, thinly sliced
- 2 tablespoons packed brown sugar
- ½ teaspoon ground cinnamon
  Lemon wedges

las! Sometimes the hens quit laying in the winter time (perhaps the rooster was too cold for romance.) Eggs became scarce. There were efforts to preserve them—in lard—in solutions—by hard boiling—and by burying them in the ground. Everybody breathed a sigh of relief, however, when fresh eggs became plentiful again.

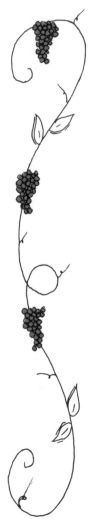

POULTRY

Toast almonds: spread in single layer in small baking pan or pie plate. Bake at 400 degrees for 5 to 10 minutes, or until golden. Note: To microwave toast almonds, add 1 teaspoon butter; spread in glass pie plate; microwave at high (100 percent power) for 4 to 6 minutes, stirring.) Bake chicken. Arrange skin side down in shallow greased baking pan (13x9x2-inch). Sprinkle with salt, pepper and paprika. Bake at 400 degrees for 30 minutes, turn chicken over and sprinkle lightly with salt, pepper and paprika. Continue baking for about 20 more minutes, until browned and tender. Meanwhile, prepare onions. In large (10-inch) heavy skillet, melt butter on stovetop on medium heat. Add onions, separated into rings, and cook uncovered, stirring often, until onions are golden and tender, about 30 minutes. (If onions show signs of browning, in the first 15 minutes, reduce heat.) Just before serving, sprinkle the brown sugar and cinnamon on the onions and stir to blend. Serve the chicken topped with the onions, the toasted almonds sprinkled over the top, and lemon wedges. Makes 4 servings. (To save time for a party, toast almonds and cook onions ahead of time, omitting sugar and cinnamon. Reheat onions in microwave, add sugar and cinnamon just before spooning over chicken. Chicken is best cooked fresh.)

CHICKEN BISCUITS CIRCA 1915 (From *Favorite Recipes of the Ladies of the Cosmos Society* of the Bradley Methodist Church, Greenfield.)

Cook chicken with plenty of broth, if not fat add ½ cup butter. Make a pan of small baking powder biscuits, cover them with the chicken broth, bake in a quick oven ten or fifteen minutes. Serve them on a meat platter, pouring over and around them plenty of gravy made from remaining broth.

PARTY CHICKEN BAKED IN CREAM

You can use either bone-in or boneless chicken breasts in this recipe.

- 3 pounds chicken breast halves (about 6 halves), skin removed
- 3 to 4 tablespoons vegetable shortening
- ½ cup chopped onion
- 1 clove garlic, minced
- 6 tablespoons brandy
- 1 cup whipping cream
- 1 cup chicken broth
- 1½ teaspoons salt
- ⅛ teaspoon pepper
- 1 tablespoon Worcestershire sauce
  Thickener for sauce: 2 tablespoons flour and ½ cup cold water

In large heavy skillet over medium high heat on stovetop, cook the chicken breasts in the shortening until lightly browned. As they are browned, remove them to a large casserole or baking pan, about 3 quart size. If chicken is bone-in, arrange bone side down in dish. In medium mixing bowl or pan, stir together the chopped onion, garlic, brandy, cream, broth, salt, pepper and Worcestershire. Pour this sauce evenly over the browned chicken pieces. Cover the casserole and bake at 300 degrees for about 2 to 2½ hours, or until pieces are very tender when pierced with fork. Just before serving, remove chicken to a platter. Make sauce: skim off any fat on top of pan juices and pour into a medium saucepan. Add the well-blended mixture of flour and cold water. Bring to a boil, stirring constantly, until mixture boils and thickens, about 2 to 3 minutes. Add a little milk to thin if necessary. Strain sauce over chicken pieces, or serve separately, as desired. Makes about 6 servings.

VERA'S HOT CHICKEN SALAD

The world lost an excellent chef when Vera Boyd McCreery, of Greenfield, took to the banking trade in the early 1900's. This was natural, however, because her grandfather, Philander Boyd, founded the Citizen's Bank in Greenfield.

Hunting was enjoyed as a pastime in Riley's day, but it also provided welcome variety for the table. Pheasants (an English import), partridges and quail were bagged and enjoyed.

3 chicken breasts, boiled and cut in chunks (2 cups chunks)
   10-ounce can condensed cream of chicken soup
¾ cup real mayonnaise
½ cup toasted slivered almonds
1 cup diced celery
2 cans (8-ounces each) water chestnuts, drained and quartered
   Juice of 1 lemon
2 large hard cooked eggs, cut up
   Crushed potato chips (about 6 ounce-bag)

Preheat oven to 450 degrees. In large mixing bowl, gently mix the chicken, soup, mayonnaise, almonds, celery, water chestnuts, lemon juice and eggs. Spoon into lightly greased 2-quart casserole, and top with the crushed potato chips. Bake about 20 minutes, until hot throughout. Makes 4 to 6 servings.

TRI KAPPA HOT CHICKEN SQUARES

Kappa Kappa Kappa is a social and philanthropic sorority with chapters all over Indiana. This recipe was made in Greenfield at a James Whitcomb Riley luncheon during Riley Days in October.

3 cups chopped cooked chicken
3 cups chopped celery
3 cans (10 ounce each) cream of chicken soup
3 cups real mayonnaise
¼ cup diced onion
3 teaspoons lemon juice
3 cups cooked rice
Topping:
2 cups cornflake crumbs
½ cup sliced almonds (about 2 ounces)

Preheat oven to 350 degrees. In large bowl, combine all ingredients except topping. Spread in well greased 13x9x2-inch pan. Blend crumbs and almonds for topping and sprinkle over top. Bake for 40 to 50 minutes, until browned and bubbly. Let stand about 10 minutes to set before serving. Makes about 10 servings.

MICROWAVE CHICKEN PIECES WITH FRESH TOMATOES

This dish mellows when stored in the refrigerator a day or two, and it reheats well.

- 1 pound fresh tomatoes, chopped (4 small)
- 1 medium onion, chopped (⅔ cup)
- ½ medium green pepper, chopped (½ cup)
  6-ounce can tomato paste
- 2 teaspoons instant chicken bouillon granules
- 2 teaspoons minced fresh garlic or ½ teaspoon garlic powder
- 1 teaspoon sugar
- 1 teaspoon dried thyme
- ¼ teaspoon dried tarragon
- ¼ teaspoon ground black pepper
- 1 chicken, cut up (8 pieces), skin removed

Into 10-inch square ceramic microwave dish (or 13x9x2-inch glass dish) place tomatoes, onion and green pepper. Cover with plastic wrap or casserole lid. Microwave at high (100 percent power) for 4 to 7 minutes, until all vegetables are hot and softened. Add tomato paste, bouillon, garlic, sugar, thyme, tarragon and pepper; blend well. Place skinless chicken pieces in dish with meatiest parts around outside edges of dish. Spoon sauce over top of each piece. Cover. Microwave at high for 14 to 18 minutes, until casserole seems hot in all areas. Rotate dish ½ turn, then continue microwaving at medium high (70 percent power) for 18 to 22 minutes, rotating dish ½ turn after 10 minutes, until meat is no longer pink near bone. Makes 4 to 6 servings. Serve with pasta or rice.

CORNISH HEN, RAISINS AND WILD RICE

This recipe serves two persons and can be expanded as necessary.

- 2 Cornish game hens, defrosted if frozen
- 6 tablespoons (¾ stick) melted butter
- ½ cup wild rice (about 4 ounces)
- 1½ cups chicken broth

*N*oodles were not hard to make, but they took patience. An egg or two was beaten until frothy in a big bowl with a pinch or two of salt. Then flour was worked in until the dough was so stiff that it could be rolled out "as thin as paper." Heavily floured, the circles of dough were rolled up and cut from end to end into the thinnest possible slivers.

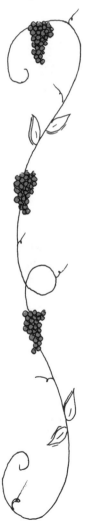

*N*oodles were a German specialty. Irish settlers called them "nodles," with a "long o" sound. Noodles were allowed to "dry out" and could be kept indefinitely. They were cooked by dropping them into boiling chicken or beef broth a few at a time, so the broth kept boiling. To boil them tender, housewives allowed a couple of hours, making sure to stir every little bit.

½ teaspoon salt
⅓ cup dark raisins
⅓ cup fresh orange juice
2 tablespoons butter
2 tablespoons flour
  Additional ½ teaspoon salt
  Dash of pepper
⅛ teaspoon paprika
1 cup half and half

Heat oven to 425 degrees. In 12x9x2-inch baking pan, arrange game hens breast side up. Brush with about 4 tablespoons of the melted butter. Bake about 45 to 60 minutes, until done, brushing with additional butter about every 15 minutes. (Note: to test doneness, cut a small but deep slit between a leg and the body of one bird. There should be no pink meat or juices at joint where leg meets body.) While birds are roasting, cook rice: In medium saucepan on stovetop place rice, chicken broth and ½ teaspoon salt. Cover and bring to boil, then reduce heat to simmer and cook 30 to 45 minutes, until rice is tender. Make raisin-orange sauce: In small saucepan on stovetop, place the raisins and orange juice. Bring to a boil on high heat, then immediately reduce to lowest heat and simmer 5 minutes. Set aside. In small skillet on stovetop, melt butter. Add flour, the additional ½ teaspoon salt, pepper and paprika and stir until smooth and bubbly. Stir in the cream and bring to boil, stirring constantly. Boil 1 minute. Stir in raisin-orange mixture. To serve: make a bed of wild rice for each serving, arrange a game hen on each bed of rice and drizzle a little sauce over each. Serve rest of sauce separately. Makes two servings.

ROASTED DUCK (1901) (from the *Ladies Society Cookbook* of the First M.E. Church in Greenfield)

If the ducks are young, they are served rare and are not stuffed. An especially delicious flavor is developed in the cooking if a cupful of chopped celery and a halfcupful of onion is placed in the body of each bird, removing this flavoring, however, before serving. Full-grown ducks should be well cooked—an hour and a quarter is usually sufficient, unless of extra size. They should be basted every ten minutes.

POTTED PARTRIDGE: Pluck and draw the partridges and wipe inside with a damp cloth. Pound well some mace, allspice, white pepper and salt, mix together and rub every part of the birds with this. Pack as closely as possible in a baking-pan, with plenty of butter over, and cover with a coarse flour-and-water crust. Tie a paper over this, and bake rather more than one and a half hours; let the birds get cold, then cut into pieces for keeping, pack closely in large potting-pot, and cover with clarified butter. This should be kept in a cool dry place. The butter used for potting game will answer for basting, or for paste for meat-pies." *The New Buckeye Cook Book (1880)*

OVERNIGHT TURKEY AND BEANS

2 pounds dry navy beans
  Salt and pepper
5 to 7 pound turkey breast, defrosted if frozen
2 medium onions
4 whole cloves
8 strips smoked bacon, cut in half-inch lengths
1 teaspoon dry mustard
1 teaspoon garlic powder
  Hot water

Soak beans overnight in water to cover. In the morning, drain and pick over beans. Place about a ⅓ of beans in a 4-quart casserole. Sprinkle with salt and pepper. Cut the onions in half crosswise and stick a whole clove in each piece, and place over the bottom layer of beans. Distribute bacon pieces evenly over onions. Add another third of the beans, and sprinkle with salt and pepper. Cut the turkey breast in half lengthwise so it lays as flat as possible in casserole. Cover with the last ⅓ of the beans, sprinkle with salt, pepper, dry mustard and garlic powder. Add hot water to the casserole just until the beans are covered. Cover tightly and bake at 250 degrees F. for 12 hours. Take out the turkey breast and remove skin and bones. Cut or gently tear meat into large pieces and gently stir them back into

Riley's poem, "A New Year's Time at the Willard's" describes the "Infair Dinner" of pioneer days. This affair, a dinner honoring newlyweds, has largely today become the "rehearsal dinner," now held before the wedding. The dinner in the poem, staged after Tomps and S'repty had been married a week, featured "turkey, all stuffed an' browned—too sweet fer nose er tooth er tongue! With sniffs of sage, an' P'r'aps a dash of old burnt brandy, steamin' hot. Mixed kin o' in with apple-mash an' mince-meat, an' Lord knows what!"

the beans. Return the casserole to the oven for 1 or 2 hours, uncovered, so the top browns before serving. Makes about 12 to 15 servings.

POT ROASTED TURKEY

Brown the turkey well, then finish in broth for moist eating. The last hour you add a choice of vegetables to serve on the side. An 8 to 9 pound turkey will serve about 6 people with leftovers or up to two more without leftovers.

- 8 to 9-pound turkey, completely defrosted
- 1 lemon
- 2 tablespoons soft butter
- ½ tablespoon salt
- 4 cups chicken broth (2 (16-oz.)cans)
- 2 bay leaves
- 1 teaspoon thyme
- 4 sprigs fresh parsley
- 1 large stalk celery, cut in chunks
- 2 pounds carrots, scraped and thickly sliced
- 2 pounds onions, peeled and chunked
- 2 pounds small red potatoes, well scrubbed

In roasting pan, place turkey. Cut lemon in halves and rub all over turkey. Place one squeezed half in body cavity, one in neck cavity. Rub all over top with butter, and rub inside and outside lightly with salt. Bake uncovered at 400 degrees for 1 hour, until well browned, basting with pan juices. Any areas which look too brown (such as wing tips) can be covered with small pieces of aluminum foil. Remove from oven and pour the broth over the turkey. Add bay leaves, thyme and parsley. Arrange celery around turkey. Cover the pan and return to the oven, reducing oven temperature to 325 degrees. Cook another ½ hour. Arrange the carrots, onions and potatoes around the turkey, cover and continue cooking for an additional hour, until meat and vegetables are tender. Remove turkey to warm platter and vegetables to serving bowl. Make gravy: Strain liquid and skim off grease. Measure liquid into large saucepan and for every cupful of liquid, stir in

iley was once entertaining friends in his Greenfield home to a feast of roast duck prepared by his sister-in-law, Julia Riley, his brother John's widow. The duck, apparently a tough bird, taxed Riley's skill as a carver. Each time he plunged a big carving knife into the bird, he sent the "gravy" splattering upwards. "It's a good thing the gravy matches the ceiling," the frustrated Riley quipped.

mixture of 1½ tablespoons flour and 1½ tablespoons water. Over high heat, stirring, bring to boil and allow to boil 1 minute. Salt and pepper as desired. See note above for servings.

TURKEY CARROT SALAD

7-pound turkey breast, roasted or simmered until tender
1 pound carrots, scraped, cut in chunks and simmered not-quite tender
1 bunch (1 pound) celery, cleaned and sliced
Black pepper
½ cup chopped fresh or dried parsley
1 cup (or more) toasted slivered almonds
Dressing:
1⅓ cups coarsely chopped onions
¼ cup (½ stick) butter
2 cups real mayonnaise
¼ cup prepared horseradish
1½ teaspoons salt
½ teaspoon ground black pepper
2 teaspoons dried dill weed

Prepare salad ingredients: Cook turkey as package directs until tender. Remove skin and any bones. When cool enough to handle, cut into bite size chunks. Meanwhile, clean and cook or microwave carrots (using high (100 percent power) for about 7 to 9 minutes), and prepare celery. In large mixing bowl, toss turkey, carrots, celery and parsley. Make dressing: In 2 quart microwave casserole, place onions and butter. Microwave at high (100 percent power) for 3 to 4 minutes, until onions are tender. Stir in remaining dressing ingredients. Toss dressing with turkey mixture. Taste and add more black pepper, (up to ½ teaspoonful.) Spoon into serving bowl and garnish top generously with almonds. Makes about 10 to 12 servings. (Note: to toast almonds, place in microwave casserole with 2 teaspoons butter. Microwave at high for 4 to 6 minutes, stirring every minute or two, until toasted.)

Ducks were welcome in villages around the Midwest. Cunning and droll, their little yellow babies made good playthings for the children. Geese were not kept inside the towns. Outside in the country they were burglar alarms, honking and squawking when strangers appeared. But in the towns they had a very bad habit of flopping on children if they got angry, which was often, and they were big tough birds. One thing they did produce was the most wonderful paté of all—goose liver paté.

SUCCOTASH STEW

In early times succotash meant a hodgepodge of whatever was in season, although succotash has come to mean a combination of corn and lima or green beans. If you don't have leftover cooked poultry, buy a 2-pound chunk at the deli for make this colorful and tasty dish.

- 6   slices bacon
- ¾   cup sliced celery
- ½   cup thinly sliced shallots or green onions
- 2   large cloves garlic, minced
- 3   cups diced cooked turkey or chicken
- 8   cups chicken stock or 4 (16-oz.) cans
- 4   large fresh tomatoes, coarsely chopped
- 2   cups fresh lima beans or 1 pkg. (10-oz.) frozen, thawed
- 2   cups whole kernel corn or 1 pkg. (10-oz.) frozen, thawed
-     6-ounce can tomato paste
- 1   teaspoon dried thyme
- 1   bay leaf
- ¼   teaspoon salt
- ¼   teaspoon coarsely ground black pepper

In 5-quart Dutch oven, cook bacon over medium heat until crisp; remove, crumble and set aside. Remove all but 3 tablespoons bacon drippings from Dutch oven and add celery, shallots and garlic. Cook and stir 3 to 4 minutes, until vegetables are tender. Stir in remaining ingredients. Bring to boil over high heat. Reduce heat to low and simmer 30 minutes. Remove and discard bay leaf. Sprinkle each serving with bacon. Makes about 8 servings.

"LITTLE ORPHANT ANNIE"

LITTLE Orphant Annie's come to our
house to stay,
An' wash the cups an' saucers up, an' brush
the crumbs
away,
An' shoo the chickens off the porch, an'
dust the hearth, an'
sweep,
An' make the fire, an' bake the bread, an'
earn her board-an'
keep;
An' all us other childern, when the supper-
things is done,
We set around the kitchen fire an' has the
mostest fun
A-list'nin' to the witch-tales 'at Annie tells
about,
An' the Gobble-uns 'at gits you
Ef you
Don't
Watch
Out!

Wunst they wuz a little boy wouldn't say his
prayers—
An' when he went to bed at night, away
up-stairs,
His Mammy heerd him holler, an' his
Daddy heerd him
bawl,
An' when they turn't the kivvers down, he
wuzn't there at all!
An' they seeked him in the rafter-room, an'
cubby-hole, an'
press,
An' seeked him up the chimbly-flue, an'
ever'wheres, I guess;
But all they ever found wuz thist his pants
an' roundabout:—
An' the Gobble-uns 'll git you
Ef you
Don't
Watch
Out!

An' one time a little girl 'ud allus laugh an'
grin,
An' make fun of ever' one, an' all her blood
an' kin;
An' wunst, when they was "company," an'
ole folks wuz there,
She mocked 'em an' shocked 'em, an' said
she didn't care!
An' thist as she kicked her heels, an' turn't
to run an' hide,
They wuz two great big Black Things a-
standin' by her side,
An' they snatched her through the ceilin'
'fore she knowed
what she's about!
An' the Gobble-uns 'll git you
Ef you
Don't
Watch
Out!

An' little Orphant Annie says when the
blaze is blue,
An' the lamp-wick sputters, an' the wind
goes *woo-oo!*
An' you hear the crickets quit, an' the
moon is gray,
An' the lightnin'-bugs in dew is all
squenched away,—
You better mind yer parunts an' yer teachurs
fond an' dear,
An' churish them 'at loves you, an' dry the
orphant's tear,
An' he'p the pore an' needy ones 'at clusters
all about,
Er the Gobble-uns 'll git you
Ef you
Don't
Watch
Out!

Breads, Sweet Rolls, Donuts and the Like

BREADS, SWEET ROLLS, DONUTS AND THE LIKE

WHEAT BREAD OR WHITE BREAD?

Through the late 1880's and early years of the 20th century, a controversy raged over the virtues of white versus wheat bread. To many, the newer, more processed flour was better because it provided more concentrated nutrition. It did not, after all, contain fibrous parts of the grain which the body could not assimilate, and had to discard.

Sometime close to the turn of the century, a paper presented to the Natural Science Association stated: "Brown breads are inferior to white bread, because they contain much less available nutriment, weight for weight, than it does. Textbooks and medical men religiously reiterate the statement disproved years ago, that the best part of the wheat grain is milled out and thrown away in the bran. There is absolutely no foundation for the wild claims made by the whole wheat "crank;" in fact all the evidence is in favor of the white article.

"It is true," the scientist continued, "that whole wheat contains more protein than white flour, but then, we live not by what we eat, but what we digest. We can eat hay, but not digest it."

In contrast, this was the period of the health spa and the curious diet. People began to eat nuts and grains and other "natural" foods to increase their longevity. This era saw the development of commercial cereals based on various grains. Bran cereal was introduced, and other whole grain cereals followed.

If nothing else were available, the pioneers cheerfully ate bread and gravy. Contrary to today's thinking, white bread was considered healthier than brown bread. When conditions were very favorable, you were "eating your white bread." Riley's poem, "My White Bread" expresses this idea in the lines: "I drap my head on de good Lord's breast, Says a-eatin' my white braid."

REUBEN RILEY'S BREAD

This simplified recipe makes 3 to 4 loaves of bread at a time—about a day's baking for a moderately sized family in Riley's day. Make the dough ahead of time and refrigerate until just before baking. Fresh bread on demand!

11 to 12 cups unsifted all purpose flour
3 packages active dry yeast
¼ cup sugar
2 tablespoons salt
½ cup water

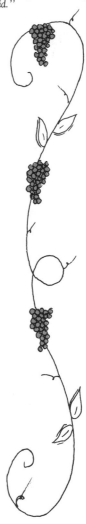

3½ cups milk
¾ cup margarine
Cooking oil

In large bowl of electric mixer, stir to blend 4 cups of the flour with the dry yeast, sugar and salt. In saucepan on stovetop or in microwave in glass casserole heat the milk and the water just until warm, not hot. Add the margarine and stir until all parts are softened or melted. Add milk liquid to the flour. Beat at high speed of mixer for 2 minutes. Scrape down the bowl, add 2 more cups of flour and beat for another minute until thick and elastic. With a wooden spoon, gradually stir in enough of the remaining flour to make a soft dough which leaves the sides of the bowl. Turn out onto floured board and knead for 5 to 10 minutes, until dough is smooth. Let rest on board for 20 minutes. Meanwhile, grease 3 (9x5x3-inch), or 4 (8x4x3) bread pans. Divide dough in 3 or 4 equal pieces, depending on pans, and shape the loaves into the pans. Brush with oil. Cover with plastic wrap and refrigerate 2 to 24 hours. About 10 minutes before baking the loaves, remove the dough from the refrigerator and also preheat the oven to 400 degrees. When oven has preheated, bake loaves for 30 to 40 minutes until done. Makes 3 or 4 loaves.

HOLYPOKES OR FRIED BISCUITS

Holypokes is an old fashioned name for a kind of doughnut ball. They are still made even today in "down-home" Indiana restaurants and are famous at Brown County's Nashville House. They're called "fried biscuits." The recipe goes something like this:
Take out some bread dough (above), as much as you need. Let the dough rise once and knead on a floured board. Form into balls the size of hazelnuts or walnuts. Place on greased cookie sheet, cover with wax paper and damp towel, and let rise in warm place until double. Preheat deep or shallow fat (see potato doughnuts recipe) to 360 degrees and fry the holypokes until golden brown. Drain on paper towels. Serve with soup or chowders, or serve with maple syrup as dessert.

BEATEN HERB BREAD

In the 1940's and 1950's beaten yeast batters were made by fortunate cooks who owned new electric mixers. These women found that using electricity to develop the gluten was much easier than kneading it by hand. The batter, being necessarily softer because of the mixing method, could be poured into the pan, and it could be baked in many shapes. Besides the traditional loaf, women baked this bread in tube pans, bundt pans and cupcakes. Eventually, manufacturers made individual loaf pans for beaten breads, and this size is charming to serve on the bread and butter plate for a special meal.

"Bread" during the early part of Riley's life probably meant one thing—hot biscuits. "Light bread" was the option, and it was not easily available in the smaller villages up to the time of the Civil War. The housewife was up early heating the coal or wood stove to cook the hot bread, which would delight for breakfast, dinner, and supper, dripping with butter and home-made strawberry preserves.

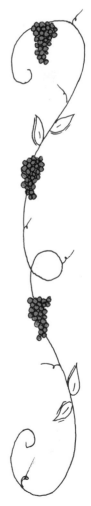

1	package active dry yeast
1¼	cups warm water
3	tablespoons cooking oil
2	teaspoons salt
2	tablespoons sugar
⅓	cup wheat germ
1	teaspoon caraway seeds
1	teaspoon nutmeg
1	teaspoon powdered or crumbled sage
2⅔	cups all purpose flour

In large mixing bowl, stir yeast in water until dissolved. Add oil, salt, sugar, wheat germ, caraway seeds, nutmeg and sage to bowl. Add half of the flour and beat for 2 minutes at medium speed of mixer, until well blended. Add remaining flour and blend with a spoon to make soft batter. Cover bowl with plastic wrap and let rise in warm place until double in bulk, about 30 minutes. Stir down batter, then pour and spread evenly in greased loaf pan (either 9x5x3-inch or 8x4x3-inch). Batter will be sticky. Pat top with floured fingers to smooth. Let rise again until about double in bulk—it will rise to ¼ inch from the top of an 8-inch loaf pan, to an inch from the top of a 9-inch pan. About 10 minutes before baking, preheat the oven to 375 degrees. Bake for 45 to 50 minutes, until browned. Immediately remove from pan to cooling rack. Makes 1 loaf.

INDIVIDUAL LOAVES: You can divide the batter among 6 greased individual pans (5x3x1½-inch). Let rise as above and bake about 30 minutes.

O ne of the real delights of Hoosier cooking from pioneer times on, and widely appreciated during the 1880's and '90's was sun-dried preserves, usually cherry. The housewife would get her sons to pick the tart cherries and would cook them with equal amounts of sugar until they were pinched and syrupy. Then the concoction would be covered with glass and would sit in a wide pan on a chair in the sun for about a week. Flavor, preservation and sunshine were baked in, to be poured out on a snowy February evening for the whole family on their hot bread.

SCRUMPTIOUS ONION ROLLS

These are made in pinwheels, like cinnamon rolls, but their scrumptious filling is savory rather than sweet.

    1   package active dry yeast
    1/4 cup warm water
    4   cups unsifted all purpose flour
    1/4 cup sugar
    1 1/2 teaspoons salt
    1/2 cup hot water
    1/2 cup milk
    1/4 cup soft margarine
    1   egg
Filling:
    6   tablespoons (3/4 stick) butter or margarine
    1   cup (1 large) finely chopped onion (part green onion and top for color, if desired)
    3   tablespoons Parmesan cheese
    1   tablespoon poppy seeds
    1   teaspoon garlic salt
    1   teaspoon paprika

In large mixer bowl dissolve yeast in warm water. Add 2 cups of the flour, sugar, salt, water, milk, margarine and egg. Blend at low speed until moistened; beat 2 minutes at medium speed. By hand, stir in remaining flour to form a soft dough. Cover and let rise in warm place until light and doubled in size, 45 to 60 minutes. Meanwhile make filling by stirring together all ingredients. Also, prepare two (1 dozen each) muffin pans by greasing well. After rising, stir down dough; toss on a floured board until no longer sticky. Divide dough in half. Roll each half to rectangle approximately 12 x 9-inches. Spread each with half of filling and roll up from wide side. Cut each roll into 12 equal parts (about 1-inch thick slices), and place in the prepared muffin cups. Let rolls rise in warm place until light and doubled in size, about 30 minutes. Meanwhile, preheat oven to 375 degrees. Bake for about 15 to 20 minutes, until golden brown. Makes 24 rolls.

"DOWN BY THE OLD MILL STREAM"

Until about 1880, when the flour mills located primarily around Minneapolis started selling quantities of processed flour, many people depended on the local mill to grind the grain for their flour. Everybody in the vicinity knew where the grain mill, and its "old mill stream" were, for they were an important part of daily life.

In her book, *Hancock County Highlights*, Dorothy June Williams tells how Earl K. Smith and Charlie Gant, two natives of Greenfield, sold their original song "Down By the Old Mill Stream" to one Tell Taylor of Chicago. For the tune, Smith received $500.00 and for the lyrics, Gant got $25.00. They were to regret this later, as several million copies of the sheet music "by Tell Taylor" were sold before 1920. The best efforts of these Hoosier songwriters became the second most popular music score of all time.

STONE GROUND WHOLEWHEAT BREAD

Breads made with only whole wheat flour have a compact and coarse texture, and close grain. They are higher in fiber than breads made with more highly processed flours.

- ¾ cup milk
- 2 tablespoons margarine or butter
- 2 tablespoons honey
- 1½ teaspoons salt
- 1 package active dry yeast
- ¼ cup warm water
- 2¼ to 2¾ cups unsifted stoneground whole wheat flour

In small saucepan over medium heat, or in microwave bowl at high power, heat milk just until small bubbles begin to break near surface (don't boil). To hot milk add butter, honey and salt; stir to melt butter. Cool until lukewarm. In large bowl dissolve yeast in warm water. Add lukewarm milk mixture and 1¼ cups of the whole wheat flour. Stir smooth, then stir in the remaining flour to soft dough. On board floured with whole wheat flour, knead the dough for about 10 minutes until smooth, In generously greased bowl, place dough; turn in the bowl until all sides of dough are greased. Cover with plastic wrap and let rise in warm place for 1 hour 20 minutes to 1 hour 25 min-

read pudding, of course, used up the last of the crusts and older pieces of bread. A pan of bread pieces was covered with a couple of cups of milk, sugar to taste and four or five beaten eggs. Raisins, dried cherries, pieces of winter apple or even dates could be added and the pan baked 45 minutes. They smothered all with whipped cream.

"*econd day bread" is something we don't remember today. Bread made with yeast had several stages from very soft and fresh, through firmer, through harder to finally "better use it today for toast or it'll mold." Most recipes called for "second day bread" as the newly baked loaf was too soft to use.*

utes, until doubled in size (takes about 1 hour). Punch dough down and shape into a loaf in greased 8x4x2-inch pan. Let rise until doubled, about 30 minutes. After rising pan should be about ¾ full. About 10 minutes before baking, preheat oven to 400 degrees. Bake bread for 15 minutes, then reduce oven temperature to 350 and continue baking for 30 minutes. If top of loaf begins to overbrown, cover it with a small sheet of aluminum foil. After baking, turn out of pan immediately and cool on rack. Makes 1 loaf.

WHEAT COUNTRY LOAVES

Rather like a coarse French bread.

    2½ cups warm water (105 to 115 degrees)
    4 envelopes active dry yeast
    1 tablespoon sugar
    4 to 5 cups unbleached all purpose flour
    2 to 3 cups whole wheat flour
    1 tablespoon salt
       Cornmeal

In large mixer bowl stir together water, yeast and sugar. Let stand about 5 minutes, until foamy. Blend in 4 cups unbleached flour and 2 cups whole wheat flour along with salt. Add more of each flour until a soft but workable dough is formed. Turn dough onto lightly floured board and knead smooth, about 10 minutes. Form dough into a ball. Place in greased or oiled bowl, turning to coat all sides. Cover with plastic wrap and let stand in warm area about 45 minutes until double in bulk. Meanwhile, prepare two 10x15-inch baking sheets by greasing a circle about 9-inches in diameter and sprinkling greased area with cornmeal. After dough has risen, punch down, turn onto floured board and cut in half. Shape each half into smooth round ball and place on prepared baking sheets, in center of greased-cornmeal area. With sharp knife, cut 3 or 4 diagonal slashes on top each loaf. Brush loaves with water, and allow to rise slightly, about 15 minutes. Place loaves in non-preheated oven and set at

350 degrees. Bake about 1 hour, until loaves sound hollow when tapped. Transfer to wire racks to cool completely before slicing and storing. Makes 2 loaves. (Note: When using heavy duty mixer with dough hook, use minimum amounts of each flour, and knead with dough hook about 7 minutes.)

SKILLET CORNBREAD

Almost all breads made with cornmeal are quick breads. Cornmeal has no gluten, which is necessary for stretching the dough when yeast bread is made. Cast iron skillets were common cooking utensils in Riley's day and they were used for cornbread. The earliest ovens were really boxes built into the wall next to the fireplace. Enclosing the heat helped cook the tops of large breads and meats. This bread is pudding-like, not dry and crumbly like those made with flour and baking powder.

- 3 tablespoons shortening
- 1 egg
- 2 cups buttermilk
- 1¾ cups cornmeal
- 1 teaspoon salt
- 1 teaspoon soda

This recipe is best baked in an all-cast-iron (handle too) skillet. You can also use a deep 8-inch square ovenproof dish or pan. Place the shortening in the skillet or dish. Place dish in a cold oven and preheat the oven and shortening to 450 degrees. Meanwhile, beat the egg slightly, then blend in the buttermilk. In small bowl, stir together the cornmeal, salt and soda; stir into the egg-milk mixture and mix very well. When oven has preheated, carefully remove the skillet or pan, pour the hot fat into the batter and mix thoroughly. Immediately pour the batter back into the skillet or pan and return to oven. Bake for 30 to 40 minutes. Cut cornbread into wedges or squares and serve immediately. Makes about 8 to 10 servings.

SWEET ROLLS, MUFFINS, COFFEE CAKE

A famous American cook-book is the Century Cook Book which advertisess "30 illustrations, over 100,000 sold." It is a collection of carefully tested household recipes by Jennie Hansey containing a Family Medical Adviser by E.N. T. Oliver. Gold Medal Flour also put out famous cookbooks, especially a Christmas edition which was reprinted in 1970 by General Mills, Minneapolis, Minn.

Harriet Beecher Stowe, famous author of the anti-slavery book, *Uncle Tom's Cabin* had a sister who was also a crusader. Catherine Stowe's cause was good cooking. In her *The Domestic Receipt Book* written in 1848, Catherine warns the homemaker that to serve poor breads is far more shameful "than to speak bad grammar, or to have a dress out of fashion."

In the 1800's sticky buns were popular. If they had a nut topping, they were usually called pecan rolls. Either way, they were made with sweetened yeast dough into which was rolled sugar and spices. Muffins were popular, especially with housewives, because they were quick to make. However, you had to have muffin pans, sometimes called "gem pans" to make these small cakes. As sweet, soft fruit breads came into popularity, homemakers used nut bread batters for muffins, too, and many of these moist, fruity batters are credited with the huge popularity of muffins today.

Scones, sweet biscuits usually enriched with egg, were also popular in the 18th century, and people used their best scone recipe as a basis for the beloved strawberry shortcake, when berries were in season.

When fruits or nuts or other special ingredients were unavailable, women used treasured spices to give their breads a special personality. It was these creative ways with seasoning and presentation which gave a distinct uniqueness, and pleasure, to each woman's baking.

WHOLE WHEAT CINNAMON ROLLS

1 package instant dry yeast
¼ cup warm water
1 cup unsifted whole wheat flour
3 cups unsifted all purpose flour

¼ cup sugar
1½ teaspoons salt
1 cup hot tap water
¼ cup butter or margarine (½ stick), softned
1 egg
Filling
½ cup butter or margarine (1 stick), melted
½ cup packed light brown sugar
Topping
1 tablespoon ground cinnamon
2 tablespoons granulated sugar

*P*OTATO PANCAKES
Peel large potatoes overnight and keep them in cool water; grate, drain and for every pint allow 2 eggs, beaten separately, ½ teaspoon salt, a dust of pepper and 1 tablespoon flour, more or less according to the quality of the potatoes. Brown in thin cakes in butter. In winter use with meat. In summer try tomato or any brown sauce. (1904 Recipe)

In mixer bowl, stir yeast and water to dissolve. Add the cup of whole wheat flour and 2 cups of the all purpose flour, the sugar, salt, hot tap water, margarine and egg. With mixer on low speed, mix to blend, then beat at medium speed 2 minutes. Add the remaining cup of flour and mix until dough is smooth. Grease or spray with non-stick spray a bowl large enough to hold more than double the bulk ot the dough. Place the dough in the greased bowl and let it rise in warm place about 1 hour, until doubled. Punch down, and roll out on floured board to rectangle about 16-inches long and 6 to 8-inches wide. Make Filling by stirring butter and brown sugar; drop mixture in mounds over dough and spread evenly. Roll up dough starting from the 16-inch side, and cut the roll into about 16 (1-inch) slices. Arrange slices in well greased tall-sided 13x9x2-inch baking pan and sprinkle with the cinnamon and granulated sugar Topping. Let rolls rise about 30 minutes, until doubled. Bake in preheated 375-degree oven for about 25 minutes. If desired, drizzle tops of warm rolls with Confectioners Sugar Icing made by stirring together ½ cup confectioners sugar with enough warm water to make pourable glaze. Makes about 16 rolls.

WHOLE WHEAT STICKY BUNS: In saucepan on stovetop, or glass cup or casserole in microwave oven, heat ½ cup brown sugar and ¼ cup butter or margarine until melted. Stir in 1 tablespoon corn syrup. Pour mixture into greased 13x9x2-inch pan, as above, and sprinkle with ½ cup pecan halves before adding the cinnamon rolls. Bake as above, and immediately invert the pan over a heatproof serving plate. Let the pan remain over the rolls to catch that last drizzle of syrup. Omit the Confectioners Sugar Icing.

DOUBLE SPICY COFFEE CAKE

There's cinnamon in both the cake and topping. You can refrigerate this overnight before baking. In the morning, heat the oven and bake the freshest cake you've ever tasted.

- 2 cups all purpose flour
- 1 cup sugar
- ½ cup packed brown sugar
- 1 teaspoon soda
- 1 teaspoon baking powder
- ½ teaspoon salt
- 1 teaspoon cinnamon
- 1 cup buttermilk
- ⅔ cup shortening
- 2 eggs

Topping:
- ½ cup packed brown sugar
- ½ cup chopped nuts
- 1 teaspoon cinnamon
- ½ teaspoon nutmeg

Grease and flour bottom only of a 13x9x2-inch pan. In large bowl, place flour, sugar, brown sugar, soda, baking powder, salt, cinnamon, buttermilk, shortening and eggs. At low speed, blend batter until moistened, then beat 3 minutes at medium speed. Pour into the prepared pan. In small bowl, stir together the topping of brown sugar, nuts, cinnamon and nutmeg. Sprinkle the topping over the batter. Cover pan with plastic wrap and refrigerate overnight. About 40 to 50 minutes before you wish to serve the cake, preheat the oven to 350 degrees. Uncover the cake and bake for 30 to 45 minutes, until golden brown. Serve warm. Makes about 12 servings. (Note: if you wish, drizzle the top of cake as it comes out of the oven with powdered sugar glaze made by stirring together 1 cup confectioners sugar with 1 tablespoon soft butter or margarine, ½ teaspoon vanilla and 2 to 3 tablespoons milk until smooth.)

BREADS, SWEET ROLLS, DONUTS AND THE LIKE

LEMON BLUEBERRY MUFFINS

1¾ cups all purpose flour
¼ cup sugar
2½ teaspoons baking powder
¾ teaspoon salt
¾ cup milk
1 well beaten egg
⅓ cup cooking oil
1 cup fresh or frozen whole blueberries
2 tablespoons sugar
1 teaspoon grated fresh lemon peel
Butter and sugar for top

Preheat the oven to 400 degrees. Grease muffin pan for 1 dozen mufffins. In mixing bowl, stir together flour, ¼ cup sugar, baking powder and salt. Make a well in the center of the dry ingredients. In small bowl or cup, combine the milk, egg and oil. Add liquid mixture all at once to dry ingredients. Stir together just until dry ingredients are moistened. Toss together the blueberries and the 2 tablespoons sugar. Stir gently into the batter with the lemon peel. Divide the batter into the prepared muffin pans. Bake for about 25 minutes, until muffins are set and golden brown. While muffins are still warm dip tops into melted butter or margarine, then into small amount of granulated sugar (or sprinkle sugar over top). Serve warm. Makes 12 muffins.

MOIST OAT MUFFINS

1½ cups all purpose flour
½ cup packed brown sugar
2½ teaspoons baking powder
¾ teaspoon salt
¾ teaspoon soda
¼ cup margarine or butter
1 cup uncooked quick or old fashioned oats
1¼ cups buttermilk
1 egg, slightly beaten

Preheat oven to 425 degrees. In large bowl, stir together flour, brown sugar, baking powder, salt and soda. Cut in margarine with pastry blender (or two knives), until mixture looks like coarse meal. Stir in oats. Add buttermilk

A contemporary of James Whitcomb Riley was Isabella Beeton of Epsom Downs, England. Born in 1836, she was the oldest in a family of 21 children. Little did anyone know she would become one of the most famous cooks in the world.

[continued]

and egg. Stir just to moisten dry ingredients. Fill greased or paper lined muffin cups about ⅔ full. Bake for 20 to 25 minutes. Serve warm with butter. Makes about 1 dozen.

INDIVIDUAL PRUNE-APRICOT PIZZAS

These are really a type of "Kolacky," which bakeries are promoting today, in various sizes, as Fruit Pizzas. Each ball of yeast dough is poked and stretched to form a shell for the good tangy filling. In Riley's day, dried fruits were frequently the only fruits available in wintertime. Today, they are the "fruit of choice" by some people because of their high fiber content.

Dough:
- 2 packages active dry yeast
- ¾ cup warm water
- ½ cup sugar
- ½ cup soft shortening
- 1 teaspoon salt
- 2 eggs
- 4 cups all purpose flour

In mixing bowl, place yeast and warm water. Stir well, and allow to stand until dissolved, about 5 minutes. Add sugar, shortening, salt, eggs and half of flour. Blend on lowest mixer speed, and scrape bowl well. Continue mixing on low speed for 8 to 10 more minutes. Stir in remaining half of flour. Let dough rise in warm place until doubled in bulk, about 1½ hours. Stir down and turn out onto well floured board. Divide into 24 equal pieces, shape each into round ball and place about 2 inches apart on greased baking sheets. Allow dough to relax for 15 minutes. Using fingertips, poke center of each ball and pull dough into flat circle with about ½-inch ridge around edges. Fill with heaping tablespoon filling. Let rise about 30 minutes, until depression remains when touched with finger. About 10 minutes before baking, preheat oven to 375 degrees. Bake for 15 to 18 minutes, until browned. Sprinkle with confectioners sugar. Makes 24 rolls.

Filling: In large saucepan, place 8 ounces (about 1 cup) prunes, 4 ounces (about ¾ cup) dried apricots and water to

In 1856 Isabella married Sam Beeton, an enterprising young publisher, and the following year, she began work on her cookbook which is now a classic. Her husband published a magazine called The Englishwoman's Domestic Magazine *for which she wrote a three penny supplement on cooking which first appeared in 1859. It was so popular that her husband put out a handsomely and strongly bound book in 1861 on which Isabella had labored for four years. Within a year 60,000 copies had been sold, and eventually it became the best selling cookbook of all time.*

cover. Simmer 30 minutes, until tender. Drain fruit; chop fine. Stir in ½ teaspoon allspice, ½ cup sugar, 1 tablespoon lemon juice and 1 tablespoon grated lemon peel.

1890 KEEPSAKE BISCUIT

From a small North Carolina collection called "Old Timey Recipes."

  1 quart milk or cream
  1½ cups butter or lard
  2 tablespoons white sugar
  1 good teaspoon salt
  1 teaspoon cream of tartar
  Enough flour to make stiff dough

Knead well and mold into neat, small biscuits with your hands. Bake well and you have a good, sweet biscuit that will keep for weeks in a dry place. They are fine for a traveling lunch.

BUTTERY RAISIN SCONES

Omit the raisins and bake this in a well greased 9-inch round layer cake pan at 375 degrees for 30 minutes as a base for strawberry shortcake. Knead the dough with a little flour and mold into about 8 balls to bake as Hot Cross Buns for Good Friday. Frost with confectioners sugar crosses.

  2 cups all purpose flour
  ⅓ cup sugar
  3 tablespoons baking powder
  ½ teaspoon salt
  ½ cup (1 stick) soft butter
  ½ cup dark raisins
  ¾ cup milk
  2 eggs, slightly beaten

Preheat oven to 450 degrees. In large bowl, stir flour, sugar, baking powder and salt. With pastry blender or fork, mix in butter until consistency of coarse meal. Mix in raisins. Combine milk and eggs, add to the flour mixture and

"What moved me, in the first instance, to attempt a work like this," wrote Isabella Beeton, the author of the famous 19th century cookbook, in 1859, "was the discomfort and suffering which I had seen brought upon men and women by household mismanagement. . . . Men are now so well served out of doors,—at their clubs, well-ordered taverns, and dining-houses, that in order to compete with the attractions of these places, a mistress must be thoroughly acquainted with the theory and practice of cookery, as well as be perfectly conversant with all the other arts of making and keeping a comfortable home."

stir just until all dough is moistened. Drop dough in 8 to 10 spoonfuls onto greased cookie sheet about 2 inches apart. Bake about 10 to 12 minutes and serve immediately. Makes 8 to 10.

ECLAIR PUFF PASTRY

Imagine this being served on Lockerbie Street to a mature, sophisticated Riley. It resembles a chocolate eclair perched atop a shortbread base.

Base:
    1 cup all purpose flour
    ½ cup butter
    2 tablespoons water
Cream Puff Topping:
    ½ cup butter
    1 cup water
    1 teaspoon almond flavoring
    1 cup all purpose flour
    3 eggs

Preheat oven to 350 degrees. Make base: Into medium bowl, place flour. With pastry cutter or two knives, cut in butter finely. With fork, mix in water until dough is formed. Divide in half; pat each portion into 12-inch long, 3-inch wide strip on large (15x10-inch) ungreased baking sheet. Make topping: In large saucepan, place butter and water. Bring to boil, then remove from heat and add the almond flavoring. Quickly beat in flour until smooth. Add eggs, one at a time, beating smooth after each addition. Spread half of mixture evenly over each strip of base pastry. Bake for about 60 minutes. Cool, then frost with Chocolate Glaze. Makes 10 to 12 total servings.

Chocolate Glaze: In 1-quart microwave bowl, place 1 square (1 oz.) unsweetened chocolate. Microwave at medium (50 percent power) for 2 to 4 minutes, until melted. Stir in 1½ teaspoons corn syrup, ½ teaspoon vanilla, 2½ cups confectioners sugar, and 3 tablespoons milk. Beat until smooth. After frosting, let glaze set about 30 minutes.

After the birth of her fourth child, cookbook author Isabella Beeton developed a fever and died at the age of 28. Her sisters thought that anxiety over her husband's speculations was the real cause of her death.

BREADS, SWEET ROLLS, DONUTS AND THE LIKE

"Frugality," preaches an old cookbook, "may be termed the daughter of Prudence, the sister of Temperance and the parent of Liberty. He that is extravagant will quickly become poor, and poverty will enforce dependence and invite corruption." Early cookbooks were full of such advice, enough to terrorize the housewife of the late 19th century, lest she waste a household resource. (Economy and frugality must never, however, be allowed to degenerate into parsimony and meanness, these books would allow.)

Housewives of Riley's era knew many ways to use up leftover food. If it did not go into the soup pot or a casserole, or if it could not be covered with sauce and served for another meal, it might be used to extend or flavor a batter or dough. Potatoes, squash, carrots, even beets were added to breads as were applesauce, nuts and dried fruits. A leftover lemon was welcome in cakes and breads and, later, canned pineapple. Cottage cheese, which was always on the table in rural areas, was a little more difficult to use up than other dairy products, but housewives managed to make bread, and even Sunday rolls, out of it.

June William's book, *Greenfield Glimpses*, tells the story of Susie Schneider's Restaurant in Greenfield, famous for its good homemade food in the 1920's. One of Susie's specialties was homemade potato doughnuts, which we tried and enjoyed very much. Not having a doughnut cutter, we cut the ends out of a flat can, about 3-inches diameter (like a tuna can), and used the smallest pimento jar (about 1-inch diameter) to cut out the holes. We got 22 large doughnuts and holes from this recipe, plus 6 crullers which were made by twisting together the scraps after all the doughnuts had been cut.

The remarkable book called Beeton's Book of Household Management was last reprinted in 1969, and is available in the Library of Congress. It contains 1112 pages and even contains legal advice. There are hundreds of items in the analytical Index. A typical recipe is on the next page.

SUSIE'S POTATO DOUGHNUTS

  1 cup unseasoned mashed potatoes
  2 tablespoons (¼ stick) soft butter
1½ cups sugar
  2 eggs plus 2 egg yolks
  1 cup milk
  2 teaspoons vanilla
  5 cups flour

1 cup milk
2 teaspoons vanilla
5 cups flour
5 teaspoons baking powder
1 teaspoon salt
2 teaspoons nutmeg
  Cooking oil for frying

In large mixing bowl, stir together mashed potatoes, butter, sugar, eggs and yolks. Add milk and vanilla; stir into potato mixture until smooth. In small bowl, stir together flour, baking powder, salt and nutmeg. Stir into potato mixture to make stiff dough. Turn dough out onto generously floured board, coating all sides with flour, and knead dough until smooth and no longer sticky. Pat out to ½ inch thick, and, with floured cutter, cut into doughnuts (see comment above). Before frying, preheat electric skillet about half full of cooking oil to 375 degrees. (If you don't have a heat regulator, drop a cube of bread into fat; when about the right temperature, the cube will brown in about a minute.) Carefully drop doughnuts into fat. When they rise to the surface, turn them over and fry just until golden on both sides. Without piercing outsides, remove to absorbent paper, and sprinkle with sugar. Makes about 22 (3-inch) doughnuts and holes and 6 large twisted crullers from scraps. (Note: To start with instant potatoes, put about ½ cup dry powdered or flaked potatoes in bowl and add hottest tap water, whipping with fork, until appearance resembles fluffy mashed potatoes. Measure out 1 cup.)

POTATO PARKER HOUSE ROLLS

These famous yeast rolls are attributed to The Parker House restaurant of Boston, which opened circa 1855. A receipt for a similar roll was given in *Miss Parloa's New Cook Book* in 1880. You can refrigerate this dough, and bake when needed.

1 package active dry yeast
1½ cups warm water
⅔ cup sugar
1½ teaspoons salt
⅔ cup shortening

2 eggs
1 cup unseasoned mashed potatoes
7 to 7½ cups all purpose flour

In large mixing bowl, dissolve yeast in warm water. Stir in sugar, salt, shortening, eggs, potatoes and 4 cups of the flour. Beat smooth, and mix in enough of the remaining flour to make the dough easy to handle. Turn onto lightly floured board and knead smooth. Place in greased bowl and turn greased side up. Cover bowl tightly with plastic wrap; refrigerate at least 8 hours, but no more than 5 days. Punch down dough. TO MAKE HALF OF DOUGH (20 ROLLS): Grease 2 (9-inch round) cake pans. Roll out half of dough about ½ inch thick and cut into 20 (3-inch) circles with cookie cutter. Brush with butter and fold in half, so top half overlaps slightly. Space in pans. Brush again with melted butter and let rolls rise until double, about 1 hour. About 10 minutes before baking, preheat oven to 400 degrees. Bake rolls about 15 minutes, until light golden brown. Total recipe makes about 40 rolls.

COTTAGE CHEESE BREAD

1 package dry yeast
¼ cup warm water (about 110 degrees)
1 tablespoon butter or margarine
1 cup cottage cheese
2 tablespoons sugar
1 teaspoon salt
¼ teaspoon soda
1 egg, beaten
2½ cup sifted flour

In small bowl or cup, stir the yeast and warm water until dissolved. In large saucepan slowly heat butter and cottage cheese until softened and combined. To butter-cheese mixture add sugar, salt, soda and egg. Mix well and mix in the yeast. Add the flour and mix very well. Turn out on floured board and knead until smooth. On board, let dough stand until double in size. Knead again to smooth and place in (9x5x3-inch) loaf pan. Let rise again until almost double in size. Bake at 350 degrees for 30 to 40 minutes, until loaf sounds hollow when thumped with

During the Gay Nineties, good bread was snacked on more than it is today. Bread and milk was often a child's supper; hot milk toast was an invalid's fare. Coming in fron a sledding trip or fall walk, a family might have slices of bread, butter and sugar. Poor families ate bread and lard, or, when margarine came in (uncolored) after the turn of the century, bread and white margarine.

middle finger. Makes 1 loaf. (Note: You can also make rolls with this recipe.)

BUTTERY BANANA BREAD

This was the way to use up bananas which were too ripe to eat fresh.

Fine bread crumbs
½ cup butter
1 cup sugar
1 teaspoon soda
½ teaspoon salt
2 eggs
1½ cups mashed bananas (3 or 4)
¼ cup sour cream
1 teaspoon vanilla
1½ cups flour

Preheat oven to 350 degrees. Grease a 9x5x3-inch loaf pan and sprinkle with fine bread crumbs. In large mixer bowl, beat butter, sugar, soda and salt until very light and fluffy. Beat in eggs. Mix in banana, sour cream and vanilla. Mix in flour until no dry areas appear in batter. Pour into prepared loaf pan. Bake for about 50 to 60 minutes until toothpick stuck in center comes out clean. Makes 1 loaf.

LEMON BREAD

Good with pork or poultry, with tea, for breakfast or brunch. Tip: After you squeeze the juice from lemon halves, freeze the rinds in a plastic bag. Frozen lemon rinds grate much easier than fresh, and they give a fresher lemon flavor than dried or frozen grated peel.

6 tablespoons shortening or butter (¾ stick)
1 cup sugar
2 eggs, beaten
1 tablespoon grated lemon peel
1½ cups all purpose flour
1 teaspoon baking powder
½ teaspoon salt

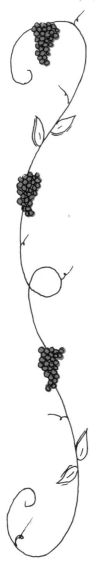

Stale coffee cake could be revitalized by the turn-of-the-century cook by putting it into a frying pan with a few drops of water and two tablespoons of butter and then steaming it very low for about ten minutes. Like a microwave treatment today.

½ cup milk
½ cup chopped walnuts
⅓ cup sugar
3 tablespoons fresh lemon juice

In large mixing bowl, beat together the shortening and sugar. Add eggs and lemon peel. In small mixing bowl, stir together the flour, baking powder and salt; add alternately to shortening-sugar mixture along with milk. Fold in walnuts. Pour batter into greased and floured 8x4x2-inch loaf pan. Bake at 350 degrees for 60 to 65 minutes. Just before bread comes from the oven, stir the ⅓ cup sugar and lemon juice together in small bowl. Pour juice mixture over hot bread and let stand in pan for 10 to 15 minutes before turning out of pan. Cool. Makes 1 (8-inch) loaf, about 10 slices.

SPICY CARROT BREAD (Microwave)

This rich bread, like many fruit and vegetable breads, can be also be served as a simple dessert. Toast the nuts by stirring with 1 teaspoon of oil in a small microwave bowl and microwaving at high (100 percent power) for 2 to 4 minutes. This step, which is optional, gives more flavor to the bread. Bake the batter in a fluted microwave tube pan for most even cooking.

Cornflake crumbs
1½ cups sugar
1 cup cooking oil
1 teaspoon vanilla extract
3 eggs
1½ cups unsifted all purpose flour
½ teaspoon salt
1¼ teaspoons baking soda
2 teaspoons ground cinnamon
2 cups lightly packed grated raw carrots (about 4 or 5)
⅔ cup chopped pecans

Prepare a 16 cup microwave fluted tube pan by greasing well and dusting with cornflake crumbs. In large mixing bowl, place sugar, oil, vanilla and eggs. With electric mixer at low speed, beat well. Add flour, salt, soda and cinnamon and beat at low speed just until blended. Fold in

carrots and pecans to make smooth pourable batter. Pour batter into prepared pan. Microwave at high for 12 to 16 minutes, rotating pan ¼ turn every 4 minutes, until toothpick inserted halfway between edges of pan comes out clean and bread begins to shrink from sides. Place pan directly on wooden board or heatproof counter about 15 minutes to allow for settling, then unmold. Makes 1 bread.

ORANGE OATMEAL BREAD (Microwave)

After grating the peel from the oranges, microwave the oranges themselves for about ½ minute, just until warm, before juicing them. The slight warmth encourages the oranges to give up more juice. Like the recipe above, this bread can be used as a simple cake.

Corn flake crumbs
¾ cup quick cooking oatmeal
1 cup fresh orange juice (add water, if necessary, to make 1 cup)
⅓ cup cooking oil
1 cup all purpose flour
¾ cup granulated sugar
¾ cup packed brown sugar
Grated peel from 2 oranges (scant 2 tablespoons)
¼ teaspoon salt
¾ teaspoon baking soda
1 teaspoon ground nutmeg
3 eggs

Prepare a 16 cup microwave fluted tube pan by greasing well and dusting with cornflake crumbs. In large mixing bowl, stir together the oatmeal, orange juice and oil. Let stand few minutes to moisten the oatmeal. Add the flour, both sugars, orange peel, salt, soda, nutmeg and eggs. With electric mixer at high speed, beat until well blended. Batter will be thin. Pour into prepared pan. Microwave at high for 10 to 14 minutes, rotating pan ¼ turn every 2 minutes, until toothpick inserted between edges of pan comes out clean. Top of cake will be moist and shiny, but area underneath should be set. Place pan directly on wooden board or heatproof counter for about 15 minutes to allow for settling, then unmold. Makes 1 tube bread.

Bruce Catton, in his fine book about Michigan life during this period, Waiting for the Morning Train, describes country Sunday suppers in the summer. Then people feasted only on fresh sliced tomatos, green beans from the garden, corn on the cob and hot fresh bread with iced tea to drink. The good old summer time!

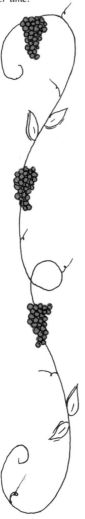

CAKES

CAKES

Cakes of yesteryear were much more varied than they are today. With the age of the cake mix and standardized recipes, a great deal of cake creativity went out the window. Like everything else, cakes were made from locally available ingredients. Molasses cakes, rather a form of gingerbread, were common, and formed the basis of the old fashioned Stack Cake. This cake was generally baked in thin layers, put together with sweetened applesauce. Young girls frequently used it as a wedding cake. Sometimes helping neighbors contributed cake layers to the wedding festivities, and a popular bride could have a very tall stack indeed. (It has even been said that the footed glass pedestal plate was brought to market by manufacters as a response to brides' wishes for tall wedding stack cakes.)

Lady and Lord Baltimore cakes were popular at Riley's time also. These were extremely fancy cakes, considered "Southern" but made all over the Midwest, and certainly in Greenfield, as our mother's mother had a recipe for this. The most extravagant Baltimore cakes used many eggs, but it was really the fancy icings, filled with dried fruits and cherries, that made the cakes special.

Geranium Cake, found in an old cookbook, called for a pound of butter to be washed and wrapped in geranium leaves overnight. Presumably, the leaves gave the cake some flavor. Pork cake used salt pork, ground, for the shortening. It, too was frequently a molasses spice cake. Today, a sausage cake survives, served for brunch or as a hearty dessert.

"Jelly Cake" referred to in Riley's poem "The Child World" could have been either a common jelly roll—a flat sponge cake spread with jelly and rolled up. Or, it could have referred to a stacked cake with cooked thickned fruit "jelly" filling like the "Lemon Jelly Cake" which follows.

In Ruth Wakefield's *Toll House Tried and True Recipes*, (1936) we read a recipe for Slop Over Cake. This used the still-common technique of breaking an egg into a cup and filling the cup with milk (Don't slop over!) This method of

"*Jelly Cake*" mentioned in "The Child World" was probably jelly roll. A yellow sponge cake was baked in a thin layer in a long, flat low-sided pan. While warm, it was heavily spread with jelly and literally "rolled up," then sliced in pinwheel fashion, end to end. It was kept moist by being covered tightly with a damp towel.

measurement controlled the total amount of liquid added to the cake.

Fruit cakes, because of their keeping qualities, were very popular. By Riley's time, candied fruits were commercially available, but some housekeepers still made their own for holiday baking and for eating as a candied treat. One interesting old time fruit cake was known as "Black Cake," and the blacker it was, the better. In the 1870's, when this was popular, some homemakers browned their flour in the oven before adding it to the cake, to darken the batter as much as possible. Also, they used heavy dark molasses, coffee, dark fruit jam, dark raisins and spices to add color. These heavily spiced, sweet cakes would keep for years and could be used to celebrate anniversaries of happy occasions year after year.

The authoritative *Gold Medal Cook Book*, put out by the Washburn Crosby Flour Mills in 1904 gave several paragraphs over to instructions on "the easiest way to make a cake." There were numerous tips on how to control the dampers and griddles on the stove, the type of fire to use and how much coal it should have, the amount of rising you should expect during each quarter of the baking period. It included advice on the quality of the ingredients, mixing instructions, tips on how and when to measure and otherwise handle each ingredient. It told you how to tell when the cake was done (it stopped hissing) and how to turn it out to cool. After all this information, the recipes themselves included sketchy instructions. Everything you needed to know was in the front of the chapter.

STACK CAKE (MOLASSES CAKE)

¾ cup shortening
1 cup sugar
1 cup molasses
3 eggs
1 cup milk
4 cups flour
½ teaspoon soda
1 teaspoon salt
3 cups thick applesauce

Cream shortening, then add sugar, a little at a time, blending well. Add molasses and mix thoroughly. Add eggs, one at a time, beating well after each addition. To this add milk alternately with the sifted dry ingredients. Beat until smooth. Place mixture about ⅜ inch deep into six (6) 9-inch greased and floured (round cake) pans. Bake at 375 degrees F. for 18 to 20 minutes. When cool, stack up layers, using applesauce generously between layers.

LADY BALTIMORE CAKE

This became popular after the 1906 novel entitled *Lady Baltimore* by Owen Wister took the reading public by storm. Its companion Lord Baltimore Cake used up all the egg yolks from the cake and orange and lemon juice for flavor. Instead of dried fruits, the icing had several kinds of nuts and even macaroon crumbs.

- ½ cup butter
- 1 cup sugar
- 1¾ cups flour
- ⅛ teaspoon salt
- 2 teaspoons baking powder
- ½ cup milk
- 1 teaspoon vanilla
- 3 egg whites

Preheat oven to 350 degrees. Grease and flour two 8-inch layer cake pans. In large mixer bowl, beat the butter and sugar until thoroughly creamed. Onto large piece of wax paper, sift dry ingredients (if you don't have a flour sifter use a wire strainer). Add flour mixture to creamed mixture alternately with milk into which vanilla has been added. In clean non-plastic bowl, beat egg whites stiff and fold into batter. Pour into prepared pans and bake for 25 minutes or until a toothpick inserted into the center of the cake comes out clean. Put layers together with Lady Baltimore Frosting. (Note: as a variation to this recipe, some people covered the cooled cake with a thick syrup made by boiling 1 cup sugar and 1½ cups water before putting on the icing.

Cupcakes were, in frontier days, literally cakes baked in cups. Up to the turn of the century many cooks used heavy, heat-proof cups to bake a variety of things, including custard.

LADY BALTIMORE FROSTING

- 2 cups sugar
- ⅔ cup water
- 2 egg whites
- 5 figs
- ⅔ cup raisins
- ⅔ cup nuts
- Candied cherries

Boil sugar and water to soft ball stage (238 degrees). Pour slowly over well beaten egg whites, beating constantly. Set aside to cool. Put figs, raisins and nuts through chopper. Add to cooled frosting. Spread between layers and on top and sides of cake. Garnish with nuts and halved candied cherries. One old-time cookbook advised: "Be lavish with frosting and decorations—the frosting is the show window for the cake."

GREENFIELD CAKE

Although the origin of this old American cake is uncertain, it is definitely appropriate for a James Whitcomb Riley cookbook.

- 2 cups sifted all purpose flour
- 3 teaspoons baking powder
- ½ teaspoon salt
- ½ cup sugar
- ½ cup butter
- 1 cup milk
- 1 egg, unbeaten
- ½ cup seedless raisins
- Topping:
- ¾ cup sugar
- 1 to 3 teaspoons cinnamon

Sift the flour, baking powder, salt and sugar into a mixing bowl. Work in the butter with pastry blender or fingertips until the mixture resembles meal. Add the milk and egg, and stir in just until the dry ingredients are moistened. Stir in the raisins. Turn into a well-greased pan about

Many of the Hoosiers Riley knew were of Southern origin. These folks liked Riley's verses "A Short'nin' Bread Song"—Pieced Out with the Chorus: "Fotch dat dough fum the kitchin - shed—Rake dem coals out hot and red—Putt on de oven and putt on de led,— Mammy's gwinter cook some short'nin' Shoirt'nin' bread."

10x14x2-inches or two 8-inch pans. Mix the sugar and cinnamon, sprinkle over the top, and bake in a preheated moderate to moderately hot oven, 375 to 400 degrees. This is good served cold, but better when served warm. Some people prefer it with butter dotted over the cinnamon and sugar.

GOLDEN LOAF CAKE

The earliest pound cakes were baked in loaves because it was practical. Housewives already had loaf pans for bread making and even the smallest or most irregularly shaped oven could hold several loaf pans at once.

1¾ cups unsifted all purpose flour
1 cup sugar
2 teaspoons baking powder
1 teaspoon salt
¼ cup white vegetable shortening
¼ cup butter
1 teaspoon vanilla
5 egg yolks
¾ cup milk

Preheat oven to 350 degrees F. Heavily grease a 9x5x3-inch loaf pan and flour it, being sure that all areas are coated. Blend dry ingredients in mixing bowl. Add shortening, butter, vanilla, egg yolks and milk. Beat 2 minutes on medium mixer speed. Scrape the bowl well and beat 2 more minutes on medium mixer speed. Spoon batter into pan and bake for 60 to 70 minutes. Cool and finish with Fresh Orange Glaze.

Glaze: This is very thin and will soak into the cake. Stir together ½ cup of fresh orange juice, 1 teaspoon or more of fresh orange rind and 1 scant cup of confectioners sugar. While cake is baking, put bowl of glaze on top of oven to keep warm. After cake has baked, remove it from the pan and set upright on wire cake rack. With a long-tined fork, punch holes into the top of the cake. Spoon the glaze, a little at a time, over cake for moisture and fruity flavor. Cool before slicing.

Before cake mixes it was no easy task to bake a cake. Today, if you actually take the time to measure all the ingredients, we say you are baking "from scratch." Just as today, it was a great disappointment if the cake didn't turn out, but in Riley's day there were more perils in delicate cake baking because of the lack of standards in ingredients and measurements.

MODERNIZED LEMON JELLY CAKE

This is smaller than the typical jelly cake, but its filling—much like lemon pie filling—is very similar. Before year-round egg production was possible, cakes were often named by how many eggs they contained. This helped the housewife to ration her egg supply. This would be a 2-egg cake, and it was also used for the old fashioned cast iron lamb cake molds.

Cake:
- 1 cup sugar
- ¼ cup butter
- 2 eggs
- ½ teaspoon salt
- 1¼ teaspoon baking powder
- 1 teaspoon vanilla
- 1½ cups cake flour
- ½ cup milk

Preheat oven to 350 degrees. In large mixing bowl, place sugar and butter. With electric mixer, beat until light and creamy. Beat in eggs, salt, baking powder and vanilla until fluffy. With mixer at low speed, add flour alternately with milk beating just until smooth. Pour batter into greased and floured 7x11x2-inch pan. Bake for 25 to 35 minutes, until toothpick stuck in center comes out clean. Remove to cake rack to cool. When cold, split cake to make two thin layers. Fill with Lemon Jelly Filling. Decorate top with powdered sugar. Makes 1 cake, about 6 to 9 servings.

Lemon Jelly Filling:
- 1 cup sugar
- 2½ tablespoons flour
- Grated peel of 2 lemons
- ¼ cup lemon juice
- 1 egg, slightly beaten
- 1 teaspoon butter

In medium saucepan, stir together sugar, flour, lemon peel and juice, egg and butter. Cook, stirring constantly, over low heat until the boiling point is reached. Take care not to allow mixture to stick to pan. Remove from heat and allow mixture to cool. It will thicken to a spreadable consistency as it cools. Spread between split layers of Two Egg Cake above.

A cake which didn't turn out was known as a "sad" cake, but really it was the people wanting to eat it who were sad. (Likewise a "sad iron" meant the clothes iron didn't do its job.) Riley's poems often mention cake. The poem entitled "Granny" says she "fetched a cake for little Jake, And fetched a pie for Nanny, And fetched a pear for all the pack That runs to kiss their Granny!" Pound cake is the kind of cake most often referred to. The ingredients were really measured in pounds.

CHOCOLATE TOPPED DATE CAKE

- 1 cup chopped pitted dates
- 1 teaspoon baking soda
- 1 cup boiling water
- ½ cup shortening
- 1 cup sugar
- 2 eggs
- 1½ cups flour
- ¼ cup cocoa
- ¼ teaspoon salt

Topping:

- ½ cup sugar
- ½ cup chopped walnuts
- ½ cup (about 3 ounces) semi sweet chocolate chips

Preheat oven to 350 degrees. In small bowl, stir together the dates, soda and boiling water. Set aside to cool. In large mixing bowl, beat the shortening and sugar until blended, add the eggs and beat until light. Stir in the date mixture, then the flour, cocoa and salt which have been combined together. Pour batter into greased and floured 9-inch square cake pan. Add topping: in small bowl, toss together sugar, nuts and chocolate chips. Sprinkle evenly over batter in pan. Bake for 30 to 35 minutes, until cake springs back when pressed lightly in center. If desired, top with whipped cream. Makes about 9 servings.

RAISIN FRUITCAKE

Take your time in making fruitcakes. Buy the fruits and nuts ahead of time, and measure them, even soak them with rum a day or so ahead. Mix the cakes later, if you wish, so fruitcake making doesn't seem such a chore. Delicious moist homemade fruitcakes really are special for the holidays. This recipe makes 2 (8-inch cakes.) They freeze very well, or give one to a friend.

- 1 pounds golden or dark raisins (or mixture)
- 1 cup candied pineapple chunks
- 1 cup halved candied cherries
- ½ cup halved candied green cherries
- 1 cup flaked coconut
- ½ cup light rum

" *Billy Goodin' "* is Riley's poem describing the little pest who was always hungry. *"Better shet your kitchen, tho', afore you go to meetin'—Better hide yer mincemeat an' stewed fruit an' plums! Better hide yer poundcake and bresh away the crumbs! Better hide yer cubbord-key when Billy Goodin' comes, A-eatin'! an a-eatin'! an' a-eatin'!"*

1 cup shortening
1 cup sugar
2 teaspoons vanilla
½ teaspoon almond extract
2 cups coarsely chopped nuts (macadamias or almonds)
6 egg whites
2½ cups sifted flour
1 teaspoon baking powder
1 teaspoon salt

Common plum cake was made as follows:
Ingredients: 3 pounds of flour, 6 ounces of butter or good dripping, 6 ounces of moist sugar, 6 ounces of currants, ½ ounce of pounded allspice; 2 tablespoons of fresh yeast, 1 pint of new milk.

(Continued)

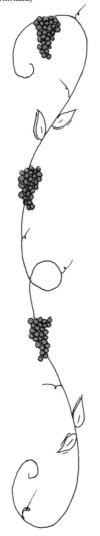

Combine raisins, candied fruits and coconut with rum, mixing well. Cover and let stand overnight. In large mixing bowl, beat shortening, sugar and flavorings until light and fluffy. Blend in raisin mixture and nuts. In small bowl, stir flour with baking powder and salt. In clean non-plastic mixing bowl, beat egg whites until stiff peaks form. Fold sifted dry ingredients into fruit mixture alternately with half of egg whites until thoroughly blended. Carefully fold in remaining egg whites. Turn into prepared molds or pans (see below—should be ⅔ to ¾ full). Bake at 300 degrees 2 to 2½ hours, until cakes test done when toothpick inserted into center comes out clean. Cool cakes and wrap in foil or plastic wrap to store in cool place. Makes 9 cups batter.

Pans for Raisin Fruit cake: Use either two 8½-inch tube ring molds (2 1/12-inches deep) or two 8x4x2-inch loaf cake or bread pans. Line greased loaf pans with greased brown paper. Line greased molds with foil then grease again. Frost, if desired, just before serving with 1½ cups powdered sugar mixed with 2 tablespoons sherry or rum the garnish with rum soaked raisins, pecans and candied fruit.

CAKE BAKING HISTORY

It was not until the 19th century that cake baking began to be done in the home. Before that time, inaccurate ovens (some ovens were called, for obvious reasons, "sad" ovens) and lack of standardization of ingredients and measures made it very difficult to follow recipes, or even repeat results from baking to baking. Even today, cake baking is one of the most delicate baking procedures, and needs the benefit of accuracy in equipment and measurement.

Pound cakes were the first cakes to be baked at home because the recipes, based on approximately a pound of several of the ingredients were somewhat easy to duplicate. After the pound cake came the invention of the angel food cake, based on many egg whites. But it took the introduction of baking powder to popularize the layer cake. Late in the 18th century, chocolate layer cake became one of the standards of baking day. As recently as the early 1940's, the one-bowl method of cake making was introduced.

In 1948 chiffon cake was named "the cake discovery of the century—the newest type of cake in 100 years." It was described as being as light as angel food cake while also being as rich as butter cake. It was also easy to make. Its secret ingredient was what was known at the time as "salad oil." Chiffon cake was invented by Harry Baker, a 64-year-old insurance salesman, who first made his unusual secret-recipe cake for movie appearances and famous Hollywood restaurants. The recipe didn't become publicly known until he disclosed the secret to Betty Crocker home economists in the mid-1940's.

It has only been about 30 years since electric mixers have been commonly available in American kitchens. This invention did much to make the mixing of heavy cake batters easier. When salad oil became a respectable cake ingredient and then in 1961, flour companies said you didn't have to sift anymore, cakes were easier to make than ever. Gradually cakes have come into their own as a favorite American dessert.

ORANGE ALMOND CHIFFON CAKE

  2 cups unsifted all purpose flour
1½ cups sugar
  3 teaspoons baking powder
  1 teaspoon salt
½ cup vegetable oil
  7 egg yolks
¾ cup cold water
½ teaspoon almond flavoring
  2 teaspoons fresh orange peel

Mode: Rub the butter into the flour, add the sugar, currants and allspice; warm the milk, stir to it the yeast and take the whole into a dough; knead it well and put it into 6 buttered tins. Place them near the fire for nearly an hour for the dough to rise, then bake the cakes in a good oven from 1 to 1¾ hours. To ascertain when they are done, plunge a clean knife into the middle; and if on withdrawal it comes out clean, the cakes are done. Time: ¾ to 1¾ hours Average cost: 1s 8D Sufficient to make 6 small cakes —Mrs. Beeton's Cookbook

A favorite 1910 dessert in Indiana was cottage pudding. Fresh yellow cake was put in sauce dishes and hot chocolate sauce or lemon sauce was poured over. Garnished with "pour" cream or ice cream. Superb!

1 cup egg whites (7 or 8)
½ teaspoon cream of tartar

Preheat oven to 325 degrees. In large mixing bowl, stir flour, sugar, baking powder and salt. Make a well and add, in order, the oil, yolks, water, almond flavoring and orange peel. Beat by hand until smooth. In large mixer bowl, place egg whites and cream of tartar. Beat at high speed of mixer until stiff peaks form. Pour egg yolk mixture slowly over whites and fold in gently. Pour mixture into ungreased 10x4-inch tube pan. Bake about 1 hour 15 minutes, until top springs back when lightly touched. Invert the pan on a funnel and let hang until cold. Remove from pan and add topping. (Note: If you don't have a funnel you may be able to use a 2-liter soft drink bottle, weighted by filling with sand or small stones, to hang the cake. Test your pan to see if the funnel will fit over the neck of the bottle before making the cake, if you plan to do this.)

Topping: In small mixer bowl, beat 6 tablespoons (¾ stick) butter with 3 cups confectioners sugar, 1 to 2 teaspoons grated fresh orange peel, 2 tablespoons fresh orange juice and ½ teaspoon almond flavor. Frost top with icing, and sprinkle with ½ cup diced roasted almonds.

PAN PENUCHE CAKE

In the early 1900's this was called "Emergency Cake," "Lazy Day Cake" or even "Lazy Susan Cake" because you served it without frills, right out of the pan.

      2 cups unsifted all purpose flour
   1½ cups granulated sugar
   3½ teaspoons baking powder
      1 teaspoon salt
      1 teaspoon ground nutmeg
    ¼ teaspoon ground ginger
    ½ cup shortening (part butter, if desired)
      1 cup milk
      1 teaspoon vanilla or rum flavoring
      3 eggs

Preheat oven to 350 degrees. Grease well a 13x9x2-inch baking pan. In large bowl of mixer, measure all ingredients. Blend well on low mixer speed. Scrape bowl well, then beat 3 minutes on high speed, scraping bowl occasionally. Pour into pan and bake for 40 to 45 minutes, until a toothpick inserted into center comes out clean. Cool and frost with Penuche Frosting below. Makes 1 (13x9x2-inch) cake, about 12 servings.

BOILED PENUCHE FROSTING

- 1 cup packed brown sugar
- ½ cup granulated sugar
- 6 tablespoons milk
- 2 tablespoons soft shortening
- 2 tablespoons butter
- 1 tablespoon white corn syrup
- ¼ teaspoon salt
- 1 teaspoon vanilla
- ½ cup chopped walnuts
- 1½ cups confectioners sugar

In saucepan, place brown and granulated sugars, milk, shortening, butter, corn syrup and salt. Bring slowly to a full rolling boil, stirring constantly, and boil briskly for 1 minute to 1½ minutes. Remove from heat and cool slightly. Add vanilla, nuts and confectioners sugar. Beat well until smooth and beginning to dull, then pour over cake to set.

"WHEN THE FROST IS ON THE POMPION....."

It is not surprising that pumpkins figured heavily in the poetry of James Whitcomb Riley, for they were a basic food of the early settlers' diet. Indians called them "pompion," meaning "cooked by the sun."

Colonists liked to bake pompions and often made pudding out of them. Using a sharp knife the pilgrims would cut the top off of a ripe pompion, hollow out the seeds and fill the cavity with milk. the top was then replaced and the pompion was baked until all of the milk was absorbed by the

Penuche (rich brown sugar flavor) was extremely popular 1890–1910. Penuche fudge was the favorite seller at Hoosier county fairs, second only to chocolate.

pulp. This treat was both tasty and nutritious and was most likely served at the first Thanksgiving celebration.

For variety, baked pompions were filled with buttery spiced apple stuffing and eaten for dessert. Alternately, they were stewed, mixed with Indian corn meal and made into bread. Today pumpkin cake and pumpkin pie, as well as pumpkin bread, are very popular.

MOIST PUMPKIN CAKE

- 2 cups unsifted all purpose flour
- ½ teaspoon salt
- 2 teaspoons baking soda
- 1 teaspoon baking powder
- 2½ teaspoons cinnamon
- 2 cups sugar
- 1 cup cooking oil
- 2 cups mashed pumpkin
  Cream Cheese Frosting
  Nutmeg

Preheat oven to 350 degrees F. Grease well and flour 2 (9-inch) layer cake pans or a 13x9x2-inch baking pan. In large mixing bowl, stir together flour, salt, soda, baking powder, cinnamon and sugar. Add the oil and mix on low speed until well blended. Lastly, add the pumpkin and mix to blend. Pour batter into the prepared pan(s), and bake for 30 to 35 minutes. After baking, let layers stand 10 to 15 minutes before inverting onto wire racks; or leave 13x9x2-inch cake in pan. Frost cake with Cream Cheese frosting below, then sprinkle nutmeg lightly over top of cake. Makes about 10 to 12 servings.

CREAM CHEESE FROSTING

- ½ cup (1 stick) butter or margarine
  8-ounce package cream cheese
- 1 pound confectioners sugar
- 1 teaspoon vanilla

In medium mixing bowl, place all ingredients. Beat very well until light and fluffy. Makes enough icing to frost Pumpkin Cake above.

AUTUMN APPLE CAKE

Cakes like these win the prize at the local county fair.

  1½ cups cooking oil
  2 cups sugar
  3 beaten eggs
  2 teaspoons vanilla
  1 teaspoon almond flavoring
  1 teaspoon rum flavoring
  3 cups all purpose flour
  1 teaspoon salt
  1 teaspoon baking soda
  3 to 4 cups diced tart apples
  1 cup chunks pecans

Preheat oven to 325 degrees. Grease and flour a 10-inch tube cake pan. In large mixing bowl, place all ingredients. Blend to combine, then beat at medium speed until well mixed. Pour batter into pan and smooth top. Bake for 45 minutes or until toothpick stuck in center comes out clean. Makes 1 cake. (Note: Batter can also be baked in 13x9x2-inch pan.) If desired, frost with Cream Cheese Frosting above.

CREAMY POUND CAKE

Start baking this in a cold oven. In James Whitcomb Riley's time, a flavored fruit brandy, such as peach brandy, was used instead of vanilla for flavoring pound cakes. It was not unusual for good cooks to beat the butter-sugar batter for 20 minutes or more by hand, just to be sure the mixture was sufficiently creamed. This updated pound cake substitutes cream cheese for part of the "pound" of butter and margarine, for flavor and creaminess.

One of Riley's poems, "The Law of the Perverse" aptly states what we today call Murphy's Law. "Where did the custom come from, anyway—Sending the boys to 'play' at dinner time, When we have company? Fancy the exiled boy in the back yard, Ahungered so, that any kind of grub Were welcome, yet with face set stern and hard, Hearing the feasters' mirth and mild hubhub, Wanting to kill something with a club!"

1 cup margarine
½ cup butter
    8-ounce package cream cheese
3 cups granulated sugar
2 teaspoons vanilla
⅛ teaspoon salt
6 eggs
3 cups unsifted all purpose flour

Grease well and flour a 10-inch tube cake. In large mixer bowl, place margarine, butter, cream cheese and sugar. On low speed, mix until well blended, then beat at high speed until light and creamy. Beat in the vanilla and salt, then the eggs one at a time. On low speed, mix in the flour just until no dry parts remain. Pour into the prepared pan and push batter to distribute evenly. Place in a cold (non-preheated) oven and bake at 275-degrees for 1½ hours (90 minutes), or until cake tester comes out clean when inserted into centermost part of cake. Remove from oven and let stand in pan about 15 minutes before inverting onto wire rack to cool. Makes 1 (10-inch) cake.

MICROWAVED PINEAPPLE UPSIDE DOWN CAKE

The thrifty housewife used both the fruit and juice from the pineapple can. You will need only about a tablespoon-ful of milk to bring the liquid measure to ½ cup.

Topping:
    1 can (8-ounce) sliced pineapple in juice
    ¼ cup butter (½ stick)
    ½ cup firmly packed brown sugar
        Maraschino cherries and/or pecan halves as
        desired (9 or more total pieces can be used)
Cake:
    1¼ cups unsifted all purpose flour
    ¾ cup firmly packed brown sugar
    2 teaspoons baking powder
    ½ teaspoon salt
    ¼ cup cooking oil
        Pineapple juice plus milk to make ½ cup

1 teaspoon vanilla

1 egg

Make topping: Drain pineapple, saving juice. In 2-qt. microwave tube pan place butter and brown sugar. Microwave at high (100 percent power) for ¾ to 1½ minutes, until butter is melted. Stir well, then arrange drained pineapple slices over butter-sugar mixture. Decorate with additional maraschino cherries and/or pecan halves (rounded side down) as desired. Set aside. Make cake batter: In medium mixer bowl, place flour, sugar, baking powder, salt, oil, pineapple juice-milk liquid, vanilla and egg. Beat on low mixer speed just until all ingredients are moistened. Stop mixer, scrape bowl well, then beat at high speed for 2 minutes. Carefully spread batter over fruit in dish. Microwave at medium high (70 percent power) for 9 to 12 minutes, rotating dish ½ turn every 3 minutes, until almost all of top is dry (a few small shallow moist spots may remain) and cake looks set. Let stand on heatproof surface for about 5 minutes, then invert over serving plate. Let dish stand over cake a few minutes to release all of brown sugar topping. Serve hot or warm. Makes 6 to 8 servings.

BUTTERMILK DEVILS FOOD CAKE

A very old Midwestern cake is White Buttermilk Cake, with a similar formula to this one (without the cocoa, of course). Buttermilk cakes keep very well—like buttermilk does.

- 1½ cups unsifted all purpose or unbleached flour
- 1¼ cups granulated sugar
- ½ cup unsweetened cocoa powder
- 1¼ teaspoons baking soda
- 1 teaspoon salt
- 1 cup buttermilk (or sour milk made by placing 1 tablespoon vinegar in measuring cup and filling the cup with milk)
- ⅔ cup cooking oil
- 1 teaspoon vanilla
- 2 eggs

Preheat oven to 350 degrees. Grease and flour bottoms only of two (8-inch) round cake pans. In large mixer bowl, place all ingredients. Beat at low speed until all flour is

"An Old Sweetheart of Mine" was one of James Whitcomb Riley's most popular poems, earning for the poet a reputed $500.00 per word—a princely sum in those days. A story set in New York City speaks to the widespread popularity of the poem in the years after its introduction. A vagabond named McGlaughlin was brought to court in New York one October day, charged with panhandling. In defending himself he said that his profession was acting, he was just out of work. "To show you I'm an actor, I'll orate any piece you choose," said McGlaughlin. The court requested "That Old Sweetheart of Mine." It is said that McGlaughlin showed such skill with the poem that the court not only let him go, but they also took up a collection to get him started again.

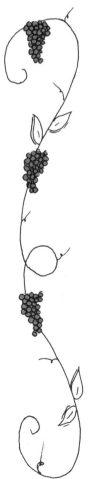

combined, then beat at medium speed for 3 minutes. Pour batter into prepared pans. Bake for 25 to 30 minutes until toothpick inserted into center comes out clean. Allow cake layers to stand in pans for about 5 minutes before inverting onto wire racks. Cool completely before frosting. Makes two (8-inch) layers.

CHOCOLATE GOBLINS CUPCAKES

They'll "get you" in a more pleasant way than Little Orphant Annie's goblins did in Riley's poem. Microwave or bake these conventionally. Use a double thickness paper baking cup when microwaving to absorb moisture. Microwaved cakes have tender top crusts, so you need a soft glaze, like the one below.

- 1 cup hot tap water
- 4 squares (4 ounces) unsweetened chocolate
- 2 teaspoons vinegar plus milk to measure ½ cup
- ⅔ cup cooking oil
- 2½ cups unsifted all purpose flour
- 2 cups packed brown sugar
- 1 teaspoon baking soda
- 1 teaspoon baking powder
- ½ teaspoon salt
- 1 teaspoon vanilla
- 2 eggs

In 1 quart microwave bowl or mesuring cup, pour hot water; add the chocolate squares. Microwave at medium (50 percent power) for 6 to 9 minutes, stirring every 2 minutes, until chocolate is completely melted. Stir smooth (mixture might look a little separated.) Set aside. In 1 cup measure, place the vinegar, then add milk to make ½ cup. Let stand until milk curdles; set aside. In large mixer bowl, place oil, flour, sugar, soda, baking powder, salt, vanilla, eggs and the curdled milk. Beat at medium mixer speed until well blended and smooth. Add the chocolate mixture and beat well. In round (6-cupcake capacity) microwave cupcake/muffin pan, place double thickness paper baking cups. Spoon chocolate batter into paper lined cups, filling about ½ full. Microwave each six cupcakes at high (100 percent power) for 2 to 3½ minutes, rotating ¼ turn every minute, if necessary and checking at minimum time. Repeat until all batter is used up (reuse the outside paper baking cups if desired). Cool cupcakes on plate or platter. When cooled, frost with Shiny Chocolate Glaze. Makes about 4 dozen cupcakes. (Note: Batter keeps if 2 or 3 days if refrigerated. Make a few at a time, if desired.)

TO BAKE CUPCAKES CONVENTIONALLY: Distribute batter into metal cupcake pans lined with single layer paper cupcake papers. Bake in oven preheated to 400 degrees for about 18 to 20 minutes. Due to differences in size of muffin cups, yield may vary; conventional pans may be larger, so yield fewer total cupcakes (about 3 dozen).

SHINY CHOCOLATE GLAZE

- 2 squares (2 ounces) unsweetened chocolate
- 2 tablespoons butter
- 2 tablespoons white corn syrup
- 1/8 teaspoon salt
- 2 cups unsifted confectioners sugar
- 3 tablespoons hot tap water, divided

In 1-quart microwave bowl or measuring bowl, place chocolate, butter and corn syrup. Microwave at medium (50 percent power) for 2 to 3 minutes, stirring every minute, until mixture can be stirred smooth. Add the salt, confectioners sugar and 2 tablespoons of the hot tap water. Beat vigorously until smooth. Stir in the remaining tablespoon hot water, to make a smooth chocolate glaze. With small spatula or knife, spread the glaze evenly over the tops of the cupcakes. Let stand until glaze sets before covering to store. Covers 4 dozen cupcakes. (Note: If you don't cook all cupcake batter at once, you can store leftover glaze, covered in refrigerator. Microwave briefly to soften before spreading on cupcakes.)

MICRO MOCHA CAKE

This recipe bakes well conventionally, too. For a large cake, double the recipe and bake at 350 degrees for 40 to

he concept of goblins may have been inspired by the many misshapen or hump-backed people, or even dwarfs of the time. In those days, tragic accidents, rough circumstances, malnutrition, and lack of medical care caused more disfigurements among people. Frequent accidents included being kicked or bit by a horse, cow or other animal, or being hit by a falling tree or a heavy limb, or by falling down a well or other open hole or pit, not to mention accidental shootings from guns which were owned by most men (many women, too).

50 minutes, until tests done. If desired, poke holes in finished cake and pour on double recipe Shiny Chocolate Glaze above. Rich!

1 ½ cups unsifted all-purpose flour
  1 teaspoon instant coffee powder
  1 cup firmly packed brown sugar
  ⅓ cup cocoa
  1 teaspoon baking soda
  ½ teaspoon salt
  1 tablespoon distilled white vinegar
  1 cup milk
  ½ cup cooking oil
  1 teaspoon vanilla

Grease a 2-quart microwave tube pan. In large mixer bowl, place flour, coffee powder, sugar, cocoa, soda, salt, vinegar and ½ cup of the milk. Beat at low speed just until well blended and smooth. Add remaining milk, oil and vanilla until well blended. Pour batter into prepared pan. Microwave at high (100 percent power) for 7 to 10 minutes, rotating pan ½ turn every 3 minutes, until wooden toothpick inserted near center comes out clean. Let cake stand directly on heatproof surface about 5 minutes, then invert the cake on serving plate. Drizzle with Coffee Glaze made by stirring together 1 cup confectioners sugar, ½ teaspoon coffee powder and 1 to 2 tablespoons hot water, to make pourable glaze. Decorate with chocolate decors, if desired. Nice served warm. Makes about 8 servings.

A number of women claimed to be James Whitcomb Riley's old sweetheart, but Riley declined to identify the real sweetheart. There was speculation, however, that it was Alice Kahle, from a family of itinerants traveling West on the National Road. During the winter, many families would stop wherever they landed for the cold months, putting the children in school as long as they stayed. The Kahle family apparently stayed in Greenfield temporarily during Riley's school years.

Lest the impression be given that Riley was a solitary figure, it should be said he kept up a voluminous correspondence in his mature years, and had many friends including Mark Twain and Joel Chandler Harris.

"AN OLD SWEETHEART OF MINE"

A N old sweetheart of mine!—Is this her presence here with me,
Or but a vain creation of a lover's memory?
A fair, illusive vision that would vanish into air
Dared I even touch the silence with the whisper of a prayer?

Nay, let me then believe in all the blended false and true—
The semblance of the *old* love and the substance of the new,—
The *then* of changeless sunny days—the *now* of shower and shine—
But Love forever smiling—as that old sweetheart of mine.

This ever-restful sense of *home*, though shouts ring in the hall.—
The easy chair—the old book-shelves and prints along the wall;
The rare *Habanas* in their box, or gaunt church-warden-stem
That often wags, about the jar, derisively at them.

As one who cons at evening o'er an album, all alone,
And muses on the faces of the friends that he has known,
So I turn the leaves of Fancy, till, in shadowy design,
I find the smiling features of an old sweetheart of mine.

The lamplight seems to glimmer with a flicker of surprise,
As I turn it low—to rest me of the dazzle in my eyes,
And light my pipe in silence, save a sigh that seems to yoke
Its fate with my tobacco and to vanish with the smoke.

'Tis a *fragrant* retrospection,—for the loving thoughts that start
Into being are like perfume from the blossom of the heart;
And to dream the old dreams over is a luxury divine—
When my truant fancies wander with that old sweetheart of mine.

Though I hear beneath my study, like a fluttering of wings,
The voices of my children and the mother as she sings—
I feel no twinge of conscience to deny me any theme
When Care has cast her anchor in the harbor of a dream—

In fact, to speak in earnest, I believe it adds a charm
To spice the good a trifle with a little dust of harm,—
For I find an extra flavor in Memory's mellow wine
That makes me drink the deeper to that old sweetheart of mine.
O Childhood-days enchanted! O the magic of the Spring!—
With all green boughs to blossom white, and all bluebirds to sing!
When all the air, to toss and quaff, made life a jubilee
And changed the children's song and laugh to shrieks of ecstasy.

With eyes half closed in clouds that ooze from lips that taste, as well,
The peppermint and cinnamon, I hear the old School bell,
And from "Recess" romp in again from "Blackman's" broken line,
To smile, behind my "lesson," at that old sweetheart of mine.

A face of lily beauty, with a form of airy grace,
Floats out of my tobacco as the Genii from the vase;
And I thrill beneath the glances of a pair of azure eyes
As glowing as the summer and as tender as the skies.

"AN OLD SWEETHEART OF MINE"

I can see the pink sunbonnet and the little checkered dress
She wore when first I kissed her and she answered the caress
With the written declaration that, "as surely as the vine
Grew 'round the stymp," she loved me—that old sweetheart of mine.

Again I made her presents, in a really helpless way,—
The big "Rhode Island Greening"—I was hungry, too, that day!—
But I follow her from Spelling, with her hand behind her—so—
And I slip the apple in it—and the Teacher doesn't know!

I give my *treasures* to her—all,—my pencil—blue-and-red;—
And, if little girls played marbles, *mine* should all be *hers,* instead!
But *she* gave me her *photograph,* and printed "Ever Thine"
Across the back—in blue-and-red—that old sweetheart of mine!

And again I feel the pressure of her slender little hand,
As we used to talk together of the future we had planned,—
When I should be a poet, and with nothing else to do
But write the tender verses that she set the music to . . .

When we should live together in a cozy little cot
Hid in a nest of roses, with a fairy garden-spot,
Where the vines were ever fruited, and the weather ever fine,
And the birds were ever singing for that old sweetheart of mine.

When I should be her lover forever and a day,
And she my faithful sweetheart till the golden hair was gray;
And we should be so happy that when either's lips were dumb
They would not smile in Heaven till the other's kiss had come.

But, ah! my dream is broken by a step upon the stair,
And the door is softly opened, and—my wife is standing there;
Yet with eagerness and rapture all my visions I resign,—
To greet the *living* presence of that old sweetheart of mine.

MILADY'S GAZETTE: FASHIONS FOR THE NEW CENTURY

GAZETTE: FASHIONS FOR THE NEW CENTURY

Women in the small towns in American in the time of James Whitcomb Riley were aware of fashion. Certainly they were! They read in the *Ladies Home Journal* what Queen Mary of England, or Czarina Alexandra wore to the balls, or for the horse races. "Dressing for fashion" for the average villager meant one, well-cut silk or wool for Sunday school and church, a nice cape or light wool coat, and a hat, a huge hat or two. It meant a pretty parasol for sun in the summer and a beaver fur muff in the winter to tuck cold hands into. (There were no heated cars; everyone walked most places.)

For the less well off there was one Sunday outfit and one or two "house dresses" and that was all. But in the wardrobes or "presses" of women in comfortable circumstances were many things in these affluent times: starchy, shirt-like blouses, full, flowing skirts, dressing gowns, even a fur piece.

On the shelf were the extras: a "rat" to pin under puffs of one's hair to get the desired height to the coiffure, ruffled collars, the new elegant glove silk hose and the gloves which were a social necessity, either elbow length or short. There was, modestly put away in a box, the corset which restrained the figure after milady ate all the good things described in this book. The stays smoothed bulges into the Gibson Girl shape, the hour-glass figure one must have, and eventually as times changed, made it flat and man-like.

The Romance
of a Petticoat

DE LONG
SNAPS

See that

hump?

De Long
Snaps

Little girls copied bigger ones and wore starchy pinafores, middie blouses and long stockings with high shoes. When they reached sixteen or so, they could put their hair up on top of their head in pins. Until then they must wait for the rain to come, catch some soft water in a bucket, wash their hair with pine tar or glycerine and rosewater and let Grandma set it in rags to make some curls. The big girls gasped and fainted in the corsets; the little ones slept on bumps all night. Such is the price of beauty.

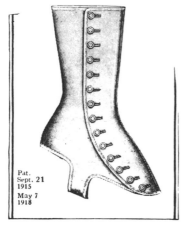

Pat.
Sept. 21
1915
May 7
1918

"More Than A Spat"

Visible Style

This trademark is
your guide and our
pledge.

EASE//ALL

Cookies

COOKIES, "LITTLE CAKES" START A DEMAND

Somewhere around the middle of this century, a jokester said he could tell how old a woman was by pointing to a plate of cookies and asking what they were. If the lady said they were sweet cakes, he knew she was over 80 years old. If she said they were tea cakes, she had to be over 60, but if she said they were cookies, that meant she was under 40.

Some say the word "cookies" evolved as "little cakes"— drops of cake batter baked in the oven to check the oven's temperature before entrusting the rest of the batter to be baked. Or, as in the story above, bar cookies were referred to tea cakes or sweet cakes. Others say the word "cookies" came from the early Dutch settlers' *koekjes*. Early cookies were hard to bake evenly in hearth ovens or over the coals of a fire. It was not until kitchen ranges became refined that cookies were commonly made. And with masses of cookies came one of the most decorative and charming of kitchen fixtures—the cookie jar!

Although in earlier times cookies seemed to have been less common and less varied than cakes, the opposite seems true with many people today. Today's cookies are the quintessential finger food—no muss, no fuss, just instantly delicious and satisfying.

During the war years, people used clarified chicken fat or even bacon fat to enrich cookies, because of the shortage of butter. Early American cookbooks told how to clarify these fats by boiling them with half as much water for 5 to 6 minutes. Cool, then chill. Skim or lift off the fat, leaving the "meat' flavor in the watery broth below.

Because of their small size, cookies are very sensitive to heat. Shiny aluminum pans, which reflect heat away, give best results with the most delicate browning, although teflon coated aluminum pans work almost as well and assure release of the cookies. Heavy, old fashioned black cookie sheets, which absorb heat, can cause burning on the bottom. Rich, delicate cookies often come off the cookie sheet more easily in one piece if you allow them to stand for a few minutes to firm up slightly, before removing with a spatula to a cooling rack.

From The Century Cook Book (1894): Stomach ache is common in dyspeptics. Carminatives are appropriate for it. One of the best of these is oil of cajuput, five drops at a dose on a lump of sugar.

173

WHAT JAMES WHITCOMB RILEY MISSED

"*Lizabuth-Ann on Bakin' Day*"

Our Hired Girl, when it's bakin'-day
She's out of patience allus,
An' tells us, "Hike outdoors an' play,"
An' when the cookies's done, she'll say,
"Land sake! she'll come an' call us!
An' when the little doughbowl's all
Ist heapin'-full, she'll come and call—
Nen say, "She'd rather take a switchin'
Than have a pack o' pesky childarn
Trackin' round the kitchen!

Although butter cookies were made in James Whitcomb Riley's time, the addition of chocolate pieces came just a little later, in about 1940. The earliest "prototype" chocolate chip cookies were created by Ruth Wakefield, owner of the Toll House Inn in Massachusetts. She chopped a bar of leftover semisweet chocolate into a favorite colonial recipe for butter cookies, and shared the results with visitors. One such visitor mentioned them to a friend who wrote about them in a Boston newspaper. Later, they were featured in a radio show called "Famous Foods from Famous Places." In the 1950's, after chocolate chips came to the market, the rights to the name "Toll House Cookies" were sold to the Nestle Company, who ran the recipe on the backs of chocolate chip packages.

CHEWY CHOCOLATE CHIP COOKIES

This recipe has been personally tested for many years, and is delicious. It makes a soft and chewy, "bendable" cookie rather than one which is crisp and crunchy. Like many old fashioned recipes, this one is large, making 6 dozen big cookies. If you do not have a large electric mixer, you may want to halve the recipe. The cookies keep well in a covered container, or may be frozen.

 2½ cups butter, margarine or butter flavored solid shortening
  1 pound dark brown sugar
 1½ cups white sugar
  4 eggs
  4 teaspoons vanilla
  2 teaspoons baking soda
  2 teaspoons salt
 5½ cups unsifted all purpose flour
 1½ pounds (two 12-ounce packages) chocolate chips or candy coated chocolate drops (like M&M's)

Preheat oven to 425 degrees. In bowl of large electric mixer, place butter or shortening, brown and white sugars, eggs, vanilla, soda and salt. Beat very well until completely blended, light and fluffy. Add flour and beat until well mixed. Stir in chocolate chips. Drop by large spoonfuls onto cookie sheets and bake for about 8 to 10 minutes. Makes about 6 dozen large cookies. (Note: When baking two sheets at a time, we recommend setting the timer for about 4 to 5 minutes, then switching the sheets, top to bottom, bottom to top, for the last 3 or 4 minutes. This gives most even baking of the cookies.)

NUTTY BUTTERBALLS

These go by many names, including Russian or Mexican Tea Cakes, or Wedding Cakes. When your recipe author was in Greenfield High School, working summers by cooking in a resort, she made dozens of these every week from this 1953 *Joy of Cooking* recipe. The cookbook called for the nuts to be finely ground, but we preferred small nutty pieces in each butterball.

- ½ cup butter
- 2 tablespoons sugar
- 1 teaspoon vanilla
- 1 cup chopped or pieces pecans
- 1 cup sifted cake flour

Preheat the oven to 300 degrees F. Beat the butter, sugar and vanilla until light and fluffy. Add the pecans and flour and stir well. Roll the dough into small balls and bake on cookie sheet for 40 to 50 minutes, just until set. While hot, roll in confectioners sugar, and reroll when cold for a snowy finish. Makes 30 to 36 cookies.

MICROWAVED CHOCOLATE CHIP SNOWBALLS

Do not overcook! Microwave only until set. These are slightly dry and crunchy rather than rich and crumbly. To make them more rich, you can omit all but 1 tablespoon of the milk and increase the butter to ¾ cup. Regular chocolate chip cookie doughs do not microwave well, but this is a good substitute. These may also be baked at 375 degrees for 10 to 15 minutes, until delicate brown.

Most hated among home remedies were the laxative castor oil (from castor bean plants) and cod liver oil, a children's tonic. At eight o'clock at night many a child could be discovered hiding under the bed, refusing to be either "purged" or "strengthened" no matter what.

½ cup butter
½ cup confectioners sugar
3 tablespoons milk, divided
1 teaspoon almond or vanilla extract
¼ teaspoon salt
2 cups unsifted all purpose flour
½ cup chopped pecans
1 pkg. (6-oz.) chocolate chips
Confectioners sugar

In large mixer bowl, place butter, confectioners sugar, 2 tablespoons of the milk, the vanilla and salt. Beat at high speed until very smooth and fluffy. Add flour and beat in at low speed, adding the extra tablespoon milk when mixture becomes too stiff to mix. Add nuts and chocolate chips and beat just to mix. Form dough into about 36 (1-inch) balls, and roll each in confectioners sugar before microwaving. Arrange 12 balls in a circle on microwave cooky sheet. Microwave at high (100 percent power) for 3 to 4½ minutes, just until surfaces look dry and cookies seem set. Let cool until they can be handled with fingers (depending on the sensitivity of your fingers, this can be almost immediately), then roll each cookie again in confectioners sugar. Repeat with remaining cookies. Makes about 3 (1-dozen) batches, about 36 cookies. (Note: These cook best on a microwave plastic cookie sheet. If you use a glass or pyroceram microwave plate or platter, you may improve cooking results if you place the plate on top of an inverted microwaveproof saucer, set inside the microwave.)

BROWNIES, BANGOR BROWNIES OR CHOCOLATE INDIANS

Old cookbooks often present brownies as a form of cake, sometimes a rich cake which falls while cooking, other times a cake so rich that it must be baked thin and cut small. As a cookie all its own, brownies came to be popular around 1910 or 1920, so perhaps James Whitcomb Riley enjoyed brownies during the opulent years near the end of his life. Some people say brownies originated in Bangor, Maine. Other early cookbooks referred to brownies as "Chocolate Indians."

ON MICROWAVING BROWNIES

Brownies are frequently microwaved in a square dish, even though the corner areas can overcook (just as with baked brownies.) Some people prefer the chewy corner cookies to softer center areas, or, to eliminate corners, bake in a round dish. Check microwave oven user's manual about brownies. It's usually true that larger microwaves bake better than smaller ones do.

TRIPLE DECKER BROWNIES

Brownies:
    2 squares unsweetened chocolate
    ⅓ cup butter
    1 cup sugar
    2 eggs
    1 teaspoon vanilla
    ⅔ cup unsifted flour
    ½ teaspoon salt
Toasted Pecan Icing and Chocolate Glaze:
    ¼ cup butter (½ stick)
    1 cup broken pecans
    2 cups confectioners sugar
    2 tablespoons milk
    ½ teaspoon vanilla
    2 ounces (2 squares) unsweetened chocolate
       Additional tablespoon butter

In small glass mixing bowl or 1½-qt. microwave casserole, place chocolate. Microwave at medium (50 percent power) for 2 to 4 minutes, until melted. Add butter and continue microwaving at medium for ½ to 1 minute, until melted and mixture can be stirred smooth. Add sugar, eggs and vanilla; beat very well. Stir in flour and salt just until well blended. Pour batter into greased 8-inch square dish. Microwave at high (100 percent power) for 4 to 7 minutes, rotating dish every 2 minutes, until cooked and center is firm.* Cool. Meanwhile, make Toasted Pecan Icing: In 1-qt. microwave bowl or casserole, place butter and pecans. Cover with wax paper. Microwave at high for 5 to 7 minutes, until both butter and pecans are very browned but not burned.* Add confectioners sugar, milk and vanilla

The "Leonainie Hoax" gave Riley, in his early youth, a damaged reputation in some quarters. After trying doggedly but unsuccessfully to have some of his early poems published, Riley concluded that people will only read poems written by well-known authors. To prove his point, Riley pretended to find a "lost" poem by Edgar Allan Poe in an old Bible, which created a sensation. (Edgar Allan Poe died the year Riley was born.) The poem was really Riley's, written in Poe's style. When the truth was learned, the gullible public was angered at being tricked. But Riley had won his audience and in the long run, the ruse paid off.

*R*iley had to work at being famous in his early years. He traveled by trains all over the United States and was paid to read his poems to audiences. (This was a form of entertainment before TV.) Some audiences paid Riley as much as $1,000 to read his poems. But the strain of travel affected Riley. He was noted for missing trains all his traveling life. Some audiences paid him the compliment of waiting patiently for him to arrive. Other audiences angrily dispersed.

and mix well. Carefully spread icing over top of brownies. Make chocolate glaze: in 2-cup microwave bowl or casserole, place chocolate. Microwave at medium for 2 to 4 minutes, until melted. Add butter and stir well. Drizzle over pecan icing. Refrigerate until cool and firm, then cut into squares. Makes about 36 rich rich cookies.

**Or, instead of microwaving, conventionally bake the chocolate brownie mixture at 350 degrees for 30 to 35 minutes, until top crust looks dull. Also, you may toast the nuts by browning them very carefully in a skillet on the stovetop.

NEW YORK BROWNIES (UNBAKED)

Although you can use any power level for melting chocolate, it's easier to control the melting at medium (50 percent) than it is at high (100 percent). Don't cover the chocolate as it melts or you might trap steam which could condense and drop water onto the chocolate.

Brownies:
  1 ounce (1 square) unsweetened chocolate
  ½ cup butter (1 stick)
  ¼ cup sugar
  1 egg
  2 cups graham cracker crumbs (about 22 squares)
  ½ cup chopped nuts
  1 cup coconut (3½ oz.)
  1 teaspoon vanilla
Chocolate Glaze:
  2 ounces (2 squares) unsweetened chocolate
  1 tablespoon butter
  ¼ cup water
  3 cups confectioners sugar
  ¼ teaspoon salt
  1 tablespoon corn syrup
  1 teaspoon vanilla

In 2-quart microwave bowl or casserole, place chocolate. Microwave at medium (50 percent power) for 2 to 4 minutes, until melted. Add butter and microwave at medium for 1 to 2 more minutes, until melted. Stir in sugar and egg

thoroughly and continue microwaving at medium for about 1 more minute, until mixture has thickened slightly and slides away from the sides of the dish. * Stir in crumbs, nuts and coconut. Press into 9-inch square pan (this pan will not be placed in microwave oven, so it needn't be microwave-safe) and refrigerate. Make glaze: In 1½-quart microwave casserole, place chocolate and butter. Microwave at medium (50 percent power) for 3 ½ to 6 minutes, until melted. Let stand few minutes to cool. Meanwhile, in microwave measuring cup, microwave water at high (100 percent power) for 1½ to 3 minutes, until boiling. To chocolate mixture add water, sugar, salt and corn syrup. Stir until smooth. Pour over brownies. Refrigerate until firm, then cut into bars. Makes about 36 cookies.

* Or, instead of microwaving, melt while stirring, the chocolate and butter in a saucepan over low heat on stovetop. Add sugar and egg and heat, stirring, until mixture has thickened slightly and slides away from sides of pan.

JUNE'S MOLASSES CRISPS

This old fashioned recipe is a Greenfield original, perfected by Dorothy June Williams when her six children were small. Unlike most households, ours had rolled and decorated cookies frequently as the children grew up, and one of "the Williams girls" won a sweepsteaks ribbon at the Indiana State Fair with these cookies. Besides various fancy decorated cookies, you can make good gingerbread men with this recipe.

   1 cup mild molasses (or honey)
   1 cup sugar
   ½ cup butter
   ½ cup lard (or solid white shortening)
   5 cups sifted all purpose flour, divided
   2 eggs, beaten
   ½ teaspoon baking soda
   ½ teaspoon salt
   ½ teaspoon ground ginger
   ½ teaspoon ground cinnamon
   ½ teaspoon ground cloves

Riley was exceptionally tender hearted. At the age of about 12, he was supposed to recite "Horatio at the Bridge" for one of the Friday afternoon school programs. When the bridge gave way and Horatio fell into the raging seas, it was such a dreadful predicament to a little boy from an area where the biggest of water was Brandywine Creek, that he burst into tears and could not finish the piece.

In saucepan, while stirring over medium heat, bring to simmering the molasses, sugar, butter and lard or shortening. When simmering, remove from heat. In large mixing bowl, place 2 cups of the flour. Carefully pour the hot molasses mixture over the flour and beat the mixture smooth. Add the beaten eggs and beat the mixture until it is smooth and well mixed. Cool. When mixture is no longer hot to the touch, stir in the additional 3 cups flour which has been mixed with the soda, salt, ginger, cinnamon and cloves. "Work" the dough until it is well mixed, then refrigerate, covered, until chilled. To bake, remove from refrigerator and cut off small pieces of dough (dough becomes very firm and hard). Roll out thin on floured surface, using floured rolling pin. Cut into shapes with cooky cutter. Bake the cookies in preheated 375 degree oven for 8 to 10 minutes, until set and cookies look just dry. Remove to wire cooling racks to cool. When cold, frost as desired with colored confectioners sugar icing, nuts and decorative sprinkles. Makes about 6 dozen cookies. Store cookies in tightly covered container.

CHURCH CIRCLE LEMON BARS

Named for the "taste testers." These are rich but not overly gooey.

Crust:
- ½ cup sugar
- ⅔ cup butter or margarine (1 stick plus 2½ tablespoons)
- 2 eggs
- 2 cups unsifted all purpose flour

Filling:
- 6 large eggs
- 1 cup sugar
- ⅔ cup freshly squeezed lemon juice
- 3 tablespoons grated lemon rind (yellow part only)
- 1 cup butter or margarine (2 sticks), softened
- 1½ cups ground almonds
- 1 teaspoon salt

Make crust: In medium mixer bowl, combine sugar and butter; beat smooth. Add eggs and beat, then stir in flour. Press mixture into 13x9x2-inch baking pan. Make filling: In large mixer bowl, beat eggs with remaining ingredients. Pour filling over crust. Bake in preheated 375-degree oven for 40 to 50 minutes, until top is soft but set. Cool before cutting. Makes about 35 to 40 squares or rectangular bars. (Note: If desired, you can decorate the tops of these bars, before cutting, by drizzling with mixture of ½ cup confectioner's sugar and enough lemon juice to make thin glaze. After drizzling, sprinkle on colorful decors sprinkles, if you wish.)

SPICY MINCEMEAT DROPS

     2 cups all purpose flour
     ½ cup cocoa
     1 teaspoon baking soda
     ½ teaspoon salt
  1¼ cups sugar
     ¾ cup solid shortening
     ¼ cup butter (½ stick)
     2 eggs
     2 teaspoons vanilla
        9-ounce package condensed (dry) mincemeat,
        crumbled
     1 cup chopped walnuts
        Candied cherries

Preheat oven to 350 degrees. Combine flour, cocoa, baking soda and salt. In large mixer bowl, beat sugar, shortening and butter until fluffy. Beat in eggs and vanilla. Add flour mixture; mix well. Add mincemeat and nuts. Roll into 1-inch balls and space 2 inches apart on ungreased baking sheets. Flatten slightly by pressing piece of candied cherry on top. Bake 8 to 10 minutes, until almost set. Cool few minutes before removing from cookie sheet. Makes about 70 cookies.

ROLLED SHORTBREAD CUTOUTS

These are delicious, and not too hard to make. They are time-consuming, though, because of the rolling out procedure.

    1   cup soft butter
    ½   cup sugar
    ½   teaspoon vanilla
    2¼ cups all purpose flour

Preheat oven to 375 degrees. In large mixer bowl, beat together butter, sugar and vanilla until light and fluffy. Add flour and mix well. Turn out onto well floured board and roll dough with well floured rolling pin to about ½-inch thick. Cut with cookies into desired shapes (or cut squares, triangles, diamonds, with knife.) With wide spatula, transfer to ungreased cookie sheet. Before baking, sprinkle with colored sugars or decors, if desired. Bake for 8 to 10 minutes, until set and lightly browned. Frost with confectioners sugar icing, if desired. Makes about 4 dozen average cookies (size depends on shape of cookies.)

PIES

PIES

It is natural that pies would be mentioned frequently in Riley's poetry because they were so common to the everyday diet in his day. In rural areas, the men and children rose early to do at least an hour's chores before eating, so there was time for the housewife to make a pie or two. In the summer, pies were protected from flies and other insects in pie safes, ventilated with tin inserts on the sides and doors. In the winter, pies could be made ahead because they kept well on an unheated back porch in freezing weather. Usually, there was more than one kind of pie in the house at all times.

When fresh fruit was unavailable dried and canned fruit was used. When that was unavailable, people resorted to pies made from common household ingredients, and came up with custard and cream pies. Sugar cream pie has an enthusiastic following in central Indiana, and is a specialty in several eating places like the historic Kopper Kettle, and the the now-closed but fondly remembered Durbin Hotel and the Log Cabin at Crawfordsville. James Whitcomb Riley probably ate Sugar Cream Pie many times during his life.

SUGAR STREUSEL PIE

- 1 (9-inch) pastry crust
- 1 cup packed light brown sugar
- ¼ cup flour
- ¼ cup (½ stick) butter or margarine
- ⅛ teaspoon ground mace
- 1½ cups heavy or whipping cream, not whipped
- 1 teaspoon vanilla

Preheat oven to 350 degrees. Prepare and roll out pastry. Make filling: In large mixing bowl, place brown sugar, flour, butter and mace. With fingertips or pastry blender, blend mixture until crumbly, and spread evenly in unbaked pie crust. Stir vanilla into cream; pour to distribute evenly over crumbly mixture. Bake for 50 to 60 minutes, until browned and set. Makes one (9-inch) pie.

Last Thanksgivin' dinner we
Et at Granny's house, an' she
Had—ist like she allus does—
Most and best pies ever wuz

Canned blackberry-pie and goose-
burry, squishin' full o' juice;
An razburry—yes an' plum—
Yes, an' churry pie—um yum!

Peach an' punkin, too, you bet
Lawzy! I kin taste 'em yet!
Yes, an' custard pie and mince!

An' - I - ain't - et - no - pie - since!

(Incidentally, the remedy for stomach ache in Riley's time was half a teaspoonful baking soda to a glassful of water.)

KOPPER KETTLE SUGAR CREAM PIE

From the famous restaurant in Morristown, Indiana, which was once a way station for the Pony Express.

- 1 (9-inch) pastry crust
- 1 cup sugar
- ½ cup flour
- 2 cups (1 pint) coffee cream or whipping cream
  Pinch salt
- 1 teaspoon vanilla
  Ground nutmeg

Preheat oven to 450 degrees F. Prepare and roll out pie crust. In medium mixing bowl, place all ingredients and mix thoroughly until smooth. Pour into unbaked crust. Sprinkle top generously with nutmeg. Bake for 15 minutes, then reduce oven temperature to 350 degrees F. and continue baking for about 30 minutes. Makes 1 (9-inch) pie. (Note: For a slightly less firm, more custard-like filling, use ⅓ cup flour instead of ½ cup.)

CREAM SUGAR PIE

A 1970 Methodist Church Cookbook in Greenfield printed this recipe from the Durbin Hotel in Rushville, Indiana.

- 1¼ cup sugar
- ¼ cup corn starch
- ⅛ teaspoon salt
- ⅛ teaspoon nutmeg
- ½ cup butter or margarine (1 stick)
- 1 teaspoon vanilla
- 2 cups milk
  Baked 9-inch pie shell

Mix sugar and cornstarch, add a little milk and blend. Add rest of milk, salt and nutmeg. Cook in double boiler until it thickens. Stir while cooking. After it has thickened, stir in butter and vanilla and cool. Pour in baked pie shell. Sprinkle lightly with nutmeg.

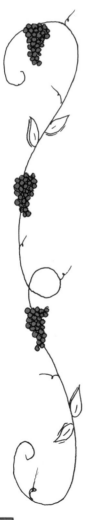

*R*hubarb was known as "pie plant" and in rural areas is still favored, tho' now usually in combination with something else, such as strawberries. How tramps regarded a "hand-out" of this variety is told in "A Hobo Voluntary." "A tin o' black coffee, and a rhubarb pie—Be they old and cold as charity— They're hot-stuff enough for the pore hobo, And it's 'Thanks, kind lady, for to treat me so.'"

FRANGIPANI PIE

Although a famous man of letters, James Whitcomb Riley never attended college. However, by his time, there were several well known colleges in Indiana.

At Indiana University, there is a Frangipani Room in the Student Union. Frangipani (pronounced fran-ji-pana), is a flower and perfume made from West Indian red jasmine. It bears no relationship to the Hoosier university, except that its name rhymes with the word "gloriana," as in "Gloriana, Frangipani, E'er to thee be true," in Indiana's popular school song. The rhyming word came out of a dictionary, but IU adapted it enthusiastically.

Frangipani was also an early Italian gentleman who lent his name to Frangipani Cream, a flavorful pudding, used to fill pastry shells, and cake layers. This is Fanny Farmer's early *Boston Cooking School Cookbook* recipe Frangipani Pie: 'Make like cream pie, using Frangipan Cream."

oney was an extremely important item on the pioneer table. Sugar cost money, but honey was a gift from the bees. An early settler hoped to lure a swarm into a homemade hive in his back yard. "Honey in the Comb" was on the table, and the children chewed the comb as gum, called "Honey-wax."

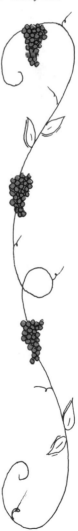

FANNY FARMER'S FRANGIPAN CREAM

- ⅔ cup powdered sugar
- ⅓ cup flour
- 2 eggs or 4 egg yolks
- ¼ teaspoon salt
- 1 cup scalded milk
- 2 tablespoons butter
- 2 tablespoons macaroons (dried and rolled)
- ⅔ teaspoon vanilla
- ⅓ teaspoon lemon extract

Make a cream filling of first 5 ingredients; then add butter, macaroons, and extracts.

LEMON CHESS PIE

- 3 tablespoons fresh lemon juice
- 3 tablespoons milk
- 3 tablespoons melted butter
- 1½ cups sugar

o Riley, honey was the epitome of sweetness, and his poem "Honey Dripping from the Comb" recalls sweet old-fashioned memories. "How slight a thing may set one's fancy drifting Upon the Dead Sea of the Past!—A view—sometimes an odor—or a rooster lifting a far off 'Ooh! ooh! — ooh!" Doc Sifers, in the poem "The Rubyaiyat of Doc Sifers" says he has "eighteen hive of bees."

    1 tablespoon flour
    2 tablespoons grated lemon peel
       Pinch salt
    3 large eggs
       9-inch unbaked pie shell

Preheat oven to 350 degrees. In large mixing bowl, place lemon juice, milk, butter, sugar, flour, peel, salt and eggs. Whisk mixture lightly just until blended (don't worry if mixture looks curdled, and don't overmix—sugar should be distributed through mixture, but doesn't have to be dissolved). Pour filling into pie shell and bake for 45 to 50 minutes, until set. Garnish tops of each serving, if desired with whipped cream and twist of lemon peel. Makes 6 to 8 servings.

EIGHT EGG LEMON PIE

This is a very tall chiffon pie, made in spring or summer when eggs were plentiful.

    1 baked 9-inch pie shell
    8 eggs, separated
    2 cups sugar, divided
    1 envelope (1 tablespoon) unflavored gelatin
   1/2 cup water
    1 tablespoon grated lemon peel
   1/2 cup fresh lemon juice
   1/4 teaspoon salt
   1/4 teaspoon cream of tartar

Separate eggs. In saucepan stir yolks, 1 cup of the sugar, gelatin, water, peel, juice and salt. Over medium heat of stovetop, cook, stirring constantly, until mixture comes just to a boil. (With overboiling, acid in the lemons can begin to thin filling.) Chill mixture in refrigerator until mixture mounds when dropped from a spoon. Then, beat egg whites and cream of tartar until frothy. Beat in remaining 1 cup sugar, 1 tablespoon at a time; continue beating until stiff and glossy. Do not underbeat. Fold in lemon mixture and pile into pie shell. Chill several hours, until set enough to cut neat slices. Makes 1 (9-inch) pie, about 8 servings.

DEEP DISH APPLE PIE

Housewives tried to serve their fruit pies as soon as possible because the juicy fruit made the bottom crust soggy if they stood too long. Deep dish pies, with no bottom crust, avoided this problem and were considered a good make-ahead pie.

    6   cups thin sliced apples (6 medium)
    ½   cup sugar
    ½   cup light brown sugar
    ⅛   teaspoon allspice
    ¾   teaspoon cinnamon
    ⅛   teaspoon salt
    1   tablespoon lemon juice
    2   tablespoons butter
        Pastry for single pie shell
        Milk
    1   tablespoon sugar

Preheat oven to 425 degrees. In large mixing bowl, mix apples, sugars, spices, salt and lemon juice. Spread evenly in 10x6x2-inch dish and dot with butter. Roll out pastry about ½-inch larger on all sides. Moisten edges of dish and adjust pastry over apples, pressing pastry to edges of dish firmly. Crimp edges of pastry, and slit top. Brush top with milk and sprinkle with sugar. Bake for about 60 minutes, until juice begins to bubble through slits in crust. Place strips of aluminum foil over crust in areas which seem to be browning too much. Serve warm. Makes about 8 to 9 servings.

APPLE STREUSEL PIE

Apple pie was made so frequently in homes of the early 20th century that it was not considered "exotic" enough to be included in recipe books. Variations like this one, sometimes called French Apple Pie, were included, however.

Filling:
    ½   cup sugar
    1   teaspoon nutmeg
    ⅛   teaspoon salt

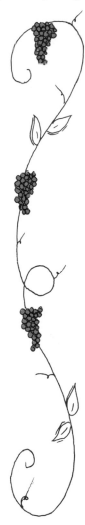

On top of rich milk, especially from Jersey cows, would form thick, rich cream that could almost be cut with a knife. This cream whipped easily, and when sweetened, was indescribably delicious as the topping for date or raisin pie. Sugar and cream accompanied tea, oatmeal, rice, corn flakes, stewed fruit, dumplings and many other goodies.

1 teaspoon grated lemon peel
4 cups thinly sliced apples (about 4 medium)
  Pastry for single pie shell
Streusel:
½ cup packed light brown sugar
¾ cup all purpose flour
¼ cup butter

Preheat oven to 425 degrees. In small bowl, combine sugar, nutmeg, salt and lemon peel. Line 9-inch pie plate with pastry being careful not to prick or tear the crust. In pastry, layer apples and filling until all are used up. Make streusel: In small bowl, rub together sugar, flour and butter to make crumbly mixture. Spread evenly over apples, patting lightly. Wrap a 2 or 3-inch strip of aluminum foil around edges to prevent excessive browning. Remove strip last 15 minutes of baking to crisp edges. Bake for about 50 minutes, until apples are tender. Makes 6 to 8 servings.

MICROWAVE HONEY APPLE PIE

This recipe features quick-to-make pastry from the food processor.

Food Processor Pastry (below)
4 cups peeled and cored sliced apples (4 to 6 medium)
2 tablespoons honey, divided
½ cup sugar
2 tablespoons flour
¾ teaspoon ground cinnamon
¼ teaspoon ground cardamom
⅛ teaspoon salt
2 tablespoons butter

Make processor pastry. On floured board with floured rolling pin, roll one pastry disc to a circle, 12 inches in diameter and ⅛-inch thick. Fit into 9-inch glass pie plate; trim edge. Over bottom of pastry arrange half of sliced apples, and drizzle apples with 1 tablespoon of the honey. In a small bowl, mix sugar, flour, cinnamon, cardamom and salt. Sprinkle honey-drizzled apples with half of sugar mixture, then repeat layers—other half of apples, the second tablespoon honey and the rest of the sugar-spice mixture.

Dot the butter over the top. Roll out the other round of pastry as the first and vent it by making decorative slits near the center. Moisten edge of the bottom pastry by brushing with water, then place the vented top pastry over the pie; trim about ½ inch beyond edge of the plate. Fold top crust under bottom crust at the rim and crimp edges together firmly.

Preheat the conventional oven to 450 degrees F. During preheating, start cooking the pie in the microwave at high (100 percent power) for about 10 minutes, rotating ½ turn after 5 minutes. After about 8 or 9 minutes, fork the apples through one of the slits in the top pastry—apples should be almost tender and you might see signs of juice starting to bubble. Also, the top crust will become puffy and will have lost most of its transluscence, and become almost opaque. At this point, transfer the pie to the preheated oven, placing it on the bottom shelf, and continue baking the pie for an additional 15 to 20 minutes, until evenly browned and you can see bubbling juices. Cool before cutting. Makes 6 to 8 servings.

FOOD PROCESSOR PASTRY: In work bowl of food processor with steel blade, place 2 cups all purpose flour (stirred 2 or 3 times to fluff up before measuring), and 1 teaspoon salt. Add ½ cup vegetable shortening which has been divided into 6 parts, and 1 tablespoon of frozen butter. Process, using short on-off procedure, until particles resemble coarse crumbs, about 20 seconds. With processor running, all at once add ⅓ cup cold water through the feed tube, and continue to process no more than 20 to 30 seconds. If dough forms a ball before that time, stop processor immediately. If ball doesn't form in 30 seconds, stop processing and shape by hand—longer processing can toughen pastry. Divide dough in half and shape each half into a smooth flat disc.

PEACH CANTALOUPE PIE

Early pies were used fruit mixtures, sometimes for variety, sometimes out of necessity when the household didn't have enough of one type of filling to complete the pie.

iley mentions powdered sugar in his poem "Bub says." "The moon in the sky is a custard pie, An' the clouds is the cream pour'd o'er it, An' all the glittering stars in the sky, Is the powdered sugar for it."

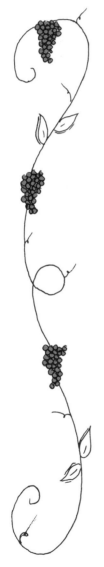

ie was a daily feature of the meals, and before holidays the "grub board" was lined with a supply. Hoosiers ate pie for breakfast, lunch, and dinner and most preferred it over cake.

Pastry for two-crust pie
2 cups slices peeled and sliced fresh peaches
2 cups thinly sliced peeled and seeded fresh cantaloupe
1 cup sugar
¼ cup flour
½ teaspoon salt
¼ cup sliced almonds
1 tablespoon butter

Preheat oven to 425-degrees. Make filling: In large bowl, toss to mix the peaches, cantaloupe, sugar, flour and salt. Set aside while preparing and lining pastry shell with pastry. Pour filling into lined pastry and arrange evenly. Sprinkle with almonds and dot with butter. Prepare top pastry and use to cover pie, sealing edges well. Slash top once or twice for steam to escape. Bake 35 to 40 minutes, until bubbly and well browned. Makes 6 to 8 servings. (Note: For a more crispy crust, if desired, top may be sprinkled lightly with sugar just before baking.)

ELLIS ROCK JACKSON'S COCONUT CREAM PIE

Mrs. Jackson was wife of Indiana's Attorney General in the 1920's and mother of Dorothy June Jackson Williams, one of the authors of this book. Her cooking was well known among her friends and her husband's political associates. This is her entire recipe for coconut cream pie.

1 rounding tablespoon cornstarch
1 rounding tablespoon flour
½ cup sugar
1 pint milk

Beat 2 egg whites and add. Put coconut over the top.

BUTTERED COCONUT PIE

1 cup firmly packed brown sugar
½ cup light corn syrup
⅓ cup butter, melted
3 eggs
4 ounces shredded moist coconut
½ teaspoon vanilla
½ teaspoon almond extract
½ teaspoon salt
9-inch unbaked pie shell

Preheat oven to 350 degrees. In large mixing bowl, place brown sugar, corn syrup, butter, eggs, coconut, extracts and salt. Stir mixture just until blended. Pour into pie shell. Bake for 45 to 55 minutes, until set. Festive when served in a pool of chocolate syrup, or with chocolate ice cream.

CHOCOLATE PRALINE PIE

2 eggs
½ cup sugar
½ cup butter (1 stick), melted
2 teaspoons instant coffee powder
1 teaspoon rum extract
2 tablespoons water
6-ounce package semi sweet chocolate chips
1 cup chopped pecans
9-inch pastry shell, unbaked

Preheat oven to 400 degrees. In mixing bowl, beat together eggs, sugar and melted butter. In small bowl or cup, stir together coffee powder, rum extract and water until dissolved. Add to beaten mixture along with chocolate chips and pecans. Pour into unbaked pastry. Place in oven, reduce temperature to 350 degrees and bake for 40 to 50 minutes, until set in the center. Cool before cutting. Whipped cream and stemmed maraschino cherry is an attractive garnish for each serving, if desired. Makes about 6 to 8 servings.

Hoosiers at the turn-of-the-century liked to make layered pies, with a rich French custard on the bottom and a sweetened, thickened, fruit layer on the top.

FROZEN FUDGE PIE

Your recipe author made a version of this pie every Saturday night for five summers, while working as a cook at a summer resort.

MERINGUE:
    Butter
- 2 egg whites
- ⅛ teaspoon salt
- ⅛ teaspoon cream of tartar
- ½ teaspoon vanilla
- ½ cup sugar
- ½ cup chopped pecans

FILLING:
- 4 ounces sweet chocolate (German's)
- 3 tablespoons hot strong coffee
- 1 tablespoon vanilla
    Pinch of salt
- 1 cup (half pint) heavy cream

Make meringue shell: Preheat oven to 300 degrees F. Butter an 8-inch pie plate. Beat egg whites with salt, cream of tartar and vanilla until soft peaks form. Add sugar, a tablespoon at a time, until very stiff peaks are formed. Fold in nuts. Turn into buttered pie plate, spreading over bottom and thickly up sides and over edges of plate. Bake for 50 to 60 minutes, until dry and crusty. Cool. Make filling: Place chocolate in glass or plastic 1-quart casserole. Microwave at medium or medium-low (50 percent) for 2 to 4 minutes, until chocolate can be stirred smooth. Stir in coffee, vanilla and salt until blended. Cool to room temperature. In chilled bowl with chilled beaters, beat whipped cream until stiff and fold into chocolate. Spread mixture into meringue shell and freeze. About 20 minutes before serving, place pie in refrigerator to make cutting and serving easier. Makes 1 pie, 6 to 8 servings. (Note, for really special dessert, make a pool of chocolate sauce in dessert plate, add a slice of pie and top with whipped cream and shaved chocolate.)

Here's to the black raspberry! It's the more humble sister of the elegant red jewel Riley and his friends loved to pick along the leisurely roads of their childhood. It's the black raspberry that's most beloved of Hoosiers, redolent with that sharp-sweet taste and the memories of early mornings when the sun slanted down through trees on blue-jeaned berry pickers and the birds of youth and promise sang. Cook a quart of them with 2 cups sugar and 4 tbls. flour till mixture boils. If you don't have time today for homemade crust pick up a pre-rolled or box mix. Lattice the top, bake at 375 30 minutes. Heaven!

PECAN MERINGUE PIE

  3 egg whites
  ½ teaspoon baking powder
  1 cup sugar
 11 graham cracker squares, rolled into fine crumbs
  1 cup chopped pecans
Topping:

  1 cup whipping cream
  1 teaspoon vanilla

Preheat oven to 350 degrees. In large mixing bowl, whip the egg whites until frothy. Add baking powder, then beat in sugar, a tablespoon at a time until very stiff; do not underbeat. Fold in the crumbs and pecans. Spread in well buttered 9-inch pie plate. Bake for 25 to 35 minutes, until dry and crusty. Cool. Make topping: Whip cream with vanilla, spread over cooled pie, and chill at least 4 hours before serving. Makes 6 to 8 servings.

FROST ON THE PUNKIN PIE

A frozen layered pie, with ice cream and spicy pumpkin filling.

      9-inch baked or graham cracker pie shell
  1 cup cooked or canned mashed pumpkin
1¼ cup sugar
  ½ teaspoon salt
  ½ teaspoon ground ginger
  ¼ teaspoon ground nutmeg
  1 cup whipping cream
  1 pint quality vanilla ice cream
      Butterscotch Sauce

Prepare, bake and cool the pie shell. In medium mixing bowl, stir pumpkin, sugar, salt, ginger and nutmeg. Whip cream until stiff peaks form and fold into pumpkin mix-

Housework was a woman-killer in pioneer times. A man might marry the first time for love, resulting in several children. To bring up the children, he might marry several more times, as we would say "for convenience." Riley's poem "My First Womern" mentions this sort of life: "Fer I'm allus thinkin'—thinkin' Of the first one's peaceful ways, A bilin' soap and singin' of the Lord's amazin' grace.—And I'm thinkin' of her, constant, Dyin' carpet-chain and stuff And a makin' up rag carpets, When the floor was GOOD ENOUGH! And I'm allus thinkin' of her reddin' up around the house; Er cookin' fer the farm hands; er drivin' up the cows.—And there she lays out yander By the lower medder (meadow) fence. W'y they ain't no sadder thing Than to think of my first womern, and her funeral last spring."

ture. In bottom of pie shell, spread the ice cream in an even layer. (Tip: Soften, if necessary by microwaving at high, 100 percent power, 10 or 15 seconds, no more.) Layer the pumpkin mixture over the ice cream and spread evenly. Freeze for at least 2 hours, or up to 3 days. Allow to stand in refrigerator about 20 minutes before cutting. Serve with Butterscotch Sauce. Makes about 8 servings.

BUTTERSCOTCH SAUCE

While you're making this, you might want to double the recipe; it keeps well when refrigerated.

- 1 tablespoon cornstarch
- 1¼ cups packed brown sugar
- ½ cup half and half (cream)
- 2 tablespoons light corn syrup
  Dash salt
- ¼ cup (½ stick) butter
- 1 teaspoon vanilla

In 1½ quart microwave casserole, stir together cornstarch and brown sugar. Stir in half and half, corn syrup and salt. Add butter and cover. Microwave at high (100 percent power) for 3½ to 4½ minutes, stirring every 2 minutes, until thickened and sugar is dissolved. Add vanilla and stir until smooth and well blended. Serve warm or cold. Makes 1½ cups.

*O*ne of the most beautiful poems in the English language is Riley's "When The Frost is on The Punkin'," the famous first lines of which are as follows: "When the frost is on the punkin', and the fodder's in the shock, And you hear the kyouck and gobble of the struttin' turkey-cock." Many farms in former times considered guineas as the watchdogs of their land. When a stranger turned in the lane, the guineas set up a tremendous howl in their high pitched, loud babble. Riley calls this "the clackin' of the guineys," in the poem.

"WHEN THE FROST IS ON THE PUNKIN"

WHEN the frost is on the punkin and the fodder's in the shock,
  And you hear the kyouck and gobble of the struttin' turkey-cock.
And the clackin' of the guineys, and the cluckin' of the hens,
And the rooster's hallylooyer as he tiptoes on the fence;
O, it's then's the times a feller is a-feelin' at his best,
With the risin' sun to greet him from a night of peaceful rest,
As he leaves the house, bareheaded, and goes out to feed the stock,
When the frost is on the punkin and the fodder's in the shock.

They's something kindo' harty-like about the atmusfere
When the heat of summer's over and the coolin' fall is here—
Of course we miss the flowers, and the blossums on the trees,
And the mumble of the hummin'-birds and buzzin' of the bees;
But the air's so appetizin'; and the landscape through the haze
Of a crisp and sunny morning of the airly autumn days
Is a pictur' that no painter has the colorin' to mock—
When the frost is on the punkin and the fodder's in the shock.

The husky, rusty russel of the tossels of the corn,
And the raspin' of the tangled leaves, as golden as the morn;
The stubble in the furries—kindo' lonesome-like, but still
A-preachin' sermons to us of the barns they growed to fill;
The strawstack in the medder, and the reaper in the shed;
The hosses in theyr stalls below—the clover overhead!—
O, it sets my hart a-clickin' like the tickin' of a clock,
When the frost is on the punkin and the fodder's in the shock!

Then your apples all is gethered, and the ones a feller keeps
Is poured around the celler-floor in red and yeller heaps;
And your cider-makin' 's over, and your wimmern-folks is through
With their mince and apple-butter, and theyr souse and saussage, too! . . .
I don't know how to tell it—but ef sich a thing could be
As the Angels wantin' boardin', and they'd call around on *me*
I'd want to 'commodate 'em—all the whole-indurin' flock—
When the frost is on the punkin and the fodder's in the shock!

Desserts and Candies

1989 RILEY DAYS APPLE COBBLER

This recipe was used by the congregation of the Greenfield Christian Church for their "Kobbler and Ice Cream Cafe" located in the church basement during the 1989 Riley Days.

 1½ cups sugar
 1½ cups flour
 1 teaspoon nutmeg
 1 teaspoon cinnamon
  Dash of salt
 12 cups thinly sliced pared tart apples (about 5 medium)
 4 tablespoons (½ stick) butter or margarine
Pastry:
 5 cups flour
 2 teaspoons salt
 2 cups vegetable shortening
 ⅔ cup water

Heat oven to 425 degrees F. In large bowl, stir together sugar, flour, nutmeg, cinnamon and salt. Mix lightly with apples. Let stand while making pastry. Make pastry: In large mixing bowl, measure flour and salt. Cut in half of shortening until size of small peas. Cut in remaining shortening until size of large peas (this procedure makes pastry flaky). Stir in water until moist enough to hold pastry together into a smooth ball. Divide dough into two portions, using about ⅔ of dough for one portion, and ⅓ of dough for the second portion. Shape ⅔ of dough into flat rectangle and roll out to fit a 13x9x2-inch baking pan. Fit loosely onto bottom and up sides of pan making sure no cracks appear in pastry (if they do, patch with more pastry tidbits, "glueing" them firmly with water). Pour filling into pastry lined pan, and dot the top with butter. Roll out the second (smaller) portion of dough into rectangle to cover the top of the pan. Slash pastry top to vent steam. Adjust top pastry over filled cobbler. Seal top and bottom edges of pastry and flute. To prevent excessive browning, cover edges of pastry with 2 to 3-inch strip of aluminum foil. Remove foil last 15 minutes of baking. Bake 40 to 50 minutes or until crust is brown and juice begins to bubble through slits in crust. Serve warm with cream, whipped cream or ice cream. Makes about 15 to 20 servings.

Here's to the lemon! Grown since Renaissance times in orangeries of the nobility and popular in America from the Colonial era on, it is the gem of the pastry maker's treasure chest. Piquant, tangy, it came across the wilderness traces in "traipsin' bags" with the pioneers. Lemon tea bread drizzled with sugary juice, lemon pound cake rich with butter lusciousness, lemon cake and cookies—its hard to choose the lemon goodie that's best. Every new bride in Riley's day knew how to handle lemons and believed she had become a true wife when she presented her husband with the ultimate, indescribably delicious masterpiece, lemon meringue pie. No summer (or winter for that matter) is complete without one.

199

OLD FASHIONED APPLE DUMPLINGS

This starts with a biscuit dough filled pinwheel-style with spicy chopped apples. Over the top goes a buttery syrup which is absorbed by the dough, leaving a moist dumpling with a crusty top.

*G*reatly prized in early times was the maple syrup prepared from the sap of the small sugar maple trees. Wooden "spiles" were inserted into a small hold bored in the trunk of a tree and a bucket was secured below the spile to catch the drippings. It took many gallons of sap to produce, when boiled over an outdoor fire, a small amount of maple syrup. Riley mentions this in his poem "When Early March Seem Middle May" in lines which go: "When through the twigs the farmer tramps, And troughs are chunked beneath the trees, And fragrant hints of sugar-camps Astray in every breeze. When early March seems middle May, the Spring is coming round this way."

2 cups finely chopped apples
1 teaspoon cinnamon
1/2 cup (1 stick) butter
2 cups sugar
2 cups water

Dough:
1 1/2 cups all purpose flour
1 1/2 teaspoons baking powder
1/2 teaspoon salt
1/2 cup shortening
1/3 cup milk

In medium mixing bowl, toss apples and cinnamon. Set aside. In 1-quart measuring cup, or small bowl, place butter. Microwave at high (100 percent power) for 1/2 to 1 minute, until melted. Pour melted butter into 13x9x2-inch baking pan and spread evenly. Into same measuring cup stir together sugar and water. Microwave at high for 5 to 7 minutes, stirring after 3 minutes (or simmer in saucepan) until sugar is completely dissolved; set aside. Make dough: Into large mixing bowl, place flour, baking powder and salt. Add shortening and cut in until mixture resembles fine crumbs. Add milk and stir with a fork just until dough forms a ball. Turn out onto floured board and knead 5 to 10 times, just to smooth. Roll dough into 1/4 inch thick rectangle (about 6 x 8-inches). Spread cinnamon apples over dough, leaving about 1 inch at long edge uncovered. Roll up dough, starting from 16-inch side which is covered with apples (opposite the uncovered edge, which should be dampened to seal edges). Cut roll into about 16 (1/2-inch) slices. Arrange slices evenly in the buttered baking pan and slowly pour the warm sugar syrup over the top. Syrup will float on top at first, but will be absorbed by dough as dumplings cook. Place in oven set at 350 degrees and bake for 60 to 65 minutes. Serve warm with cream or ice cream. Makes 8 servings. (Note: Blackberries, black raspberries, cherries or peaches can be substituted for apples. Save any juice to substitute for part of the sugar syrup.)

MICROWAVE CANDY APPLE BETTY

Made with graham cracker crusts, this is super easy and very tasty. Use red cinnamon candies for part of the sugar to flavor and sweeten the betty. Granny Smith are good apples for this.

- ½ cup butter
- ¼ cup sugar
- 2 cups graham cracker crumbs (about 26 squares)
- 5 cups slices (about ¼ inch thick) from washed cored unpeeled apples
- ¾ cup candy red hots (6 ounces)

In 2-quart microwave casserole or bowl place butter. Microwave at high (100 percent power) for 1 minute, until melted. Add sugar and crumbs and mix well. Place about half of mixture in 9-inch pie plate and pat evenly over bottom and sides. With fingers arrange apple slices in flat layers over crumbs, alternating cinnamon red hot candies between layers. Be sure red hots are completely covered by apples in filling—any which aren't covered won't melt as the dessert bakes. Top betty with rest of crumbs and pat top firmly in place so dessert slices well. Microwave at high for 10 to 14 minutes, until bubbly and apples have "cooked down", rotating pie ½ turn after 5 minutes. Let stand a few minutes until serving. Makes 6 to 8 servings.

SOUR CREAM BLUEBERRY PUDDING CAKE

Serve this as dessert, with whipped cream, or as a morning coffee cake, drizzled with powdered sugar glaze, if you wish.

- 1 cup soft butter
- 1¼ cups sugar
- 2 eggs
- 1 cup sour cream
- 1 teaspoon vanilla
- 2 cups all purpose flour
- 1½ teaspoons baking powder
- ½ teaspoon baking soda
- 12-ounces frozen blueberries, thawed

*A*pples are the most frequently mentioned of any food item in Riley's poems. Apples are mentioned 40 times in Riley's complete poetic works. Practically every home had apples which ripened at various seasons from Maidenblush to Harvest. Riley most often mentions the Rambo. Perhaps the most famous apple of Rileyana, a variety known as Rhode Island Greening, is found in "An Old Sweetheart of Mine." "Again I made her presents, in a really helpless way, The big 'Rhode Island Greening,' I was hungry too that day! But I follow her from Spelling, with her hand behind her—so—And I slip the apple in it,—and the Teacher doesn't know!''

¹/₂ cup sugar
1 teaspoon cinnamon

In large bowl of electric mixer, place butter, sugar, eggs, sour cream and vanilla. Beat well until very creamy. Stop mixer and add flour, baking powder and soda. Very slowly beat mixture, until well blended. Batter is stiff. Spread evenly in greased and floured 13x9x2-inch pan. Sprinkle top evenly with thawed (drained if necessary) blueberries. In small cup or bowl, mix together sugar and cinnamon, and sprinkle over blueberries. Place in a cold oven and bake at 350 degrees for 45 to 55 minutes, until toothhpick stuck into non-fruit area comes out clean. Makes 8 to 10 servings.

INDIANA PERSIMMON ALMOND PUDDING CAKE

This dessert attributes its exceptional moisture to persimmon pulp and buttermilk.

¹/₂ cup (1 stick) butter
1¹/₄ cups sugar
2 eggs
1³/₄ cups all purpose flour
1¹/₂ teaspoons baking powder
¹/₄ teaspoon salt
¹/₂ teaspoon baking soda
1 cup sieved persimmon pulp
¹/₄ cup buttermilk
1 cup ground, unblanched almonds
Powdered sugar

Preheat oven to 350 degrees. In large bowl of electric mixer, place butter and sugar. Beat together until very light and fluffy. Add eggs, one at a time, and beat smooth. In small bowl, stir flour with baking powder, salt and soda. Add dry ingredients alternately with persimmon pulp (made by putting about a pint of ripe persimmons through ricer or mashing and sieving) and buttermilk to the creamed mixture, mixing until smooth. Stir in ground almonds. Pour into greased 10-inch tube pan. Bake for 45 to 55 minutes, or until a toothpick inserted into center of cake comes out clean. Cool in pan about 15 minutes before

ere's to the transparent apple! Harbinger of summertime and fruit of June. Riley's friends and relatives liked to carefully peel about five cups of them, slice thick with two cups of sugar and add a teaspoon of cinnamon and one of butter. The crust was double. Heavy whipping cream on the warm pie would make them wish for more!

turning out. If desired, dust each slice with powdered sugar and garnish with fresh red and green grapes. Makes 12 servings.

"Foreign grapes may be had at the fruit stores throughout the winter. The Malaga leads all foreign grapes, and comes packed in cork-dust, which is a non-conductor of heat and absorbent of moisture, and so is always in good condition. If left in the cork-dust this fruit will keep three months in prime order. When used rinse well in ice-water, and place on a glass dish or dishes surrounded by fine ice; if plentiful do not divide clusters, but serve a bunch for each guest."
The New Buckeye Cook Book (1880)

SATIN PUDDING, FLOATING ISLAND OR "FLOAT"

When the hens were laying and cows producing there were plenty of ingredients for custard, topped with a light meringue. As Satin Pudding, the custard was put into a heat-proof casserole and the meringue spread on top, to be browned in the oven. Floating island was made by dropping meringue in mounds (islands) over the top. The meringues were often left uncooked (the heat from freshly-boiled custard would cook and set them). Sometimes the meringues were poached on top of boiling water in an enclosed kettle, then spooned over the custard. The custard was always served chilled. One flowery cookbook writer said the pudding "was as smooth as a medicine man's spiel."

Custard:
   1 quart milk
   1 cup sugar
   3 tablespoons cornstarch
  ½ cup cold milk
   5 eggs yolks
      Pinch salt
1½ teaspoons vanilla
Meringue:
   5 egg whites
  ⅓ cup sugar

Riley's age believed transparent apples made the smoothest, most subtle-flavored applesauce of all. They quartered and boiled them and put apples and all in a fine-sieved colander. Sugar to taste.

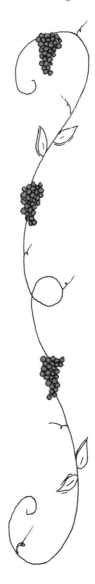

Into heavy saucepan, place milk and sugar. Over medium heat bring almost to a boil. Meanwhile, in small bowl, stir cornstarch with ½ cup cold milk until smooth; add the egg yolks and beat until smooth. Add this to the hot milk and cook on medium heat until mixture coats a silver spoon. Remove from heat, add the salt and vanilla and pour into a heatproof casserole dish. Make meringue: in grease free, non plastic bowl beat the egg whites, gradually adding sugar until very stiff and glossy. Spread meringue over top, or drop in mounds (see above). If desired, brown the top of the meringues in 375 degree preheated oven, watching constantly, until pale golden, about 5 minutes. Makes about 8 servings.

One of the standard dishes of years ago was called "Float" or "Floating Island." A custard was prepared by cooking egg yolks, milk, and sugar until the mixture "coated a spoon." After the mixture was flavored (with precious vanilla) and cooled, a meringue of egg whites and sugar was spooned on top. It made a very attractive dish, the white "islands" on the yellow custard. Riley's hired girl, Floretty, "made a hasty crock of 'float,'—poured thence into a deep glass dish of irridescent hue and glint and sparkle, with an overflow of froth (the meringue) to crown it, foaming white as snow."

BUTTERY SHORTCAKE

This shortcake has a crumbly, cake-like texture designed to catch all the juices from fresh strawberries and other favorite fruits.

- 2 cups all purpose flour
- ½ cup sugar
- 3 tablespoons baking powder
- ½ teaspoon salt
- ½ cup butter (1 stick)
- ¾ cup milk
- 2 eggs, slightly beaten

Preheat oven to 375 degrees. Grease well an 8-inch square pan or a 9-inch round pan. In large bowl, combine first 4 ingredients and stir to blend. Using pastry blender or fork, cut in the butter until consistency of coarse meal. Combine the milk and eggs; add to the flour mixture. Stir just until dry ingredients are moistened. Spread dough in greased pan and bake 25 to 30 minutes, until golden brown. Serve warm, split and filled with sweetened strawberries, or serve with Fresh Peach Sauce (below), and whipped cream. Makes 8 servings.

INDIVIDUAL SHORTCAKES: Preheat oven to 450 degrees. Drop dough by rounded tablespoonsful onto greased cookie sheet about 2 inches apart. Bake about 10 to 12 minutes.

FRESH PEACH SAUCE

3 large peaches, peeled and sliced (about 2 cups slices)
¼ cup honey
2 tablespoons white rum
1 tablespoon confectioners sugar
1 teaspoon lemon juice
¼ cup blanched slivered almonds

Measure ½ cup of the peach slices; puree these in the food processor, or by rubbing through a sieve. In heavy saucepan, place the puree along with honey and rum. Over low heat, stir sauce until a few bubbles start to form. Add the remaining peach slices, confectioners sugar, lemon juice and almonds. Let stand few minutes to warm fruit throughout. Serve over ice cream, custard or shortcake with whipped cream. Makes about 2 cups.

"The ripest peach is highest on the tree." Riley.

MAPLE FRANGO

Around the turn of the century in central Indiana, people tapped maple trees for their sweet sap. That was when there were more trees, and people had more time to boil down the syrup.

3 egg whites
¾ cup maple syrup
1 to 2 cups whipping cream

Have ready: electric mixer with egg whites in largest mixer bowl and beaters attached. In saucepan on stovetop, bring the maple syrup to a boil, and boil until a little dropped from a spoon makes a fine hair-like thread. Remove from heat and immediately begin beating egg whites until stiff peaks form. Slowly pour the hot maple syrup over the whites and beat until completely dissolved and creamy. Cool to room temperature, then whip the cream and fold in. Place in a metal pan (10 to 13-inches long, depending on amount of cream used, or use metal pie plate(s) and freeze until firm without stirring. Serve in squares or

trawberry shortcake was looked forward to through all the long winter and spring. For real short-cake, very ripe berries were crushed and generously sweet-ened, maybe the night before using them. Baked pie pastry was broken into large pieces, and the fruit and juice poured over, then a second layer of pastry and berries were added. A big gob of sweetened whipped cream went over all.

wedges with more maple syrup, if desired. Makes 8 to 10 servings.

AYRES DATE TORTE

The *Duncan Hines Dessert Book* (1955) gives this recipe from the L.S. Ayres Tea Room in Indianapolis.

- ½ cup egg whites
- 1½ teaspoons water
- ⅝ cup (10 tablespoons) sugar
- 1 cup unfrosted cake crumbs
- ¼ teaspoon baking powder
- ½ cup walnuts or pecans
- 1 cup chopped seedless dates

Preheat oven to 325 degrees. In largest bowl of electric mixer, place egg whites. Beat until stiff, gradually adding water. Continue beating while gradually adding sugar. In small bowl, combine crumbs, baking powder, nuts and dates. Fold into egg whites. Pour mixture into ungreased 9-inch square baking pan. Bake for 30 minutes. If desired, serve with whipped cream flavored with vanilla.

CANDIES

Candy used to be made throughout the year, but especially at Christmas time. When making chocolates, a home-maker tried to have as few "bursters" as possible. A burster was what you got when you dipped the candy too thinly in some places, so the filling burst through the finished chocolate. Bursters could be identified by the tiny bubbles on the surface where the sugary filling seeped through. Cream fillings or crystallized fruit were known to be especially susceptible to "bursting," homemakers were warned.

As recipes came to be perfected by professional home economists and cooking schools, such terms as "soft ball stage," "hard crack stage," and so on helped further the making of candies by giving somewhat more specific direc-

erenades were common in Riley's day. Riley played the violin, mandolin, guitar, banjo and anything else he could lay his hands on. Girls at a fudge party were the recipients of the music. If a song did not please, they were apt to throw a bucket of water down on the luckless boys' heads.

tions. Today, serious cooks use candy thermometers to tell when the candy has reached the proper finished temperature.

BOURBON PECAN CHOCOLATES

Filling:
- 1 cup pecans
- ¼ cup bourbon
- 1 pound confectioners sugar
- ½ cup butter
- 1 teaspoon vanilla

  Extra pecan halves, optional

Soak pecans in bourbon several hours or overnight. Mix sugar, butter and vanilla with hands until creamy. Drain bourbon from nuts and add bourbon to the creamed mixture. Make fondants by molding about a heaping teaspoonful of bourbon-sugar mixture around a nut half. Chill at least an hour before dipping. Dip into chocolate (see below) and top with additional pecan half, if desired. Makes about 50 chocolates

COCONUT FONDANT CHOCOLATES

Filling:
- ¾ cup mashed potatoes (see method below)
- 1 pound (16 ounces) flaked coconut (about 4 cups)
- 1 pound confectioners sugar (about 4¾ cups, sifted)
- 1 teaspoon almond extract

To Make Mashed Potatoes: You will need about 1 large potato, peeled and cut into 1-inch cubes (this should equal about 1¼ cups of cubes). In 1½-quart casserole, place cubes and 2 tablespoons water. Cover with lid or plastic wrap. Microwave at high (100 percent power) for 5 to 8 minutes, until centermost cube is tender. With electric mixer or potato masher, mash potatoes until smooth. Measure ¾ cup mashed potatoes. To potatoes, add coconut, confectioners sugar and almond extract. Beat until well mixed; mixture is stiff. Drop mixture by heaping teaspoonfuls onto wax paper. Let cool until mixture can be rolled

affy was a simple candy often made. Twice as much sugar as water and maybe a little butter were boiled together until the practiced eye detected by a drop of the mixture in a cup of cold water that the "pullin' stage" was reached. Flavoring was added, then the candy poured out on a well buttered plate, to be parcelled out in handfuls to all those present. When pulled with buttered fingers, it finally became a hard rope that could be cut into squares. Riley's poem "The Child World" tells us, "Floretty (a hired girl) came to call The children in the kitchen, where they all went helter-skeltering with shout and din—for well indeed they knew that summons meant, Taffy and pop-corn—so with cheers they went."

between palms of hand to form into balls. Refrigerate at least an hour before dipping. Dip into chocolate (see below). Makes about 5 dozen (60) balls.

CREAM MINTS

Filling:

   8 ounces cream cheese

  ¼ teaspoon oil of peppermint (2 or 3 drops)

1½ pounds confectioners sugar

    Food coloring

This fondant is very stiff and may be made in a food processor or a heavy duty electric mixer. In workbowl of processor (with steel blade) or bowl of mixer, place cream cheese and peppermint. Mix to cream the cheese until smooth. Add confectioners sugar in portions until mixture is very stiff. Mix in food coloring to tint desired pastel. With fingertips, pinch off small portions of mixture, about a teaspoon, and mold into smooth flat patty. Let stand on wax paper lined cookie sheets several hours until dry and firm. Dip partially into chocolate to expose some of the colorful filling. Makes about 6 dozen mints. (Note: Store these in the refrigerator up to 2 or 3 weeks, in the freezer for longer storage.)

TO DIP CHOCOLATES

Chocolate Coating:

  6 ounces semi-sweet chocolate chips

  4 ounces (4 squares) semi-sweet chocolate

  ⅓ paraffin bar (regular size bar, 5 by 3-inches), cut into small chunks

Melt the coating: In 1½ quart microwave casserole, place chocolate chips, semi-sweet chocolate and paraffin. Microwave at medium (50 percent power) for 9 to 13 minutes, until ingredients can be stirred smooth. (Note: paraffin does not melt by microwaves, but from the heat of the chocolate. Cutting it into small chunks exposes more of the paraffin's surface to the warm chocolate, helping it melt quickly.) With forks or tongs, dip each candy into

arly sugar was coarse. We can assume that it was granulated sugar that is meant in "The Rubáiyát of Doc Sifers" in the passage "Doc's the first man ever swung a bucket on a tree Instid o' troughs, and first man brung grained sugar—so's 'at he could use it fer his coffee and fer cookin', don't you know— Folks come clean up from Pleasauthland 'fore they'd believe it, though!" Brown sugar was available before white sugar, and was bought in the bulk. There were lumps in it which the housewife smoothed out with a rolling pin.

melted chocolate. Remove to wax paper or cooling rack. Refrigerate until hardened. Store finished candies in tightly sealed container. Coats about 50 to 60 chocolates.

MODERNIZED FUDGE

In the early 1900's making fudge could be the centerpiece of a date between two young people. Parents liked this idea because they could "supervise." This timesaving recipe, which is a microwave shortcut, wouldn't have been so popular.

    1   can (5.3-ounces) evaporated milk
    2¼ cups sugar
    ½   cup (1 stick) butter
    2   tablespoons (1 ounce) vanilla
    1½ cups walnuts
    12-ounces semi sweet chocolate chips
    6-ounces milk chocolate chips

(Note: for more of a "candy bar" flavor, substitute equal weight of milk chocolate candy bars for the semi sweet and milk chocolate chips). In large mixing bowl, put butter, vanilla, walnuts and both kinds of chips. Set aside. In 3-quart glass or microwave plastic casserole, stir milk and sugar well. Microwave at high (100 percent power) for 6 to 8 minutes, stirring every 3 minutes, until boiling. Stir, and continue microwaving until sugar is completely dissolved. Immediately pour over the butter, nuts and chocolate chips in first bowl. Stir until thoroughly mixed. Pour into well buttered 13x9x2-inch dish or pan and refrigerate until set. Cut in squares. Makes about 2 pounds candy.

MISS FURR'S CARAMEL ROLL

In the early and middle 1900's, Miss Mary Furr taught Home Economics to the girls of Greenfield High School. Students had to learn to make this recipe, based on modern-day canned evaporated milk, in order to pass the class.

O Henry was the name of one of the earliest candy bars. Riley pays tribute to the new treat in his poem "O. Henry" as follows: "O. Henry, Afrite-chef of all delight!—Of all delectables conglomerate That stay the starved brain and rejuvenate the mental man—it's (hunger's) pangs thou dost abate And all so amiably alleviate."

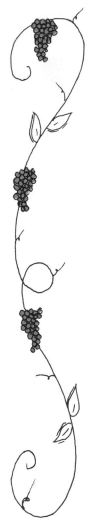

3 cups granulated sugar
1½ cups (12-oz. can) evaporated milk
1 cup white corn syrup
½ cup butter (1 stick)
⅛ teaspoon salt
2 cups (½ pound) chopped pecans
1 teaspoon vanilla

Butter an 8-inch square pan. In heavy saucepan, stir sugar, evaporated milk, corn syrup, butter and salt. Stir over low heat until sugar is dissolved, then cook without stirring until "hard ball" stage (250 degrees) has been reached. Candy is done when a little dropped into cold water forms a hard ball). Remove from heat. Add pecans and vanilla. Beat by hand until candy holds together and loses its gloss. Quickly pour into buttered pan and spread evenly. When cold, cut in squares. Store in an airtight box. Makes 3 to 4 dozen small squares.

DIVINITY CREAM

Our mother and grandmother, Ellis June Rock Jackson, made this recipe in the 1800's. Despite its calories from sugar, it has no fat whatsoever.

2½ cups granulated sugar
½ cup corn syrup
½ cup water
2 egg whites
¼ teaspoon salt
1 teaspoon vanilla

Just before boiling the syrup, beat the egg whites and salt to stiff peaks. In heavy saucepan, stir together sugar, syrup and water. Stir over low heat until sugar is dissolved, then cook without stirring to "firm ball" stage (260 degrees on candy thermometer). When done, a little of the hot syrup dropped into cup of cold water will form a firm ball. Remove from heat and pour, beating constantly, in a fine stream into the beaten whites. Lastly, add the vanilla, and continue beating candy until mixture becomes stiff enough to hold its shape and slightly dull. Quickly drop by spoonfuls into individual mounds on wax papaer. Or, if desired, spread evenly in buttered square 8-inch square pan or dish and cut into squares

A nother popular early candy was known as wax, a sort of unpulled taffy. In the fall, it was customary to gather nuts in the woods nearby in bushel baskets for these treats. A big buttered platter was heavily spread with nutmeats, then over it a syrup was poured of sugar, butter and water boiled to the "medium ball" stage, a point just before it would "spin a thread" off a spoon. Pieces of the chewy result were pinched or cut off.

when firm. Makes about 48 pieces. (Note: if you wish, you can add about ½ cup chopped pecans to this recipe.)

DISHPAN CANDY

From *Favorite Recipes Compiled by The Ladies of the Cosmos Society of The Bradley Methodist Episcopal Church*, Greenfield, Indiana (1914), which bears the introduction: "Within you will find more of relish than of wisdom. The recipes herein have all been tested and recommended by the ladies whose signatures they bear."

"Put a cupful of light brown sugar and a half cup of butter into a saucepan and place this on the fire, stir constantly. Let it boil until it is ready to burn, then empty into a buttered dishpan. Let this stand for two or three minutes. Then take hold of the edges of the candy and spread it up on the sides of the pan until it is thin as gauze. After it has all been spread out until there are no thick places in it, break in bits. This is fine."

CRISP TOFFEE

The above recipe for Dishpan Candy is actually a form of toffee. Note the similarity with this recipe.

- 1 cup toasted chopped almonds
- ½ cup butter
- ¾ cup brown sugar
- ½ cup semi sweet chocolate chips (about 3 ounces)

Grease well an 8-inch square pan. Distribute the nuts evenly in the pan. In saucepan, boil together butter and brown sugar, stirring constantly, until hard crack stage is reached (a little of mixture dropped into cold water forms brittle thread). Pour mixture over the nuts and, while hot, lay the chocolate chips over the candy. When melted, swirl chocolate to spread evenly. Refrigerate until cold, and break in pieces. Makes about 1 pound. (Note: you can also microwave this recipe. Cook butter and sugar at high 100 percent power, for about 5 to 7 minutes, until hard crack stage is reached.)

The study of elocution was very popular during Riley's day. Many young ladies could emote to such poems as Riley's "The Bumble Bee," "Extremes," "Tradin' Joe," and others. Especially good for this purpose was "Prior to Miss Belle's Appearance." Willie says, "What makes you come HERE, fer, Mister, So much to OUR house?—Say? Come to see our big sister! An Charlie he says 'at you kissed her—but we p'omised Belle An' crossed our heart to never tell—'Cause SHE gived us some o' them·er Chawklut drops 'at you br·inged to her!"

opcorn was a great treat in Riley's time. As the Hired Man puts it: 'Now when I wuz a boy, we wuz so poor, my parunts couldn't 'ford pop-corn no more to pamper me with; so I had to go WITHOUT pop-corn— sometimes a year or so! Many and many a time I've dreamt at night About pop-corn, —all busted open white And hot, you know and jest enough o' salt and butter on it fer to find no fault—Oomh! And I have PRAYED whatever happened, it 'ud eether be pop-corn or death!" In "John Alden and Percilly," at the Christmas celebration, "The preacher 'nounced (announced) 'A ball o' pop-corn Free fer each and all.'

PEANUT BRITTLE

1 cup sugar
½ cup white corn syrup
⅛ teaspoon salt
1 cup raw peanuts
1 teaspoon butter
1 teaspoon vanilla
1 teaspoon baking soda

Make this either in a black iron skillet ("spider"), or microwave it. In the skillet, place the sugar, syrup, salt and peanuts in the skillet and stir constantly over medium heat until mixture makes a thick light brown syrup. (In the microwave, use 1½-quart glass or glass-ceramic casserole; place sugar, corn syrup, salt and peanuts in casserole and stir thoroughly. Microwave at high (100 percent power) for 7 to 9 minutes, until mixture makes a thick light brown syrup.) With either recipe, to this syrup add the butter and vanilla, and continue cooking about 1 to 2 more minutes. Peanuts will have browned and syrup will be very hot. Stop cooking and add the baking soda. Mixture will foam up and become very light. Carefully and quickly pour and spread evenly onto a buttered cookie sheet. Allow to cool, then flex sheet to remove. Cool at least 1 hour, break into pieces and store in airtight container. Makes about 1 pound.

MOLASSES POPCORN BALLS OR CARAMEL CORN

This old time favorite is being revived today in gourmet foods catalogues. Some companies offer chocolate-covered bites of caramel corn for more than $15.00 per pound. (Use dipping chocolate above if you wish to make your own.)

3 quarts popcorn (¼ to ⅓ cup corn before popping)
1 to 2 cups salted peanuts
Syrup:
1 pound brown sugar
½ cup (1 stick) butter
½ cup molasses
1 tablespoon water
2 teaspoons baking soda

Pop popcorn on stovetop and remove all unpopped kernels. Place in large bowl or kettle (about 6-quart capacity—a spaghetti cooker, etc.) along with peanuts. Microwave the syrup. In 4-quart glass mixing bowl, stir together brown sugar, butter, molasses and water. Microwave at high (100 percent power) for 10 to 14 minutes, stirring every 5 minutes, until completely dissolved and thickened. Quickly add the soda and stir to distribute to all areas of candy. Pour the syrup over the popcorn and nuts and toss to coat evenly. Spread on aluminum foil until cool enough to make popcorn balls. Or make Caramel Corn by separating into bite size pieces. Wrap balls in plastic wrap, or store loose corn in airtight container. Makes about 3 quarts, about 12 popcorn balls.

Maple candy was made even through the 1930's by pouring boiled-down syrup on the snow. It was a throw-back to fondly-remembered "sugarcamps" of pioneer times. Latter-day Hoosiers have always seemed to have a collective memory of frontier days, and even today find ways to cherish that past. The reason for Riley's popularity then and now is that he struck the chord of fond remembrance of an earlier Indiana and did it so well.

ABOUT RILEY'S HOME . . .

As the tourist crosses Indiana—his eye on the map—his attention is attracted to the city of Greenfield, known far and wide as the birthplace of the beloved Hoosier poet James Whitcomb Riley. Ah, here it is, accessible from either Interstate 70 or from US 40, the old National Road over which pioneers poured into Indiana.

As a boy James Whitcomb Riley loved to sit on his steps and watch the flow of traffic which went endlessly by—those going west to the Gold Rush in California, those going east to sell noisily bellowing stock, those going southwest to free lands offered by the government. Greenfield, founded in 1828 and a thriving village in Riley's time, was a way-station on the road to progress in America.

James Whitcomb Riley's parents were Reuben Alexander Riley and Elizabeth Marine Riley, who had come to Greenfield after their marriage in Randolph County. Reuben, a strong, sturdy pioneer, built the Riley home. He had little use for the dreamy son who wrote poetry. It was Riley's mother, Elizabeth, a poetess herself, who became the inspiring force in the life of the poet James Whitcomb Riley.

One day young Jim (also called "Bud"), was hoeing in the garden, a job he could not do to suit the eagle eye of the father. The boy became angry enough to throw down the hoe and leave his father's roof forever. It was much later, after life had tamed Reuben, and "Bud" Riley had passed through a career as a newspaper reporter to status as a respected Indiana poet, that the two were reconciled. Meanwhile, Reuben had lost the house he had built, due to unwise land speculation, and it had passed through the hands of several citizens of Greenfield.

James Whitcomb Riley in 1893 was prosperous enough to buy the home of his childhood, which he had always held in fond memory, as a gathering place for his brothers and sisters. Riley's brother John and his wife Julia lived in the Riley home and and kept its traditions. John died in 1912; Riley himself in 1916. The heirs were willing to let the city of Greenfield purchase the house and maintain it as a shrine to the Hoosier poet.

By the time of his death, Riley was internationally famous, one of the three or four best known American poets. Even queens and kings of Europe read "When the Frost is on the Punkin," "Little Orphant Annie," and "Child's World," which is modelled on the Arabian Nights and the Canterbury Tales.

A group of Greenfield citizens led by the Mayor, Arthur Downing, and the Mitchell family, spearheaded an effort to secure the home and make it available to the public. Today it continues to be maintained through the personal devotion of the city of Greenfield: its board of trustees, volunteer tour guides, and even many crews which repair it from time to time, are all local citizens.

The Greenfield Riley Home is open April 1 to Christmas 10 a.m. to 4 p.m. Tours are requested to make reservations, 317-462-8539. The Riley Lockerbie Street home in Indianapolis is open Tuesday through Saturday 10-4, Sunday 12-4. Closed Monday.

READING LIST AND
SOURCES—JWR COOKBOOK

Beard, James A. *American Cookery*. Boston, 1972. 877 pp.

Beeton, Isabella. *Mrs. Beeton's Book of Household Management*. 1969 (reprint).

Beecher, Catherine. *Miss Beecher's Domestic Receipt Book*. New York, 1846. 293 pp.

Connor, Phyllis (collected by). *Old Timey Recipes*. Bluefield, W. Va. 1973. 64 pp.

Farmer, Fannie Merritt. *Boston Cooking-School Cook Book*. Boston 1896. 682 pp.

Fletcher-Berry, Riley. M. *Plantation Christmas Cakes*. New York, 1915. 15 pp.

Flexner, Marion. *Out Of Kentucky Kitchens*. New York, 1949. 319 pp.

Gold Medal Century of Success Cookbook, Minneapolis, 1979. 112 pp.

Washburn Crosby Co. *Gold Medal Flour Cook Book*. Minneapolis, 1917. 74 pp. (Also 1904 Christmas edition.)

Good Housekeeping's Book of Meals Tested, Tasted and Approved. New York, 1930. 256 pp.

Hansey, Jennie A. *The Century Cookbook*, Chicago, 1894.

Hill, Sallie F. *Progressive Farmer's Southern Cookbook*. Birmingham, 1961. 470 pp.

Hines, Duncan. *The Duncan Hines Dessert Book*. New York, 1955. 361 pp.

Ladies of the Cosmos Society of the Bradley Methodist Church. *Favorite Recipes*. Greenfield, Ind. 1904. 138 pp.

Ladies of the First Methodist Church. *Ladies Society Cookbook*. Greenfield, Ind 1902. 148 pp.

Neil, Miss E. *The Everyday Cook Book*. (Circa 1900, exact date and location unknown). 315 pp.

New Buckeye Cookbook, The. Dayton, 1880. 1288 pp.

Tri Kappa Cookbook. Greenfield, Ind. 1928. 92 pp.

Vaughn, Beatrice. *Yankee Hill Country Cooking*. Brattleboro, Vt. 1963. 202 pp.

Wakefield, Ruth Graves. *Tried and True Recipes*. New York, 1937. 212 pp.

Williams, Dorothy June, *Greenfield Glimpses*. Greenfield, Ind. 1989. 195 pp.

Williams, Dorothy June, *Hancock County Highlights*. Greenfield, Ind. 1986, 96 pp.

About the Authors . . .

Dorothy June Williams

Diana Williams Hansen

Dorothy June Williams writes:

"As I grew up, and listened to my friends' many ambitions, I had only one: to write a book. It took me many years to realize my goal."

"I was born on October 26, 1908 in a house on the main streets of Greenfield, Indiana. I started to school at the age of five and graduated from Indiana University at the age of twenty—a little too young, perhaps. Upon graduation, I went to Yellowstone Park for a summer's employment as a "heaver" (waitress). The big silver dollar the rangers gave us at our first meal was the first real money I had ever earned (my father, in whose law office I had answered the phone and typed, didn't count as a bona fide employer.)"

"I taught English for five years and was just beginning to like it, when I married a long time friend. His mother said he had declared in the second grade that he was going to marry the girl with the black curls. He had been to Purdue, Carnegie Tech, and Ohio State though, before this came to pass. I always thought his mother made up that story, but I liked it. While my husband was climbing the corporate ladder of the Pure Oil Company, now merged into Union, I was at home tending to six children and trying to keep up some vestige of a social life, which was very important to me. Being a true Hoosier, I was a joiner. All you had to do was to ask me to join something, and that organization had a new member. After his retirement, we traveled."

"I lived with Tom for fifty two years before death took him away and left me, for the first time in my life, 'on my own.' Working at the James Whitcomb Riley birthplace in Greenfield since 1956, (the year in which one of my treasured three boys, Danny, died at the age of six,) has kept my mind on poetry and the better things of life. I counsel everyone to find something he or she likes to do which will nurture his soul and make life worthwhile."

*Diana Williams Hansen is the second child, and second daughter, of Dororthy June and Tom Williams. She was born in Rushville, Indiana and grew up in Greenfield. During her years at Riley Grade School and Greenfield High School, she participated in many annual Riley festivals with appropriate readings from the works of the Hoosier Poet. She graduated from Purdue University in Lafayette, Indiana; and has an MBA from Bellarmine College in Louisville, Kentucky.

Professionally, Diana has worked in food and recipe development jobs for over 25 years. Employers include the Betty Crocker Kitchens, California Raisin Advisory Board and General Electric Co., where she was manager of the Range Department Test Kitchens. Since developing her own consulting company named "Diana Hansen's Kitchens" in Louisville, her clients have included Rubbermaid, Inc., Campbell Soup Co., Magic Chef, Inc., Dole Pineapple Co., and many others. She has written cooking columns for the *Los Angeles Time Syndicate* and the *Louisville Courier Journal* and has had food articles published in many national home magazines. This is her second cookbook, the first being *Creative Microwaving*.

Tour guides at the Riley Home including Front row (l to r) Edna Jacobs and Ruth Williamson Back row (l to r) Lucilla Boyd, Peggy Kingen, Lucinda Arthur, and the author Dorothy June Williams.

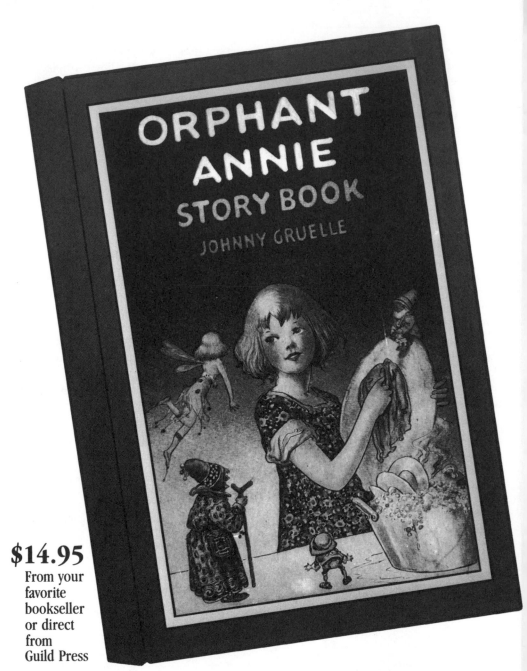

James Whitcomb Riley's poem "Little Orphant Annie" was written in the 1880's, but it found its most wonderful expression in a book published by Bobbs Merrill in 1921.

Orphant Annie Storybook was written and illustrated as a tribute to Riley by Johnny Gruelle, the creator of Raggedy Ann and Andy. In this charming children's book Annie tells tales of grouchy but lovable goblins, odd gnomes who live in little towns in the wood, pumpkins that fly and ladybugs who talk. All of these stories are guaranteed to charm nostalgic grandparents and parents and a whole new generation of children.

STANDARD TRADE AND LIBRARY DISCOUNTS

Guild Press of Indiana   6000 Sunset Indianapolis, IN 46208

I (we) would like _____ copies of *Orphant Annie Storybook* by Johnny Gruelle at $14.95.
Indiana residents add 5% state sales tax.
Please add $1.50 postage per book on individual orders.
☐ I have enclosed a check payable to Guild Press of Indiana (required for individual orders)
☐ Bill us (Stores and Libraries)

Name _____

Address _____

_____

_____

To:

Greenfield Chamber of Commerce
City Hall, Greenfield, Indiana 46140

I WOULD LIKE INFORMATION ON THE FOLLOWING:
1. The Riley Home
2. Other sights around Greenfield, Indiana
3. Books of poetry by James Whitcomb Riley which are for sale, and cost
4. Other souvenirs available at the Riley Home.

Name _____

Address _____